Silk Dreams, Troubled Road

Jonny Bealby was born in 1963.
Canada, he developed a passion
journeyed extensively in Australa
has earned a crust in a variety o
horse rider, circus roustabout, mo
to name but a few. As a writer and traveller he has visited more than
seventy countries and has had features in a variety of publications
including the *Daily Telegraph*, *Observer*, *Elle*, *Global* and *Traveller
Magazine*. He is also the author of *Running with the Moon* and *For a Pagan
Song* and now runs the adventure travel company Wild Frontiers
(www.wildfrontiers.co.uk). While not travelling, he lives in London.

Praise for Jonny Bealby
Silk Dreams, Troubled Road

'A truly enthralling book.' – *Daily Mail*

'An absolute page-turner... I found myself firing through the
"travelling" passages so that I could get to the latest camp-fire dust
up... Wonderful descriptions of the Mountains of Heaven and the
ancient city of Samarkand.' – *Wanderlust*

'Fascinating reading, an amazing travel adventure, [and] an account
of a human relationship as it is tested to the limit.' – *Brentwood Gazette
Series*

'Reads like a cross between Ray Mears' *Extreme Survival* and *Streetmate*.
An incredible adventure.' – *OK! Magazine*

Running with the Moon

'Honest and passionate, one of the best travel books I've read.' – *GQ*

'Bealby handles this tragic tale with endearing honesty and tenderness.
It is the romantic's naivety, not to mention his irrepressible energy,
optimism and courage, which charm the reader.' – *Daily Telegraph*

For a Pagan Song

'Entrancing... compelling... completely engaging... The very best of
the summer's travel books.' – *Daily Mail*

'A rollicking tale... No one has written a better travel book about the
region since Eric Newby came down from the Hindu Kush.' – *Daily
Telegraph*

Silk Dreams,
Troubled Road

Love and War on the Old Silk Road:
On Horseback through Central Asia

Jonny Bealby

/ arrow books

For two great friends,

J.B.S. and A.J.H.

with thanks

My heart of silk is filled with lights,
with lost bells with lilies and bees.
I will go very far, farther than those hills,
farther than the seas, close to the stars,
to beg Christ the Lord to give me back the soul I had
of old, when I was a child, ripened with legends,
with a feathered cap and a wooden sword

Federico García Lorca

Contents

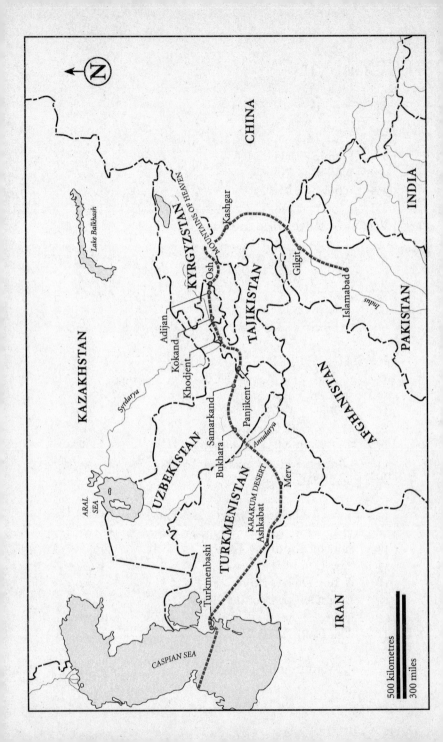

PART ONE
A Suitable Girl

'Life is what happens when you're busy making other plans'
John Lennon

1 False Dawn

The first time I met Rachel I knew I was in trouble.

Passing through Islamabad on my way north to investigate the possibility of setting up a travel company offering adventure holidays in the Karakoram and Hindu Kush mountains, I'd been invited to spend the weekend with an old friend, Hen, and her partner, Johan, who both worked for the UN. When Hen told me a female colleague would be joining us for dinner I thought nothing of it. After all, I was in Pakistan, hardly a place I'd imagined meeting a potential girlfriend. But Rachel enthralled me. Seating ourselves at one end of the table, we soon became absorbed in conversation. On the surface it was simply superficial connections: we shared favourite books (*The Alchemist, Captain Corelli's Mandolin*), films (*Cyrano de Bergerac, The Apartment*), music (Radiohead, Morcheeba); enjoyed similar recreations (travel, photography, wine), parts of the world (India, Provence, New York); even cherished the same dream (to own a little farmhouse in France), but beneath that there seemed to be a more base connection. Much of the conversation took place without words.

If it makes any sense, Rachel was the most feminine woman I'd ever met. The way she sat, held her head, her slender arms, elegant hands, sexuality oozed from every pore of her body. Not only that, but she was very beautiful: fine dark hair, a wide and sensual mouth, delicate nose, and deep brown eyes that sparkled with mischievous fun. And, whether intentionally or not, she used her eyes cunningly. While she listened to what I was saying she locked her gaze not on my mouth, as is usual, but on my eyes, seeming to search inside to read the words that I wasn't using as surely as her ears heard those that I was. Whether she smiled, laughed, became suitably serious, amazed or annoyed, I was left with the warm sensation that I'd got it right, that whatever I'd said really was funny, intelligent, poignant or wise. There was never simply a polite little chuckle or impatient 'umm'. When she listened, she really listened. In short, Rachel had the ability to make me feel like I was the only man alive in the world and she was the only woman. Intoxicating Bewitching. And very dangerous. Towards the end of the evening she asked if I wanted to accompany her driving a Land Rover back to England at the end of the year. Without a moment's hesitation, I agreed at once.

Big deal? Well to me it was. Recently, relationships had been things that happened to other people, not me. Following the death of my fiancée, Melanie, almost a decade earlier, and one bizarre and short-lived episode – which saw me stumble through an extra-ordinary marriage – I hadn't had the slightest interest in becoming seriously involved with anyone I'd met. I'd had flings, of course, but these had usually been drunken affairs lasting days and weeks rather than months and years, and on the whole had been far more dispiriting than fulfilling. With Melanie things had always been so easy and for five years we'd shared a wonderful relationship – flat-mates, bed mates, best mates, soul mates – but while travelling to-gether in Kashmir, just two months before we'd planned to marry, I'd awoken to find her breathing her last. She'd suffered – so an autopsy report later informed me – an asthma attack brought on by high altitude and a bout of bronchitis, and after a brief struggle she'd died in my arms. Since then a basic connection had always seemed to be lacking; the ability to feel totally natural with someone I found physically appealing, the feeling of being at one.

Until now?

It certainly seemed so three days later while out horse riding on the edge of town. Rather than driving a Land Rover home, Rachel suggested we ride instead. That we happened to be in Pakistan at the time, with home lying 5,000 miles away across some of the world's meanest mountains and cruellest deserts, through lands struggling with economic stagnation and political unrest – at least one still reeling from the crippling effects of a vicious civil war – and among people whose reputation for thieving and banditry was almost as fabled as their generous hospitality, didn't seem to concern her in the least. If I'd been interested before, now I was hooked. No one had ever suggested such an outlandish – and patently crazy – adventure to me before. Usually it was the other way around.

Turning my heels into my horse's side, I trotted up beside her. 'Are you serious?' I asked, doubting whether she knew the answer or not.

'Maybe . . .' Her dark eyebrows rose defiantly. 'Last night I just got thinking and the more I thought about it the better an idea it seemed. If James wants me to ship his Land Rover back to England, leaving us nothing to drive home in, why not ride?' She gazed beyond the path and across the lake to where an amber sun was setting; the Punjabi dusk was turning golden calm. 'Once I finish out here next spring,' she continued reflectively, 'I don't think I'm going to work abroad again, at least not for a while, and before I settle back down to London life I just want to do something special. That's all.' As her horse passed beneath a sprawling jacaranda, a low branch brushed her hair, sending a cloud of violet blossom tumbling to the ground. She looked up and smiled mischievously. 'Could we?' she asked again. Her forehead was creased with expectation, her bright eyes bold and daring. 'Do you think it would be possible?'

'Definitely,' I beamed, and I meant it. As I looked into her impassioned face the world felt rich with endless possibilities: drive home, ride home, fly on a carpet, what difference did the details make? Had she asked, I'd have happily walked.

'Great,' she answered with a pretty grin. 'You do know about horses, don't you?'

'What I don't know ain't worth knowing,' I bluffed.

'Good,' she said, 'then I think we should do it.'

The journey quickly began to fire my imagination. I knew immediately which route to take, east to west along the old Silk Road. 'For most travellers, and all merchants,' wrote Peter Fleming in his travel classic *News from Tartary*, 'the road from China to the west lies as it has lain for centuries, along that ancient Silk Road which is surely the most romantic and culturally most important trade route in the history of the world.' As a traveller of quixotic disposition I'd always hoped that one day I'd find myself bound on its story-strewn path. I just never imagined I'd find the excuse.

In my mind's eye I saw Rachel and myself dressed like Cossacks on heavenly horses, riding the mountain steppes just as Genghis Khan and his Mongol hordes had done; crossing the same shadowy passes and lonely valleys as the imperial players of the old Great Game; visiting the ancient cities of Samarkand, Bukhara, Khiva and Merv; travelling in the hoof-prints of Alexander the Great, Tamerlane, Marco Polo, Ibn Battutah and a thousand other warriors, merchants, poets and pilgrims who had carried their dreams along the old Silk Road. Accompanied by a beautiful woman, what more wonderful adventure could there possibly be?

'Do you know which route you'd like to take?' I asked carefully, knowing. I already did.

'Not really,' she replied.

'The Silk Road would be the obvious way to go. It –'

'Oh yes.' Her smiling eyes shone even more brightly.

'Yes? Excellent.' My mind was racing now, an imagined map before me. 'Well, Kashgar would be the natural starting point from here. We could travel by road up the Karakoram Highway to China, buy horses in the famous Kashgar Sunday Market and ride the Silk Road all the way to, to . . . the Caspian Sea.' I was so excited I stood in the saddle and gestured flamboyantly towards the lake. 'What do you reckon?'

'Fantastic.'

'Yes, it'll be pretty easy to reach home from there. And it has a cool ring to it as well, don't you think . . . Kashgar to the Caspian Sea?'

'It sounds just perfect.' And with a beaming smile lighting up her face, she broke into a canter. 'Come on,' she shouted over her shoulder, 'I'll race you back to the stables.'

If it's possible to pinpoint a moment that one falls in love, that was it. How could anyone be so fantastically blasé about such a huge undertaking? After nine lonely years, I felt I'd finally discovered the person I'd been looking for. And, what's more, it seemed to be reciprocated. Three nights later we found ourselves kissing; a short while after that, romping in a bed.

The better I got to know Rachel – as friends, lovers and 'partners in crime' – the more impressed I became. She was bright, witty, intelligent, talented, and whether playing Chopin on the piano, galloping wildly through a darkening wood or chatting easily in flawless French, she carried a beauty and grace I'd seldom seen.

Employed by various aid agencies, she'd worked all over the world and now had an interesting job with the UN. But there was also a sensitive vulnerability to her. On the surface she was confident, assured, in control, but the more we talked, and the more layers I managed to peel away, the more I discovered an uncertain, insecure person. To fall in love with a woman I have always had to be able to see the little girl behind the adult mask. Rachel's childhood alter-ego was always apparent just below the surface. And the more time we shared, the more in tune we seemed.

Consumed by this passion for both Rachel and the trip, I began to read up on the area, study maps and make basic plans. I quickly realised just how exciting the journey would be. The route would take us through the very heart of Asia, through cultural and physical extremes, from the ancient towns with their teeming bazaars, Islamic mosques and palaces, peopled by the sedentary Uzbeks, Tajiks and Uyghurs, to the surreal landscapes of mountains, steppes and deserts, in turn inhabited by the nomadic Kazak, Kyrgyz and Turkmen tribes.

Sitting up late, with glasses of wine, we worked out the route. Having travelled overland by bus from Islamabad to Kashgar and the Chinese province of Xinjiang, we planned first to ride over the Torugart Pass and into Kyrgyzstan. From here we'd make our way due west, taking a course directly over the Tian Shan range – the much-fabled Mountains of Heaven – to Osh at the northern end of the 200-mile-long Ferghana Valley. Once there we'd cross the border into Uzbekistan, travel south through the valley, Central Asia's rich agricultural heartland, take a short cut across a thin corridor of Tajikistan, before re-emerging on the Uzbek plains. Here, sticking wherever possible to small tracks and nomadic trails, we'd journey through some of the most culturally wealthy and historically important towns in Central Asia: Khodjent, Samarkand, Bukhara and Merv. Then, having crossed the Amu Darya – formally the River Oxus – and entered Turkmenistan, a gruelling 800-kilometre slog across the bleak and baking Karakum – or Black Sands – Desert would carry us to the Caspian Sea. It was a journey of approximately 2,500 kilometres and would take, we figured, some four months to complete. If we left in early June, we'd arrive on the Caspian's eastern shores by mid-October latest.

'The trouble with journeys these days,' wrote Peter Fleming in the 1930s, 'is that they are too easy to make and too hard to justify.' Maybe so, but with Rachel there seemed to me plenty of reasons for making the trip. Not only did it venture through a part of the world I wished to explore, and use a method of transport I'd always wanted to take, but it offered me the perfect opportunity to bring my story full circle. Having written two books about my travels and life after Melanie, I saw now a chance to write the closing episode of this traveller's tale: from love, through loss, to love again. Not only could it prove another cracking adventure, packed with exciting characters and the challenges of an ancient road, but also with a little luck it might end up providing the concluding chapter to a story that began in Kashmir more than nine years ago. The last part of a decade-long trilogy, I thought grandiosely.

Over the course of the following nine months, both as a journalist and with my new adventure travel company – now called Wild Frontiers – I managed to spend a good deal of time in Pakistan, and my relationship with Rachel developed. But for all the charismatic edge she possessed, it didn't take long for me to discover a darker side lurked just behind – perhaps that was what made her so intoxicating – and as far as our relationship was concerned, I spent a great deal of the time rather confused. With a smile and a kiss she'd lead me in one direction, and a few minutes later drag my emotions in quite another. With great precision she'd define the road ahead, only to leap from its course to another path entirely. She would love with a passion and then push away, hold on tightly and then let go. She was the type of person Milan Kundera, John Fowles or Leo Tolstoy based their characters on. She was the most exciting woman I had ever met; she was also the most dangerous. I knew very well what a vulnerable position I was in and yet seemed totally powerless to do a thing about it. Retract from Rachel to win her love? I could as soon have kissed the moon.

There were often other men craving her attention – at parties, hanging around the house, even flying in from New York or London specially to see her. Though she pretended not to, it was obvious she enjoyed the attention. One day, while I was staying at her house, she came home and casually announced that some guy had proposed to her over the phone. I had no doubt at all that he had been serious. It was just the kind of reaction men had to Rachel. Only after a few moments did she realise I might be hurt by such a statement. 'Don't worry,' she said, placing a reassuring hand on my arm, 'I turned him down.' I just laughed anxiously and carried on. Rachel was a drug to me. And I was addicted.

Occasionally, persuaded either by her own anxieties or by me, she did try to talk about us. For various reasons, she didn't feel ready for a full commitment, to me or anyone else. There were painful experiences with ex-boyfriends she still had to resolve, there were worries over the fact that she lived in Pakistan while I didn't, and much to my dismay she read *Running with the Moon* – the book I wrote about a journey around Africa, relating in part to my life with Melanie – which, as I thought it might, made her concerned about living in the shadow of a seemingly perfect person who had now passed on. Did she want a relationship at the moment or did she want to be single? She said she wasn't sure. Excuses? Undoubtedly – there were probably many more – but while I had more or less what I wanted, it was relatively easy to bury my head beneath the soft and cosy blanket of intimate friendship, sex and laughter, and dream of the epic journey that was to come. After all, if there was one sure-fire way of resolving the affair, surely it was to spend four months of both extreme adversity and soul-surging pleasure together. I focused my hopes and fears on the journey.

An innocuous telephone call I made from London one night ruined everything. Some throw-away comment she made about being unable to take a short beach holiday we'd planned – 'Oh yeah, we've got to talk about that' – was all it took to have the demons of despair leap from nowhere to spit acid in my face. Following that, everything changed. The e-mails and telephone calls that had flooded in at a rate of two or three a day dwindled to a miserable trickle and their tone was hardly encouraging. 'I'm worried you're expecting too much out of this trip,' she wrote in one correspondence, 'I think it would be better if we go on it as devoted friends, rather than anything else.' Right.

It took a month of denial and self-delusion before I finally accepted the shattering reality. I was given little choice. A few days before I was due to fly out to see Rachel again, two months before we were set to leave for Kashgar, I logged on to pick up my e-mails only to discover that I'd finally been dumped. I sat staring at my computer screen, my mouth dry, my hands shaking, my heart pounding like timpani drums. I read the words again. I stood up. Sat down. I felt hot. I felt cold. I read them for a third time, looking for some shred of hope. There was none.

A few days later, feeling pitiful, I flew out to Pakistan. When I saw her – looking, it has to be said, painfully gorgeous with a sun-kissed face setting off those sparkling eyes – she cried. She told me she was sorry, that she still loved me, that she'd never connected with anyone more deeply in all her life, that she was always so happy when she was with me, that she didn't know what she was so scared of . . . and that she was seeing someone else. I put a brave face on the proceedings, didn't cry . . . much . . . and, still entranced as I was by her powerful presence, departed wishing her well. The next day, miserably tearing up all plans for adventures on the old Silk Road and a life together with the woman I loved, I flew back home to England.

2 Coming or Going?

Sitting on the plane home with easy tears rolling down my cheeks, I naturally assumed that was it, not only in terms of my relationship with Rachel but also regarding the journey. Without Rachel there was no quest, with no quest there was no story, and with no story there could be no book . . . therefore what was the point in going? Whatever crazy dreams I may have harboured of a romantic odyssey on the old Silk Road, of bagging a story as well as a wife, they would, it seemed, just pass me by. In a way, I was relieved. Somewhere deep inside I'd suspected all along Rachel wasn't going to fall my way – our relationship, though intense and at times passionate, had never been balanced – and I figured it was probably better to have discovered this now, rather than two months into a four-month trip.

Still, it wasn't easy. Being traded in by a girl I loved left me feeling utterly crushed, lacking self-confidence and motivation. I found myself questioning every aspect of the life I led. Did I really want to keep flogging my arse around the world eking a meagre existence from writing books that few bought and even fewer read? Wasn't it time I got a proper job or concentrated on my new travel business – I'd already taken three successful trips to Pakistan – made some money, found a stable home? Over the last ten years I'd spent so much time abroad that while in England I'd had nowhere to call my own. I'd simply moved from pillar to post, to wherever a cheap and convenient abode could be found. I couldn't remember the last time I'd slept in a place that had my pictures hanging on the walls, my pots and pans in the kitchen, my books on the bookshelves. Wasn't it time now to stop invading other people's lives and find one of my own? At thirty-five, wasn't it finally time I started growing up?

A lonely London was, however, a sorry replacement for the wonders and excitement of the Silk Road and, as it happened, probably a good deal more dangerous. I moved temporarily into an abandoned flat in Brixton owned by a friend. He wouldn't live there, neither would anyone else: a paranoid schizophrenic, questionably released from a mental institution on a 'care in the community' scheme, inhabited the flat below. Being threatened with grizzly forms of mutilation, forced sexual depravities, even death, every time I entered or left the property, only served to push me further into an unshaven state of hideous self-pity. Consumed by painful thoughts of Rachel and her new lover, I drank too much and slept too little. However, as Fate would have it, I wasn't going to be left to mope for long. Two weeks after returning from Pakistan I received an extraordinary telephone call.

'Lion TV have come through,' bubbled Mark, my agent. 'All you've got to do is a short screen test, something on horseback down in the country, and you'll get the gig. They're really very keen.'

I could hardly believe what I was hearing. At the beginning of the year, when Rachel had still been interested in the journey, I'd written a book treatment for my publishers. Eager to build me an income he thought I'd be unlikely to gain purely from writing travel books, Mark had handed the proposal on to newspapers and a leading independent television production company; not only would a TV series obviously pay very well, it would increase my book sales and profile enormously. Though the publishers and papers had loved the idea and offered deals immediately, I'd heard nothing about any TV spin-off. I'd assumed they weren't interested. However, here was Mark informing me that not only had they not lost interest but also that they were very keen to move ahead. I hardly knew what to say.

'Mark,' I stuttered in a tired voice, 'what are you talking about? You know the situation, what's happened with Rachel. So what's the point of doing a screen test? It isn't going to happen.'

'I know, Jonny,' he answered, switching in a moment to his soothing avuncular voice, 'and I'm very sorry that things with her didn't work out. Very unfair. But it doesn't mean that *every*thing has to stop. You just never know.' Whether he hoped Rachel might suddenly be consumed with remorse and do a screeching U-turn, or had some other plan up his sleeve, he didn't say. I hoped the latter; the former seemed very unlikely. 'The point is if you tell them "no" now, you'll go back to the bottom of the pack and it might be a year or more before you get another chance. But if, on the other hand, you do this screen test and they like it, like you, you just don't know where it might lead. They're a big firm, worth getting to know. Even if you can't do this journey, they might find something else for you to do. I think you should at least have a chat with them.' He paused. 'What have you got to lose?'

What indeed?

So I called them up, and two days later – having biked over a 'video diary' I'd made, primarily of myself, while travelling in the Hindu Kush – I found myself sitting in the office of Jeremy Mills, the head honcho at Lion TV.

It was an embarrassing meeting. 'We've watched the video and think it's great,' said Jeremy, positively cooing with enthusiasm. 'But more importantly we think the proposal is fantastic as well, and we want you to do it. A video-diary series filmed by yourselves for the Beeb or Channel 4 – we'll sell it later – on a journey down the Silk Road. We all have confidence you'll make a fabulous success of it.' They wanted it, he said, to spearhead their travel section.

How could I tell him I'd just been dumped? Not only would this have been embarrassing and humiliating but I would be throwing away the biggest career break to come my way. Besides, he seemed so keen. 'God, it'll be spectacular,' he went on. 'Kashgar to the Caspian Sea: the Mountains of Heaven, the Kyrgyz steppes, the Karakum Desert . . . never heard of half the places but they all sound great.' I laughed nervously. 'No backup, no sat phone, crew or any of that nonsense. Just the two of you travelling the old Silk Road as it used to be travelled.' Staring vaguely at the ceiling there was a wistful air to his words, as though, in his mind's eye, he was already watching the film. 'On horseback. Yeah, love it. *Video Diaries, Travels with my Camera*. It's a wonderful idea. Bound to be a hit. Of course we'll finance it.'

Bound to be a hit? Of course we'll finance it? Not even a mention of a very tricky screen test? What else could I do but lie?

That evening I sat disconsolately in the pub with Mark and my editor, Victoria, discussing various ways to salvage the plan. Mark was really pissed off. 'Rachel can rip out your heart and use it as a football,' he protested angrily, 'she's perfectly entitled to do that – as we know, all's fair in love and war – but screw your career? It really shouldn't happen!' Victoria wondered if I could do it alone. 'Maybe pick someone up as you drift along?' she mused with a smile. But it was at a party full of strangers a couple of days later that the cards began to turn.

Swaying comfortably with a warm glow of alcohol, I suddenly found myself asking an attractive, happy girl if she was free for the next few months and fancied accompanying me on a horse journey across Central Asia.

She giggled. 'That's the best chat-up line I've heard in a while. Definitely beats "D'you wanna join me an' some mates in the pub on Friday night, luv?"' Barely pausing for breath she added, 'Of course I'll come with you.'

'You will?' I was . . . well, staggered, sceptical and frankly a little freaked out.

'Of course and so would half the girls at this party . . . at least the single ones.' She gestured towards the packed room. 'Most of us are bored senseless by jobs we'd rather not have, mortgages that tie us down, cars we don't need that cost us a fortune, wankers that offer us horse trips across . . .' She punched me playfully in the stomach. 'Only joking. An adventure in Central Asia? Are you kidding?' She sucked on her lower lip and shrugged apologetically. 'Problem is, I can't ride.'

The effect of being picked up by a warm-hearted, desirable woman was simply miraculous. A night with her, putting at least a sexual divide between Rachel and myself, and I felt like a new man. I could suddenly see a future free of long, dark shadows and I charged towards it like a fevered bull.

Victoria and Mark both agreed that going with a stranger was a great idea, tailor-made for TV. In fact they thought it could be better and certainly more unpredictable than the original: would we get on or would we hate each other, or, more basely, would we or wouldn't we shag? All very tabloid, but, in this era of docu-soap voyeuristic TV, I could see they had a point. Jeremy took the news about Rachel in his stride and agreed wholeheartedly with the others that the new idea was excellent. His only criteria to continue to finance and supply the film's production were that we stuck to the original plan and travelled all the way from Kashgar to the Caspian Sea and that when I chose the girl 'romance had to be a possibility'. They seemed simple enough requests and, just as Mark had predicted, he was soon singing the new plan's praises. 'The important thing in films like this is to get everything on camera: the anger, the joy, the love, the pain, laughter and tears. Yes, make sure you get the emotion, that's what'll make it special.' Victoria even thought she might have a couple of friends who would be perfect for the role. Sadly, they weren't – one, though stunning, had just landed a part in a major movie, another, a new job in Paris, and a third, unbeknown to Victoria, turned out to be pregnant – but it didn't matter, there were plenty more to choose from.

Once word was out, much to my surprise offers came in from all corners. Most, as my friend from the party suggested, were women in their late twenties to early thirties, bored with London life and looking for adventure; they were between jobs, had recently split from their boyfriends, wanted to make a film, get into TV, journalism, artists or were simply inveterate travellers. There can be few better remedies for a grieving heart than having to interview a bunch of strangers of the opposite sex for such a post; sometimes I was inviting out as many as three in a day for a drink, offering them, I soon realised, quite an extraordinary dream. It had its embarrassments, too. Explaining that this was in effect an elaborate blind date often had me squirming in my seat. One twenty-one-year-old girl called Julia, who was steered my way by a friend at the publishers, was so beautiful that the whole idea of an amorous liaison seemed patently ridiculous – sad, even – and I couldn't bring myself to explain the crux of the gig. I simply laughed to myself and walked away, meekly explaining that she was too young.

There were times, however, sitting alone in that strange flat with thoughts of Rachel tormenting my mind, when I found myself questioning the sanity of the whole plan; times when all I wanted to do was close the door on the editors, agents, television executives – this corporate life in which I'd suddenly entangled myself – and hibernate for a while, lie low and lick my wounds. The ten-month episode with Rachel had affected me deeply, as deeply as anything I'd known for a very long time, and the embarrassing, sometimes facile, meetings with some of these new girls only accentuated this. After all, what was I really looking for? Another Melanie? Another Rachel? It had taken me ten years to find Rachel. What on earth made me think I'd discover someone else in less than ten weeks and gain a happy ending? And if not that, then what? There were times when I felt I'd lost control of my life, that I'd somehow allowed it to be taken over by others, for the good of others. To them this was just another project: a television programme, a series of articles, a book. To me it was my life. Did I really want to be taking off around Central Asia for months with a total stranger just because it was 'a good story'. What of all my previous thoughts of trying to settle down, find a home, grow up?

In the end, however, I decided that though it wasn't perfect – in fact I felt fairly sure it was probably insane – it was a way, perhaps the only way, of turning a nightmare into something positive, and I couldn't help fantasising that, if I did find the right girl, things might just work out.

Still, having spent two hard weeks interviewing friends of friends, workmates of friends, acquaintances of friends, acquaintances of acquaintances – even grabbing and asking a startled young woman in Regent's Park – the perfect companion still proved elusive, and time was running out. It was already mid-June, two weeks after the time Rachel and I had planned to leave. If we were to stand any chance of succeeding in the original mission of riding all the way from Kashgar to the Caspian Sea, we had to be saddled up and on the road by early August. If we left Kashgar any later, the Mountains of Heaven would be getting cold and it would be winter by the time we entered the Karakum Desert where temperatures can plummet to 30 below. Realising drastic measures were called for, one week later I found myself standing over the kitchen table, reading an advert in the travel section of the Saturday *Independent*.

'**PERSONAL AD-venture**.' My shout line leapt from the page. 'Quixotic travel writer seeks happy adventuress for horseback jaunt through Central Asia. Must be 24 to 35, intrepid, enthusiastic and happy to rough it. For more information please call . . .'

3 New Day Dawns

Sarah was the first to respond.

The phone rang while I was still drinking my coffee, staring in nervous anticipation at the newspaper before me. The advert suddenly seemed rather pathetic and desperate. It was meant to be tongue in cheek, a spoof of a lonely hearts ad. I now wondered if it read that way. I raised myself from the chair, and sheepishly made for the phone.

'Hi,' said a deep, rich voice, 'I'm calling about the advert.' I could tell in an instant the girl was smart, privately educated and from south of the Watford Gap. She also sounded young.

'Yep, great, well you've got the right number. I'm who you need to speak to. My name's Jonny.'

'I know,' she answered smoothly.

'You do?' I was taken aback. 'How come?'

'I heard through a friend of a friend – they have something to do with the television company you're working with. They told me you were placing an advert today. I'm responding. I'm really very keen to come with you.'

'Wow . . . right. So you know then that part of the deal is making a video diary of the trip, possibly for the BBC or Channel 4?' I hadn't seen the point in putting this information in the paper, as the last thing I needed was a hundred wannabe presenters wasting my time.

'I do. As a matter of fact I know quite a lot about it, and about you.' She was now sounding rather smug in a playful kind of way, teasing me slightly. Feeling nervous, I was a little put out by her apparent calm. We'd only been speaking for fifteen seconds, and she was already in complete control. 'And I bet that's not the only surprise I can give you.'

'U-huh.' I answered cautiously.

'Last night you were drinking at the Enismore Arms. Guinness, I think.'

I nearly fell off the sofa and hung up. This was too weird, even by my warped standards. Who the hell was this girl?

'Don't worry,' she added hastily, 'I'm not some screwball stalker or anything. I was there too, having a drink with a friend of mine. You might remember him, he has green hair.'

I did, he was carrying a guitar. 'Sure . . . difficult to miss. I'm afraid I can't remember who he was with though.'

'No bother, he does tend to steal the limelight.'

'Even so, how did you know who I was?'

'I've read your book, *Running with the Moon*. There's a photo on the sleeve. And by the way, I just loved it. What a fantastic adventure; it's just the kind of thing I've been longing to do. I couldn't believe it when I heard that you were looking for someone to accompany you on a similar trip. You, a writer and everything . . .'

'Really?' What idiot was it who said flattery will get you nowhere? In less than a minute, without so much as a glimpse of this girl, I'd flipped from an anxious sceptic into a drooling buffoon.

We agreed to meet the following evening, back at the Enismore Arms.

When I arrived at the pub just before six I found a bespectacled woman, in her mid-twenties, fumbling with a lock and chain and a very old bicycle. She was trying to loop the chain through the front wheel and around a set of railings, and was struggling to make the ends meet. 'Oh hi,' she said rather vaguely, and dropped the chain. 'Jonny, I'm Sarah.' As she stood to shake my hand she somehow managed to knock the bike's handlebars, sending the rusting contraption crashing to the ground. 'Shit,' she cursed, looking at the carnage, and proceeded to rub an elbow.

I bent down to help her. Close up I could see she was not beautiful, at least not in any conventional sense. Her jaw was wide and nose large, her eyes were set close together, her hair – short, dark, highlighted blonde – was as scruffy as an Irish terrier's, and her lips were round and rather fat. But I could see in an instant she had something, a kind of easy charm, a confidence of knowing exactly what she was, who she was, and being happy with it. I realised also that I was grinning like a fool.

The bike sorted out, we stood back and looked at each other. It was a sultry afternoon and she'd been cycling. Beads of sweat glistened on her top lip. Beneath her chin her neck was damp, shimmering slightly in the yellowing light, and dark patches of sweat smudged her stripy T-shirt. She pushed her glasses back up her nose and, with her hands on her hips, breathed in deeply . . . then sighed and smiled. I suddenly realised it was a lovely face, everything seemed to fit just right. 'Hello,' she said, beaming happily, and after a moment's pause leant forward and kissed my cheeks.

We walked into the pub.

'It's a very weird situation this, huh?' she said as we approached the bar. 'I mean, forget the film and all that, the trip and who you're going to take, what I mean is I know so much about you and you know nothing at all about me.'

'Having read my book, you mean?'

'Exactly.'

'Well, that book refers only to a part of my life – albeit a fairly pivotal one – and most of that is a long time ago. A great deal's happened since then. Besides, I don't give everything away.'

'Almost,' she grinned. 'Sleeping with an African prostitute, indeed!'

I smiled back. 'Do you want this job or not?'

She held up her hands in mock surrender.

'Anyway, I'm halfway through this one as well.' From her bag she pulled a copy of my second book, *For a Pagan Song*. She was evidently doing her homework.

'Well then, this session had better be largely about you.'

As it had been with Rachel, talking was easy; it was as though we already knew each other. At first, I let her tell me about herself, which she seemed happy to do. She was twenty-five, had grown up in France, and was now living in Worcestershire with her dad and step-mum and, when working, in London with her mother and step-dad. She'd travelled on her own for four months in Turkey during her gap year, had studied fine art at Edinburgh University, and after that had tried working in films but hated the fact that just to get a break you were obliged to work for nothing – 'a bloody con,' she spat angrily, 'I think it's slave labour.' She said her biggest dream was to be an explorer. 'I think I was born several centuries too late and quite probably of the wrong sex,' she lamented. 'Penis envy, daddy calls it. I don't know, I just feel trapped living in London, sucked into a deepening cycle of shitty nine-to-five jobs, predictable and drunken weekends and a computer age I don't understand and have no interest in learning.' She shrugged and lit a cigarette. 'It's a repetitive cycle – many of my friends have already fallen into it – and I don't want to. As soon as I heard about your trip I knew it was my chance. My chance to apply my . . . my . . .' – studying the glowing end of the cigarette, she concentrated hard – 'I don't know, zealous and energetic approach to life for a good reason. I want to climb mountains, ride across deserts, battle against extreme weather conditions and use all that to ultimately seek, I don't know, I suppose some sort of "spiritual fulfilment".' Having placed her cigarette in her mouth, with the first two fingers of each hand she placed the last expression in inverted commas.

'I'll raise a glass to that.'

'Don't get me wrong, I like the finer things life has to offer as well,' she said with a smile. 'Dinner at a nice restaurant, a group of friends out on a trip, lying on a Caribbean beach – not that I've ever actually done that, you understand. It's balance that's the key.' Again I agreed.

She had her own camera and had even written a video-diary proposal of her own. 'It's a great idea, really it is, to follow in the footsteps of Freya Stark, travelling all over Iran, Turkey, Afghanistan and the like.'

'That might prove a little tricky.'

Clearly on a roll, she dismissed the interruption with an irritated flick of the hand. If she knew what she was talking about she certainly had pluck. 'But will these bastard TV production companies listen, will they give you a chance? Will they hell. They're all so arrogant, stubborn, everything has got to be so formulated, so . . .' I realised I was not really listening to her, I was simply enjoying watching her talk; the enthusiastic and assured, even powerful, way she spoke was captivating: her energy, her confidence, the way she clenched her teeth and sucked in her breath between sentences, how she pushed the delicate square-rimmed specs back up her nose when they slid down too far – I've always been a sucker for girls in glasses – the way she crossed her legs and leaned across the table. The whole spectacle I found very alluring. I, too, was leaning forward, sitting on the edge of my seat, trying to get closer, eagerly nodding in response to almost everything she said, whether I agreed with her or not. 'But then of course it's not like that for you, is it?' She breathed out and visibly deflated. 'You're established, they'll listen to you.'

Flattered once more, I mumbled something about the deal with Lion TV simply being a lucky break.

'Nonsense,' she said, running a soft hand across my arm and smiling sweetly, 'you totally deserve it.'

Like a schoolboy after his first real kiss, I felt confidence rushing through my blood once more. If Rachel had left me battered and bruised, my self-confidence in tatters, there was no doubt at all that Sarah's charming words were now dressing the wounds.

She pointed to my pint. 'Drink up,' she said. 'I'll get us both another.'

She disappeared towards the bar, and I looked out of the window. As I stared vaguely into the golden light, discarded fragments of my dream leapt back into sequence and focus. Once again in my mind's eye I saw the mountain steppes, the heavenly horses, two travellers dressed as Cossacks with the first shy signs of something more than friendship in the air between them. Could it really be done, I pondered, just as I'd originally planned?

When Sarah returned from the bar we chatted about the trip, the reasons for it happening, travel, her art, my writing, life in general, and the more we talked the more I was taken with her. We seemed totally in tune. But there was something else, something much more poignant, that really drew me in. She, like myself, had experienced a defining event in her life that had coloured all subsequent moments. A few weeks before her twenty-first birthday she had been involved in a head-on car crash that had seen her scalped, unconscious and banging hard on heaven's door; she parted her hair to reveal the long, thin, purple scar running from temple to temple just behind the hairline. As so often seems to be the case with people who experience such a pivotal moment, once recovered she had vowed to do something special with her life. This journey she saw as a major step along that road.

Added to that, she told me she had ridden since she was a young girl (though by her own admission was a little rusty), she was experienced with a video camera, she was a good artist, which, I mused, would be great for illustrating a future travel book and, most importantly, she was free for the next few months.

'Yes, I've been dossing around doing this and that for too long already. It's time I got on. This is perfect.' She sat back. 'And with my boyfriend working so hard, it'll be a good time to get away.'

My heart hit my boots. 'Your boyfriend?' I tried, but failed, to sound casual.

'Oh yes, my boyfriend, he's a banker – I hardly ever see him though, he works so hard – but, yes, my boyfriend.' I couldn't tell if it was something she'd accidentally let slip or something she wanted to make clear. Either way, given my own rather fragile and hopeful state of mind, and the television company's insistence that 'romance had to be a possibility', there was no denying it represented a rather major blow.

'Oh, only I'd imagined I'd be doing this trip with a single person. To be honest, it hadn't occurred to me that someone attached would want to come.' Nervously, I took one of her cigarettes and lit up. 'Shit, I'm not sure I'd be too happy letting a girlfriend of mine go off with a stranger for four months. Does your boyfriend know you're here? Doesn't he mind?'

'Of course he knows,' she stammered defensively, also diving for a fag. 'I don't get in the way of his career, and I don't expect him to get in the way of mine.'

Lost for a relevant response, I told her that I'd have to think about it, that there were other people who I had to see. That was no lie. Before I'd gone out that evening, five more girls had answered the advert. When I returned there were seven more messages waiting.

Realising that some of the most interesting moments for a television viewer would be my initial meetings with the girls, I decided, somewhat reluctantly, that I should not meet them in the pub but in a place where I could capture the scene on film. From Lion's point of view this was, after all, supposed to be a fly-on-the-wall docu-soap about how two strangers got along on an arduous and demanding journey; the meeting and choosing were surely a crucial and interesting part of the process.

I arranged to borrow a friend's flat where this could be achieved

(I saw little point in having my demented Brixton neighbour terrify them before we'd even met), borrowed two cameras from Lion, and invited the candidates to appear, at forty-five minute intervals, the following Saturday. After many long, amusing and confusing telephone conversations – an eighteen-year-old called asking to be considered for the 'holiday', only for her hysterical mother to grab the phone and accuse me of being a dirty old perv – there were twelve candidates who agreed to the filmed interview.

The trouble was I couldn't stop thinking about Sarah. Two days after our first meeting she'd sent me a beautiful ink drawing on parchment paper of five fine horses gathering at the start of a race – a copy of a Degas apparently – with a very sweet poem written on the back. She'd called twice, principally to explain some connections she had at the British embassy in Almaty, but both these conversations had become more expansive, and we'd chatted with great enthusiasm about the journey, ourselves, and the history of Central Asia that she was already busily researching.

I was careful to stress that I had not made up my mind yet, that there were still the interviews to go through, and that she would have to take part in them. And there was still the little matter of her attachment.

Deeply confused, I asked friends for their advice. Most saw the boyfriend as a minor problem. This girl is at the beginning of her adult life, they said, what you're about to show her will blow her mind; forget the boyfriend, she soon will. As I had, they asked how anyone could leave someone they loved in order to travel for months on end with a total stranger . . . especially in circumstances such as these. All were agreed it showed either an unbelievable trust and understanding, or a fading affair sliding inexorably towards a sorry conclusion. What easier way could there possibly be to end a tired relationship than to take off and avoid its termination? But others were not so sure, especially my old friend Hen, who had now moved back to London. 'Think about it, Jonny,' she said. 'What is it this girl wants? A TV break, that's all. If you were going into this purely and simply as a business venture then that would be fine, but I don't think you are. You're too bloody trusting, that's your problem. Honestly, you're like the clichéd naïve young woman, always falling for the bastard. I warned you about Rachel' – she had, but I hadn't listened – 'and I'll warn you again here. I'm afraid you're being used.'

One thing I did realise was that I needed greater clarification on the state of her relationship, for the backers' sake if not my own. We met the following evening.

'Listen,' I said, wondering quite how I was going to approach what was obviously a delicate subject. After all, what it really boiled down to was whether or not there was a chance of a shag. 'I've tried to be as open as I can be about this, but I think you'll agree it is tricky.'

'Yes,' she said. 'I understand.' There was a cheeky smile playing on her lips; she seemed to be enjoying the situation.

'I think you're great and in every way perfect for this . . . this . . . job.' I threw up my hand, unsure what else to call it, and then cast my eyes down. 'But the problem is your boyfriend. Whilst I appreciate that it might sound a bit unreasonable, it is the reality. I've been told by the television company who are financing this project that, and I quote, "romance has to be a possibility".' I could feel myself blush and so moved on fast, without looking up, frightened of her reaction. 'Now, although I realise that it's a pretty ludicrous thing to ask of you while we're sitting here in a pub in London, having known each other just a couple of hours and given the fact that neither of us can possibly know for sure what will happen once we're up in the mountains of Kyrgyzstan,' – I just managed a peak at her face, she was nodding – 'if you *are* about to get married or something, or if your relationship is, like, very long term and secure, I feel you should let me know about it, so I can make an informed decision . . . and probably choose someone else.' I sat back feeling physically drained. 'I mean Lion TV would probably throw a fit if they knew I was thinking of taking someone with a boyfriend.'

'We don't have to tell them.'

'No, we don't, but that's not really the point. Besides, I do have a responsibility to them.' Again I stole one of her cigarettes and hastily lit up. 'Look, personally I'm not too bothered about all this.' Was that a lie or not? 'As I've explained, I've just come out of a fairly painful situation, so if nothing happens between you and me, so be it. That's fine. But two things worry me: firstly that you'll suddenly decide a week before the off that you can't face the time away from him and pull out of the trip, and secondly that you'll miss him so much while we're away it'll be a right bore for both of us.'

Her anger surprised me. 'Do you honestly think that I haven't thought about all this? Of course I have. I've thought about it bloody hard and I know what I have to do. My boyfriend is a workaholic. I hardly ever see him: he's out of the door and off to work before I get up in the morning and doesn't return until past ten, when he's so knackered all he wants to do is go to sleep. At weekends he wants to see his friends while I want to see mine; he's a banker while I want to be a traveller.' She pulled determinedly on her cigarette. 'What do you think?'

'Well . . . then I guess everything's fine.' I grinned timidly. 'Just fine.'

'Good.' The muscles in her jaw eased, transforming her mouth into a coquettish smile. She leant across the table and squeezed my hand again. 'But it was fun watching you squirm.'

4 Choices, Choices

I took a sip of coffee, and checked myself in a large gilt-framed mirror that hung above the fireplace: a little pasty around the eyes, a spot beneath my chin, but not too bad considering. Trying to explain the story to camera, I'd spent all the previous day, and many beforehand, filming myself – at home, on the street, around town – and I was beginning to feel a little pressurised and hassled by the intrusion. It was rather like making my own *Truman Show*, or being the star of another *Ed TV*. The previous evening, relieved at having completed that stage of the project, and nervous about the following day's interviews, I'd gone out and got fantastically drunk. I rather regretted it now.

Sarah was in the penultimate slot. I knew it would take someone special to beat her, but I still harboured concerns. The way she had answered my embarrassed enquiries certainly implied that her life was moving on – away from any current commitments – but taking her was a gamble. Unsure as I was, I prayed someone else would turn up and blow me away. I wasn't very hopeful.

At my side a digital video camera was perched on a tripod, its lens aiming at the sofa; behind, another pointed at the armchair opposite. I turned and paced the room, rubbing hard at my sweating palms. What on earth was I going to ask them, these twelve girls I'd never met, never seen, only spoken to for a few minutes on the telephone? What's your favourite book? Favourite film? What music are you into? A little trite, surely. What star sign are you? Like that would tell me a lot. Where have you travelled? Does that really matter? I checked the cameras, the microphones, and glanced up at the clock. The first of the girls was due to arrive in five minutes. Rob, a friend in the film business who I'd commandeered for the day, was sitting on the windowsill, casually reading the paper. Without looking up, he told me to calm down. It was all right for him: he only had to turn the cameras on and off, make some tea and coffee; he was not the one being filmed, asking the questions, choosing the companion and setting off on this crazy journey. Get it right and it could be wonderful; wrong, and a four-month trip to hell was waiting.

A moment later the doorbell rang.

Pushing my hand through my hair, I picked up the third camera and made towards the flat door. Rob had suggested I filmed the girls as they arrived, echoing *The Commitments* band-audition scene. I hurried down the stairs and stopped in the hall. Through the front door's frosted glass window I could just make out the blurred image of a short, neat figure with dark hair falling to the shoulders, framing an oval face. I took a deep breath and opened the door.

'Fiona . . .'

'Hi. Jonny.' She appeared calm, incredibly so, and smiled warmly. Her eyes were green and kind, her nose small and neat, and there was a mole just above her right lip; she was wearing an elegant black trouser suit. Then her eyes darted quickly from me to towards the camera. For a instant there was uncertainty, nervousness, insecurity . . . a desire to run? And in that single moment the reality, and the lunacy, of the situation hit me. What was I doing? *Really*, what *was* I doing? Advertising for a woman, filming the greeting, the meeting, the choosing, the discarding. In less than three weeks I would be on the other side of the world with one of these strangers – perhaps the woman now standing before me – cooped up in a small hotel room, looking for horses to buy, guides to hire, a story to write and a film to make. Suddenly, I was the one desperate to be elsewhere.

'Come in,' I said.

As I spoke, Fiona tilted her head to the side, widening her eyes in a questioning manner. I smiled uncertainly and ushered her past me into the hall, unsure if my expression had betrayed me. Though certainly attractive, she had to be five years older than me and I knew already she wouldn't be the one.

Upstairs, Rob introduced himself and showed her where to sit down. I picked up a pen and some paper, thinking that notes would help later when the time came to choose, thinking that I've got to look professional – *be professional, Jonny* – and pick the one most suited for the task. But deep down I knew that that was nonsense, that I was only kidding myself. Like any normal bloke given the chance to choose a girl for a four-month journey, I'd take the one I fancied most.

The cameras rolled.

'So,' I said unnecessarily.

'So,' she answered coyly. Having regained her composure, an easy expression now rested on her lips.

'You found the place all right then?'

'Yes.' She rocked her head from side to side in a gesture that said, *obviously*!

'Good, good.'

Sensing my nerves, Fiona continued. 'Tell me, because I am intrigued to know, what exactly is this all about?' She sat straight backed and spoke with a polished, clear voice. I found her confidence a little unnerving. 'You said on the phone that you were looking for a woman to accompany you on a journey by horse across Central Asia and that you'd be making a television programme about it.' She gestured towards a camera. 'What you didn't say is what kind of television programme you intend to make. From where I'm sitting it looks like the most glamorous, exotic *Blind Date* ever made.' She pouted slightly, for me or for the cameras I wasn't sure, and with her right hand she flicked her hair behind her ears.

'Well, more *Castaway* I think.' Hoping to hide my face should it decide to turn scarlet, I looked away and repositioned myself on the chair. 'Not that I see myself as some desperate Oliver Reed character, you understand, and I'm sure there will be many more interesting stories to film and write about besides how we're getting on, but yes, that's about the size of it: "*Castaway* on horseback".' With images of a fat-bellied and bearded Oliver Reed forcing himself on the delicious Amanda Donahoe, I tried to soften the blow. 'You know, nothing too intense; just how two strangers get on in such conditions and for such a length of time. How we piss each other off, how we make each other laugh . . .' I paused. 'It *will* be warts and all, though, which means filming everything, living under the pressure of the camera a great deal of the time . . . does that put you off?'

'No, not at all. As a matter of fact, I think it's a brilliant idea.'

We talked for a while, but it was never very fluent: I found it hard to think of questions, and her answers were rather stilted. Ironically, she was a literary agent, specialising in children's books, and now had her company in a position to run itself for a few months and was keen to have an adventure while she could. She knew little about Central Asia or the Silk Road, and hadn't travelled that much, but she didn't see this as a problem. On the contrary, she thought her naïvety might, in a filmic sense, make an interesting foil for my more experienced travelling ways. I agreed she had a point. Her favourite book was *Birdsong*, her favourite film, *Casablanca*. Both were excellent choices to my mind, but I knew it was no good and it was as much as we could do to keep the interview going for the allotted time. After thirty-five minutes I said goodbye, telling her I'd let her know the following evening. We both knew what the answer would be. It didn't feel good.

Claire had flown in from Dublin.

She had a warm, open face, shoulder-length, dark wavy hair, bright eyes and pale skin. But it wasn't her face that grabbed my attention. Her skimpy white T-shirt happily exposed a pair of well-shaped, well-sized breasts; there was no bra, so her nipples showed through. 'Hi. Hi. Jonny, yeah,' she said, while tittering anxiously. 'Wow, great, shall I come in?' I shook her hand and watched her scamper past. As she climbed the stairs I couldn't stop myself from watching her rear. In a tight pair of silver pants, it looked perfect. I decided she must be wearing a thong.

She sat down and again the cameras rolled.

'This is not some kind of joke, is it?' She folded her arms defensively across her chest, then opened them up again and held her hands in her lap. 'Only I've come a long way.'

'No, no. All completely serious, I promise you.'

'Not too serious, I hope.' She laughed – cackled, really – in a pleasant, cheeky manner and repositioned herself on the sofa. She was now out of shot, so Rob told her to return to her original position. Again I wondered what the hell I was doing.

Claire was a finance secretary with a Dublin law firm. She'd travelled – South America, the States, most of Europe – had recently split from a long-term boyfriend, wanted to do something different, something special. Once talking, she totally lost her anxiety, became natural, vivacious even. She told hilarious stories about a horrendous bout of diarrhoea in Chile, being mistakenly arrested for streetwalking in Paris, being mugged on the New York subway. I liked her. She made me laugh.

'To be honest I haven't even heard of half these countries we'll – oops, sorry, you and whoever you choose – will be travelling through. Ker-gis . . . what was it?'

'Kyrgyzstan.'

'Well, exactly, I mean who the hell's ever heard of that? I bet you can't even spell it. No, no, I'm joking. But I certainly couldn't. Now, the Silk Road, I have heard of that. Marco Polo, isn't it? The Romans, Chinese, ancient trade routes and all that?'

I then explained that as we'd be travelling through Islamic areas for much of the journey, it would be preferable to pretend to be husband and wife. 'Does that bother you?'

'No, not at all, not at all; hell, it'll be a gas. But hang on' – her eyes narrowed – 'does that mean, like, we'll have to perform husband-and-wifely duties, then?'

'What? Like doing the shopping on Saturday mornings, you mean?'

'I was thinking more in terms of consummating the relationship.'

'Not compulsory . . . an optional extra.' We both laughed. Again I felt my face blush.

Her favourite book was *A Journey to the Frontiers of Anarchy*, her favourite film, *Dreams* by Kurosawa. Regretting the fact that the next girl was already due, I let her go. Things were definitely improving and, what's more, I was starting to have fun.

Jane was next; she was short, tubby, with a shock of twisted hair, and she wouldn't stop talking. I found myself worrying about tired horses, tired ears, and was hugely relieved when she revealed she was chronically allergic to horses. I wondered why she'd bothered turning up.

Charlie was very sweet, an artist, and we chatted like old friends. Unfortunately she'd never really travelled.

Lucy was tall, attractive and, having studied in Beijing, was fluent in Mandarin and knew China like the back of her hand; however, she'd never sat on a horse.

Nicky, who lived in a caravan in the New Forest, spent all day with horses, taught riding, could even shoe them; unfortunately, I simply didn't fancy her.

Jenny couldn't take as long as four months off work.

Abby didn't show up.

And Suzanna bit my head off. She was blonde and trendy, worked in television making promos for bands and had travelled almost as much as I had. Surprising me greatly halfway through the interview, just as I had explained the personal angle of the programme, she stood up and told me bluntly that I was pathetic, that as a travel writer of some renown – I liked that bit – I should have known better than to have become tempted and corrupted by cheap and tacky tabloid TV. 'Where's Cilla Black?' she demanded. 'Hiding behind the sofa?' She told me it was beneath me. Was it, I wondered?

I hadn't time to ponder before Ella arrived. Ella, with golden hair, huge blue eyes, porcelain skin and a mouth I longed to kiss, could have leaped from the cover of a glossy magazine. She was only twenty-one.

'You see, I've just left uni and I don't want to do the normal gap-year thing like all my friends; you know, lie on a beach in Koh Phangan, smoke dope in Kullu, rave in Goa.' She dragged the place names out, as if bored by their very sound. 'I want to do something bigger, better, more interesting.' 'Don't you mind doing this with a total stranger?' Like a dangerous driver suddenly switching lanes, she swerved from one theme to another.

'Well, of course I'd much rather be doing the journey with someone I know. Better still, someone I know very well indeed, but that isn't going to happen and if this is the only way of making it happen,' – I gestured to the cameras and to her – 'then so be it. This journey, this part of the world, is somewhere I really want to travel, so whatever happens with books and films, relationships and things . . . well, that's all secondary. It's the journey I really want to make.' I sat back.

Looking at Ella I knew I was lying, but only to a degree.

As with all the others I told her about the possible dangers of the trip – marauding Kyrgyz hooligans, Tajik henchmen, wolves and wild bears – and her face turned pale. I told her that in all probability she wouldn't have a shower for weeks on end, and she shrieked out in despair. Damn, I thought . . . if only.

Two to go and I was feeling tired.

Again the doorbell rang.

This time it was Sarah.

'Hi,' she said, and looked down at a piece of paper she had crumpled in her hand. 'Is this number 18?' For the sake of the programme we were supposed to be strangers. Rather elaborately she was hamming it up for the camera. I told her it was and ushered her up the stairs.

She looked good – she was wearing a tight-fitting T-shirt and long dark skirt – and, though on camera her glasses did hide her large dark eyes, I could see on the monitor that she was photogenic. She didn't appear particularly nervous and was natural as ever.

'Last year I went with my father to the States,' she said, when I asked her about her travels. 'My father had this dream that before he died he wanted to shoot a lizard. You see, he really loves snakes and things, all kinds of reptiles. We used to have a huge python as a pet –'

'You mean shoot with a camera or shoot with a gun?' It was a story I hadn't heard.

'With a gun.'

'Loves snakes, shoots lizards?' It seemed like a rather unusual fantasy to hold.

'Yes, he's like that,' she went on, 'wonderful. He's seventy-five and does have some rather strange –'

'And you're his eldest child?'

She nodded. 'I've got a younger sister whom I'm very close to. Some people say too close to, but I think that's cool. It's . . .'

I wasn't really listening. Staring at the ceiling, I was doing some mental calculations. 'Goodness,' I burst in rudely, 'so that means your father was a father for the first time at –'

'Fifty,' she interjected.

'Yes, fifty. Wow, so there's hope for me yet.'

'Certainly. Anyway, don't interrupt.'

'He must have spoilt you rotten.' I laughed.

'Not at all. Now do you want to hear this story or not?'

'Sorry.' I held up my hands. She smiled.

'So we hired a convertible Buick and . . .'

This was one of the things I liked about Sarah. She certainly wasn't afraid to say what she felt, whether people liked it or not. I hate confrontations and will do almost anything to avoid them. The truth is I've had very little experience of them – no workplace politics to deal with, few relationship problems to confront, I haven't even shared accommodation for a while – but I was also aware that there were times when this lack of steel on my part had led to my being walked all over and taken advantage of. Perhaps Sarah's more determined stance would be good for me and the journey as a whole.

'. . . we camped out there for a week, in the desert. It was just the most beautiful place. Dad got ill, though, drinking some bad water from a creek. I didn't. I never get ill.'

'Really?'

'Yes.'

'But he still managed to shoot his lizard?'

'Oh yes. A big black and green one.' She wrinkled up her nose.

'And what about experience with a camera?' I asked. 'Have you had any?'

'Yes, I worked in film for two years, and have recently been making a short film following the crop circles in Wiltshire on horseback.'

'Blimey.' That was something else she hadn't told me. It seemed rather a bizarre thing to get up to.

Sarah liked Frank Sinatra and anything 'swing', her favourite book was *Watership Down* – either that or *The Odessa File*, she couldn't decide which – and her favourite film was *The Thomas Crown Affair*. 'But not the new one,' she stormed indignantly. 'The old one with Faye Dunaway and Steve McQueen. I ask you, why do they bother remaking one of the best films ever? There must be hundreds of good new scripts out there.' She told me she was unsure of her star sign and thought me strange for asking.

As I had done with everyone else, I explained the dangers, the hardships, the programme and the book. 'Everything we say and do can be used to tell this story,' I said, thinking I sounded like a policeman. 'It's warts and all, Sarah, good and bad, when we're happy or sad; you're sure you're OK with that?'

'Of course.'

'And you'll have to sign a contract to that effect.'

'No problem.' She leaned forward and smiled. 'I'll do anything to do this journey.'

A few minutes later my mind was thrown somewhat into confusion by the last girl. Also called Sarah, she had flown in from Spain specially for the interview. A marine biologist, she'd lived for nine months in a remote part of Borneo, for four months on the Red Sea, and had just finished a year on the Falkland Islands studying the marine life of the Antarctic Ocean. I asked her if she realised that Kashgar was furthest from the sea than any other city on the planet. She didn't, and threw her head forward, bellowing with laughter. 'How fantastic,' she cried. 'I'm sick and tired of the bloody sea.' As a contrast to the other Sarah whose clothes were simple and plain, this Sarah was trendy. Baggy jeans, tight, long-sleeved Ministry of Sound T-shirt, air-pump trainers; she was a girl you'd think more at home at a London rave than studying plankton patterns in the South China Seas. She was blonde and, like Sarah, twenty-five, full of energy and had a lovely face.

Used to well-organised expeditions, however, it wasn't long before she began to ask awkward questions about the plans for the trip: precisely which route we would be taking, how would we feed and water the horses in the desert, what would we do about the language difficulties, the police, the bureaucracy? They were all legitimate enquiries, the answers to which I did not have. Since the bust-up with Rachel I'd been rather slack about the precise arrangements and, beyond the basics, was quite poorly organised. Not that this was entirely an oversight. As usual I was planning to travel by the seat of my pants, relying on instinct and luck as much as any organised preparation. In fact I'd done very little modern-day research at all, gaining almost all my knowledge of the region, and interest in it, from history books rather than current guides. Which is just how I prefer it. But Sarah was looking for more certain guarantees, and I could not give them. Her favourite book was *Trainspotting*, her favourite film, *Star Wars*. I told her the *Star Wars* films bored me rigid. Again we laughed, but when she told me she was not overly bothered about getting the job, that a free summer would give her a chance to spend more time with her boyfriend, I knew the game was over. For better or worse, I'd made my choice.

With the last interview over, I opened a bottle of wine, filled a couple of glasses and slouched back on the sofa, utterly beat. Rob turned off the cameras and sat opposite me. Rather annoyingly, he didn't agree with my choice. He thought I'd become confused, was not thinking straight and was making the cardinal sin of trying to mix business with pleasure. 'To hell with Lion's *Castaway* idea,' he said. 'Look how the original turned out. You should be using this chance purely and simply as a means to an end, to make a good film about the Silk Road and further your career. If anything else happens, great, but if you go into it expecting, hoping, it probably won't and then it'll be a nightmare.' Like Hen, he thought Sarah had too many ulterior objectives, that all she wanted was a break in TV, probably travel writing as well, and that I'd simply fallen for her duplicitous charms.

'Her smile,' he said, drawing his eyebrows together, 'it's cunning.'

'Bollocks,' I retorted, refusing to listen. My fantasy wasn't simply about writing another book or shooting a film, whatever they might do for my career. It wasn't about setting out on another adventure, even one as spectacular as a journey along the Silk Road. Nor was it solely about finding another girl and falling head over heels in love. Ever since the idea had first started to take shape while out riding with Rachel, the beauty of it lay in the fact that it gave the opportunity to combine all of these elements into the perfect package: a romantic epic that could lead me across the mountains and deserts of Central Asia to a published book and broadcast TV documentary, and finally off into the sunset to live and love happily ever after. As Lion's head honcho had pointed out, for the sake of a good story romance had to be a possibility. I agreed and as far as that was concerned there simply was no other choice. With Sarah I could see the possibility of passion, romance, of a relationship developing, and continuing where Rachel had left me stranded; with the others I could not. It was as simple as that. Sarah fitted into my dream. She could fit into Lion's film as well.

'I can't explain it,' I sighed finally, knowing that if I tried, I'd muddle it all up and sound rather foolish. 'It just has to be her.'

'Well, it's your funeral,' replied Rob, raising his glass. 'But just remember what they say. "When man makes plans, God laughs."'

Three weeks later I found myself aboard a plane with Sarah, heading towards Asia and the complete unknown.

PART TWO
High Road to China

'I'll let you be in my dream, if I can be in yours'
Bob Dylan

5 Arranged Marriage

Despite the summer hurrying past, I had decided that we should stick to the original plan and travel to Kashgar overland from Pakistan rather than fly from London via Beijing and Urumchi. It was cheaper and simpler but, most importantly, travelling to Kashgar by any means other than the soles of your feet – with a little help from buses and vans, of course – was, to my mind, cheating. Kashgar was, after all, one of the most important staging posts on the old Silk Road, a place thousands of travellers had struggled to before us. If we'd simply flown into the airport, seeing nothing of the surrounding lands, with no sweat on our brows or tales in our hearts, I would have felt like a fraud. This way we could arrive at the start having already experienced something of the southern branch of this ancient trade route and feel . . . well, worthy.

Added to that it would give Sarah and I a chance to find our feet, both with each other and the trip in general, before the real journey started. Over the course of the past three weeks we had managed to spend some time together and, on the whole, I was pleased with my choice of partner. My mind had been thrown into something of a spin when, a week before I was due to leave, a friend had introduced a lovely-looking, *single*, girl to me, called Lucy. She'd been so keen to accompany me she'd given me an address and telephone number with the simple message, 'If it all goes wrong, call me up and I'll be on the first plane out.' I'd almost wrung the friend's neck! Still, tucking the note into my money belt – nothing wrong with taking out a little insurance – I'd pushed her from my thoughts and concentrated on Sarah. We'd run around obtaining visas, having jabs, buying equipment, testing cameras, generally preparing for the trip, but we still hardly knew each other. If we were going to get through this adventure, it was important we started to form a real friendship as soon as possible. The journey north would give us that opportunity. Therefore, I planned for us to travel by bus up the Karakoram Highway through Gilgit, Hunza and Sust, over the Khunjerab Pass into China, and on to Kashgar: a journey of about a week.

As the plane circled over Islamabad, however, I wasn't so sure how wise an idea it had been. Somewhere down there beneath the clouds was Rachel and her new man. Islamabad is a small, intimate city, especially for the expatriates, and the chances of us bumping into one another were not so small. We hadn't spoken since our painful bust-up three months earlier and, as far as I was aware, Rachel had no idea I was even doing the journey, never mind with someone else. A part of me fantasised about Rachel catching me and Sarah in some wild embrace, and that I would break off to say, 'Oh yeah, hi. *We're* just off to Central Asia, actually. Didn't *you* fuck up!' – but when I thought back to all those intimate nights we'd shared, planning our adventure along the Silk Road, I knew if I saw her I'd simply crumble.

As the plane began its final approach, my thoughts turned to Sarah. She hadn't talked much on the flight but had listened to her Walkman and watched four films. I put this down to nerves, to leaving loved ones at the airport and all that was familiar far behind. She was heading off for four months with a man she hardly knew; I figured silent nerves were only to be expected.

Within seconds of leaving the plane, both of us were drenched. The air was steamy, humid and unbelievably hot; trapped beneath murky skies and the damp ground it was the kind of heat that warms you from the inside out, like a microwave oven. It was the last day of July and the monsoon had just broken.

'We'll take a taxi to a hotel I know,' I told Sarah while waiting for our luggage. 'We can rest, have some breakfast, whatever. Then, if you want, we can go and look round the Sunday Market. It's eight o'clock now; it won't really get going until two.'

'Don't they have such a thing as air conditioning out here?' She gasped, peeling her T-shirt away from her skin.

'Not in many of the public buildings.'

'Jesus, I can hardly breathe. I'm sweating like a pig.'

She wasn't the only one. Especially when customs stopped us and checked two of my bags. From my rucksack they pulled two pairs of khaki combat trousers, my Afghan waistcoat, my boots, bandanna, and knee-length, brown suede chaps I planned to wear while riding. However, to my great relief, they got bored before examining my sponge bag. Though I had little idea what might happen between Sarah and I regarding the possibilities of a burgeoning romance, I'd figured taking a six pack of condoms was only prudent. I was pleased not to have to explain them to Sarah at this early stage of the journey.

Emerging from the arrivals hall we were immediately set upon by a mob of dishevelled taxi wallahs. 'Vhere you going?' they demanded. 'Vhat hotel? I take . . . I take . . . very cheap, very cheap.' They were mostly unshaven, with broken teeth, and smelt of local cigarettes. One tried to charge five times the normal rate, another only three. I enjoyed showing off both my knowledge of Urdu and local costs. Smiling broadly, I asked them why they imagined we should want to throw our money away. We took another driver, the first to offer the real price. Wading through the sticky air, we reached his battered Suzuki Mehran and threw the luggage in the boot. Once we were aboard, the tiny yellow trash can spluttered though the entrance gates and joined the morning traffic.

Sarah lit a cigarette, opened her window and looked around. 'Wow,' she shrieked, as we passed a brilliantly painted multicoloured Bedford truck. 'All those chains, mirrors . . . the black scarves, what are they for?'

'To ward off the evil eye.' I turned round and grinned. Again she gasped as we overtook a horse-drawn tonga. Three women in the trap were covered by *burqas*, the enveloping Islamic female garb. It was rush hour, and an army of workers was making its way into the capital from Islamabad's twin city of Rawalpindi. People hung from buses, were crammed into vans, rode motorbikes, push-bikes, and walked beside the road. Sarah laughed as four on a scooter went sailing by.

'Pakistan's small family car,' I explained with a smile.

I took the camera from its bag, held it out of the window and trained the lens back on us. In the small colour monitor I could see our smiling faces, both buzzing at the prospect of the adventure ahead.

We arrived at the Ambassador Hotel and unloaded our bags. There were quite a few; eight to be exact. Taking advice from a friend who'd ridden a horse round the world, we had two small rucksacks each, which, when strapped together, could be thrown over the horses' flanks, saddlebag style. Added to that we had my large rucksack, full of camping gear, and three bags for cameras, sound equipment, cables and tapes. I had no doubt that the luggage would prove to be a nightmare.

The Ambassador is the hotel to which I had brought my tourist groups, and the staff knew me. 'Ah, Mr Jonny, how very pleasing to see you.' Not wanting Sarah to feel left out I introduced her to them. '. . . And you too, madam,' they politely added. While Sarah inspected the double-barrel, hammer-action shotgun of the doorman – apparently it was very similar to one her father owned – I approached the desk. Sarah and I had not yet discussed sharing rooms and I was worried the situation might prove a little embarrassing. Maybe she'd want, was expecting, a room of her own. I reminded myself how ridiculous that would be. Our budget was as tight as the two-man tent we were carrying – a tent we had picked together, which we'd have to share soon enough. Still, I wasn't sure.

'A double room please, Akram,' I said in a voice loud enough for Sarah to hear and intervene if she wished. There was no protest and we climbed the stairs together. Halfway up I suddenly remembered what a 'double room' was: a room with one double bed. I'd meant to ask for a twin. As we opened the door, for the second time in under an hour I found myself preparing for an awkward moment. Again it didn't happen: we'd been given a twin. Whether Akram didn't approve of my choice of bed-fellow, or had simply made a mistake, I wasn't sure. Still, I was relieved. As I took a shower, Sarah unpacked.

When I emerged from the bathroom a few minutes later, feeling a little self-conscious with only a small white towel wrapped around my waist, she told me her camera had been stolen. She'd packed it into the side pocket of one of her two small rucksacks; it must have been taken at the airport.

Despite the fact that this was obviously a massive blow – not only would she have used it to record the trip, but also, she explained, it was important for her art: if she didn't have time to complete a picture she simply took a snap and finished it later – she was remarkably sanguine about it.

I asked room service to bring us two Cokes and we crashed out on the beds.

Two hours later we were out on the street, where Sarah was set upon by a dirty little wastrel. With a runny nose and lugubrious eyes, he pulled at her shirt sleeve. 'Rupee, rupee!' he whined.

'Go away,' Sarah said flustered. Unused to beggars, she appeared confused about what to do. Sensing Sarah was an easy touch the boys persisted, standing before her, making it hard for her to pass. 'M*aaaar*-dam, M*aaaar*-dam. Rupee, chapati . . .'

'Don't you understand,' said Sarah with growing impatience. 'I haven't got any money . . . I only have dollars.'

'I'm sure he won't mind that.'

'What?'

I gave the urchin two rupees.

We reached the market and I began to film.

A street corner that is perfectly content to remain quiet six days a week metamorphoses on the seventh into a thriving tourist bazaar. Stalls – some simply a table on the road, others carpet-walled caverns, forty-feet deep – sell everything from guidebooks, piano music and pirated computer software to rugs, furs, jewellery and woodwork. Much of it is Afghan – the old muskets, swords, helmets, coats, Buddha statues, carvings, boxes, bottles and coins – and what isn't is usually sold as such. The hawkers understand only too well the appeal and romance of the country beyond the Khyber Pass. Afghan sells, Pakistani does not.

Behind her glasses, Sarah's eyes were wide with delight. I knew it was tame, a sanitised version laid on for Westerners and affluent locals: Sarah did not. A stepping stone, I thought; wait till she sees the real thing. At first I was nervous, anxiously checking over my shoulder, expecting, dreading, to see the elegant sight of Rachel pushing through the crowd. We'd often come here, wandered around, bought this and that. But soon I relaxed and began to enjoy it. Mashooq, the Afghan knife-seller, greeted me like a brother; Isa Khan, a glass merchant from Herat, offered us tea.

And I overheard little Dost Mohammed, a twelve-year-old Kabuli topi wallah, ask Sarah, 'Is Mr Jonny take you to Peshawar?' To hell with it, I thought with a smile, this is my town too.

Sarah bought a few things – a couple of boxes, a wall hanging – thought about a silk Uzbek coat but sensibly decided to wait until we were there, and then sat down and started to draw. Within moments a crowd formed around her. Having filmed the scene I joined Isa Khan a little way back and crouched down to drink more tea and chew the fat. Only then did I realise how great an advantage it was going to be that Sarah was an artist. Not only would her talent for drawing be interesting to film, but it allowed Sarah to become involved with people. In Islamic countries where women are seldom seen or heard, this can be a problem, especially for women as forthright as Sarah. Drawing was a perfect way for her to make her mark. She was also very talented. The picture she sketched of a small Punjabi boy drew gasps of admiration from all around. Watching from afar I could see she was enjoying herself. In her black top with its mandarin collar, and combat trousers, I thought she looked fantastic.

Lying on our beds reading after an early dinner, I felt like a cigarette. Normally I hate smoking in bedrooms but I was tired after the all-night flight and couldn't be bothered to go downstairs and out into the garden. I was used to travelling on my own when such decisions are easily made. Now, I had someone else to consider. But if I asked, I worried Sarah might feel obliged to say yes or appear a bore, while secretly hating it. Talk, Jonny, said a voice in my head. It's what you've got to do on this trip. If you don't you'll never get anywhere.

'Sarah?' I leaned over in her direction. She put down her book. 'Please say if you don't like it because I really don't want to if you don't, but would you mind if I had a cigarette?'

'Ha!' she exclaimed and burst out laughing. 'That's just what I've been thinking but didn't dare ask!' She sat up and reached for her packet. 'Shall we have another little whisky as well?'

We didn't leave the next day as I had planned. Sarah needed to buy some things and though we still had the long and arduous journey through and over the Karakoram mountains before the horse trek could even begin, I figured an extra day wouldn't hurt. This was Sarah's trip as well, not only mine. If I bumped into Rachel it was just too bad.

During breakfast Sarah disappeared to call England, to check she hadn't left her camera at home. She figured if she had, she could have it sent to her. She came back into the dining room with a decidedly long face.

'Everything OK?' I asked, looking up from the paper.

'That was horrible,' she replied, and took a sip of coffee. 'All he could say was, "I thought I wasn't going to talk to you for four months." That's nice, isn't it?'

'Boyfriend?'

'Umm . . .'

'I'm sure he didn't mean anything by it.' I tried to read in her eyes whether, by telling me this, she was implying something. Reaching no conclusion, I continued rather lamely, 'Long-distance calls to girlfriends, boyfriends, can often be weird.'

'Maybe,' she said, but I could tell she wasn't really listening. She turned and gazed out of the window.

Sarah wasn't as pleased about travelling to Kashgar overland as I was. In fact she thought me mad. 'Aren't we going to be doing a big enough journey anyway without adding another thousand miles to it?' she asked, rather irritated, as we climbed into a taxi half an hour later. It was hard to deny that she had a point.

Worrying that my explanations of dodgy flight connections or cheating the travellers of the past might appear rather lame, I tried a different tack. 'Don't worry,' I told her with a smile, 'it's a beautiful journey and besides we really do need some practice with the camera equipment before the horse trek begins. If we mess things up here it won't matter so much . . . later on it might.'

This was not an empty excuse. Because it had been arranged so late in the day, this whole element of the trip was worrying. Back in England we'd been given very little tuition on either the technical side of film-making – using all the flash equipment we were now carrying (two digital video cameras, wide-angle lens, filters, a tripod, boom mikes, a radio mike, tie mikes and Christ knows what else) – or how to direct.

A Lion TV cameraman had been assigned to give us a crash course in how the equipment worked and to impart vital tips. 'The most important thing is to tell the story,' he'd told us. 'Not the overall one, that will take care of itself, but each individual tale: buying the horses, getting them shod, what happens when they go lame, and so on. And to do this you must capture the beginning, the middle and the end. It isn't like writing a book, Jonny, where you can simply remember what happens and fill in the blanks later. With film, especially documentaries, if you don't catch it while it's happening, you probably won't get it at all.' This, he told us, would mean shooting a great deal of tape. 'Of every scene you want to shoot,' he went on, 'always get a wide-angle establishing shot to show us where you are – the house, the market, the mountain trail – a medium shot to show us the characters, and then close-ups, to give details. Always shoot in sequences of three – one shot is a single, two are just two single shots, but three together make a narrative sequence – and avoid using the zoom. Use a tripod when-ever possible. Hold each shot for a minimum of ten seconds and, very importantly, with whatever action you have been filming, always get cut-aways; without them it's very hard to edit.' Added to that there were a number of rather quirky requests, such as me shaving every day – something I seldom do – so that a scene from one day could be cut with another four days later without thick stubble suddenly appearing. For the same reason we were advised to wear the same clothes as much as possible. He told us chewing gum looked silly on camera – just watch football managers – and to try not to smoke or swear too much. And on little more than that we were expected to go out and record a six-part television series. Was I worried? Certainly . . . but I was also fantastically excited by the prospect.

Having always taken a keen interest in cinema, I saw this rather grandly as my opportunity to make a film. In my mind's eye I already knew many of the shots I wanted to achieve: the horses being saddled at dawn silhouetted against the rising sun, close-ups of the stirrup irons clanking, the horses' mouths chewing the bit, steam bellowing from their quivering nostrils; pictures of nomads at their yurts, dogs howling, eagles flying; Sarah and I eating simple meals by roaring camp fires, riding through forests, across wild rivers and mountain steppes. I realised it was supposed to be a video-diary series, a factual televisual record of what actually happened on the trip, but I saw no reason why we shouldn't take a leaf out of the David Lean school of film-making, or borrow the odd Sergio Leonne idea, and try to make a film worthy of this epic adventure. After all, we were here to ride horses all the way from Kashgar to the Caspian Sea, just as travellers had done a thousand years earlier. To my romantic way of thinking it was vital that as many aspects of the journey as possible – the horses we rode, the clothes we wore, the places we stayed, the meals we ate – and hence the film we made, matched up to my golden image of the past.

Still, I knew if we were going to stand any chance of making even a half decent film or series we needed practice, and we wouldn't gain much by flying directly to Kashgar.

Sarah wasn't convinced. Her horrendous car accident had apparently left her a nervous passenger, especially on dangerous mountain roads and, though she was all for practising with the new equipment, she wondered if there was any form of compromise. Thinking about it, I explained that there was a spectacular flight over the mountains from Islamabad to Gilgit that would cut the bus journey in half. I also figured it would look rather cool in the film. Scenes from *Indiana Jones and the Temple of Doom* flashed before my eyes – a red line tracing a course across a map with the old twin-prop Focker Friendship lumbering through the air superimposed over it. This would still give us plenty of time to experiment with the film equipment and arrive in Kashgar overland. Sarah was visibly relieved. I organised the tickets.

We spent the rest of the day wandering the shops, market and various bazaars for Sarah who wanted to buy more stuff – pashminas for her mother and sister, something Afghan for her dad – then packing them up and sending them from the post office. She also wanted to have a *shalwar kameez* – traditional cotton trousers and long shirt – made up. But that wasn't all.

'Jonny.' She grinned, sheepishly pulling at my arm as we left the tailors. 'I've got to buy some knickers. Just normal, everyday knickers. Stupidly, I forgot to pack any.'

'Forgot to pack any?' I was astonished.

'I know it's ridiculous but in England I seldom wear them. Especially when it's hot.' With the summer sun once again dampening her blouse, it was a comment that had me twitching. 'I find them so . . . so . . .' She left the sentence hanging.

'Claustrophobic?'

'Exactly.'

'I'm sure it won't be a problem.'

It was, though. Trudging through the slimy heat from one boutique to another, examining every kind of undergarment the city had to offer, soon calmed whatever ardour might have rushed through my blood. It would seem Islamabad's wealthy were very into orange lace, which was not exactly what was required for a four-month horse trek. In the end Sarah had to settle for four pairs of black, high-sided, matronly pants. She wasn't the only one who was disappointed.

The plane was cancelled – too much cloud for the twin-prop warhorse to negotiate safely the Karakoram's mighty peaks – leaving us no choice but to take the bus. Even this was not problem free. At the city's main bus stand a sour-faced Punjabi told us that the daily coach to Gilgit had been cancelled – its clutch plate needed replacing. Squeezed for information, he reluctantly informed us that the best we could do was take a minibus to Bisham, 300 kilometres up the Karakoram Highway, stay the night there and continue on to Gilgit in the morning. A journey that would have taken forty minutes by plane would now stretch through more than forty uncomfortable hours.

The minibus was almost full, with seats free only on the bonecrunching bench at the rear. Having secured the luggage on the roof rack, we scrambled aboard and soon found ourselves out of town and on the main road, thundering north towards the hills. Crammed pleasantly close, legs and arms pressed tight together, enjoying the scenery, the atmosphere and each other, things seemed fine to me. Whatever reservations Sarah might have had about travelling by road she seemed to have left in the capital. I could tell she was enjoying herself.

'Please be excusing me,' said a man two seats in front a couple of hours into the journey, 'but is this woman your wife?'

The question took me by surprise, and I glanced at Sarah a little uneasily. Back in England we'd decided it would be best to travel as a married couple while in remote Islamic areas, but now that we were in tourist-friendly Pakistan I was unsure how to respond. To answer in the affirmative might seem presumptuous and cocky; in the negative, and it could imply that things weren't going too well.

Sensing my momentary confusion Sarah slipped her arm through mine, faced the man with a defiant and happy grin and said, 'Yes, I am his wife.'

I straightened my back, puffed out my chest and smiled broadly, foolishly feeling rather proud.

'Then you are being a most fortunate man.' Our fellow traveller continued addressing me. In his hand he held one of Sarah's art books that had been handed round. The entire minibus had taken a look, and all had been suitably impressed. 'Your wife is actually not only very beautiful, she is also being quite talented. Allah be praised. May I please be lending your pen?'

After a moment's confusion, Sarah handed him one and I looked out of the window. Beyond Manshera, we were now well into Hazara district and the foothills of the mighty Karakoram – or black rock – mountain range that would carry us into China. Majestic pines clung to craggy cliffs, split by wandering terraces that climbed like steps towards a distant sky. Small mud homes, some raised on stilts, defied gravity as they hung precariously, one on top of another, on the hillsides. Again Sarah folded her arm through mine, and pressed more tightly to me. It was hot and sticky in the crowded van. Her skin was tanned and sweat glistened in her cleavage. Her hair was warm and fine, with a musty fragrance, and I was sorely tempted to rest my head on hers. Instead I turned away, forcing myself not to rush in. There'd be plenty of time for that.

'They're all so polite . . . and kind,' Sarah said, clearly flattered by the man's words.

'Let's wait and see what he writes in your book.'

'No, I mean everyone's just been so friendly to me. Here, in Islamabad.'

'That's only because of your husband. Best stick close to me.'

'Yeah, yeah . . .'

With a sheepish grin, eyes lowered, the man handed back the art book to Sarah. On the opening page, next to the picture of the small Punjabi boy in Raja Bazaar, was written: 'In his most merciful way, Allah has blessed and praised you both with beauty and joy, freedom and love. May He protect you on your travels.'

Had He? I wondered. Only time would tell.

As we climbed higher into the mountains the weather turned; the clouds descended and rain began to fall. At a *chaikhana* – or tea house – two lads offered Sarah and I their seats at the front of the bus. With much gratitude, Sarah jumped at it. As the vehicle wove its way round the savage bends, the cliff edge leading hundreds of feet to the river below, she held my arm, then tucked her feet up under my legs, closed her eyes and dropped her head onto my shoulder. I felt strong, in control, helpful to her, but also confused. Could her reaction really just be a result of her accident? Was she just scared?

Behind us our fellow passengers were traders and farmers but there were also two newly wed couples on their way to Hunza to take their honeymoon. One of the grooms, whose name was Ahmed Riaz, told us their marriage had been arranged. His family elders had decided that at the age of twenty-four it was time for him to marry. Word had gone out and a suitable girl found. They had met and spent a few hours together before making up their minds. Coming from different towns, they hadn't known each others' family or friends. But, despite this, both couples seemed to be enjoying the situation. Though coy at first, the brides beneath their veils eventually smiled and one traded rings with Sarah. Unfortunately Sarah didn't realise that the bride meant the exchange to be for keeps – as is the local custom – and it was an embarrassing moment undoing the swap.

As we drove on, it occurred to me how similar our situations were. None of us really knew or understood anything about our partners. All six of us were travelling in the dark. I smiled to myself, pondering just how ironic life can be. The last time I had had a wife it had also been a journey through the unknown.

For two years after Melanie's death I wandered aimlessly along, consumed by heartache and grief, with little purpose and even less understanding. But eventually waking to the knowledge that little was to be gained by wallowing in a bog of self-pity, I pulled myself together and forced myself to look forward; if the world of marriage and kids was to be denied me then I'd simply have to go and find myself something new. So I bought a motorbike, packed my bags and headed south towards Africa.

Amazingly, halfway across the Sahara at a small hotel, I met and fell in love with a young Algerian girl. Amel was lively and vivacious and very beautiful. And though after only three days I had to leave her – she had neither the passport nor visas to accompany me – the more I battled my way around that harrowing continent, the more I saw in her my salvation. I suppose a part of my deranged mind felt that by taking Melanie's life, the gods, fate, whatever, had stolen something so sacred from me that they owed me. And if I was brave enough, maybe reckless enough, to go out alone and meet the unique hazards they placed before me on the long and lonely African roads, perhaps it would be enough to earn that reward. If Africa was the challenge, Amel was the prize.

The reality of course was that Amel was a girl with her own ideas, her own fantasies and fears, and not simply a bandage with which to strap my broken dreams. In addition, she lived in Algeria and I lived in England, she was a Muslim and I was Christian, she spoke no English, while the full expanse of my Arabic began and ended with 'hello' and 'goodbye'. We communicated in limited French. It could hardly have been more ridiculous.

Still, not one to be deterred by such details, more than a year after we'd first met, and two months after spending a wonderful week together in Tuscany, I flew to Algeria to see her knowing that only two courses of action lay open to me: either to propose to her or to give her up for good. Which really left only one. How could I turn my back on her? To do so would have been to stick a finger up at the gods and possible redemption.

Amel arrived in England, much to my surprise, chaperoned by her father; apparently it was their custom to deliver the daughter to the intended groom. Driving home to a small cottage in rural Sussex – a place I'd borrowed to write my first book – I couldn't help wondering what on earth I'd done. In the front and rear of my 2CV, which spluttered and coughed as though in protest, I carried two people who I really didn't know and could hardly communicate with. At home that night I cooked them a special meal of roast lamb; they couldn't eat it, it wasn't *halal*. Amel slept with her father.

When her father left, things didn't improve. For most of the day, terrified by what I'd landed us in, I hid myself away writing my book while Amel sat in the living room watching television programmes she couldn't understand. In a cowardly way, I guess I hoped that if I ignored the problem it would simply go away, that as the magic between us seemed to have vanished just as mysteriously as it had appeared, Amel would just go home.

But it wasn't quite so simple. In Algeria the vicious civil war that would, in time, cost the lives of some 100,000 people, had just erupted in a orgy of bloodletting. Muslims were killing Muslims, slitting each other's throats, blowing each other up with car bombs, setting fire to their neighbours' homes, even cooking enemies' babies in electric ovens and hammering nails into their women's heads. Why? Who knows . . . but the excuses given were that people, families, whole villages, were simply not 'righteous' enough. It would have been unthinkable to have sent Amel back into this maelstrom of sectarian violence. She was now a girl who'd been abroad to the West, was known to have lived with a Christian man; if she returned she would be seen by many as someone who had brought shame upon her family and her religion. It's no exaggeration to say that to have sent her back would almost certainly have been to sign her death warrant.

With this knowledge and the belated realisation of the genuine responsibility I had towards Amel, we both pledged to try again and moved to my parents' farm in Lincolnshire where Amel could work running a 'pick your own' strawberry field and I could continue to write. And, for a little while at least, things did improve. But deep down we both knew we were living a sham and so finally, nine months after Amel moved to England, we finally split up.

Very bravely, Amel gained a job working as a nanny in London and began to find her own life. Still, she was not out of the woods yet. Her visa was running out, and unless she could claim political asylum by proving categorically that her life was in danger should she return home – with the government's record on such matters, a challenge we considered too risky – there was only one option left that would allow her to remain in the country: marriage. So at Wandsworth Town Hall on a cold January afternoon, to the music of Monty Python's *Always Look on the Bright Side of Life*, we tied the matrimonial knot.

Like any other couple in such a situation we had to go through the whole 'green card' routine, but being at least nominally genuine we passed without any bother. A year later Amel became a citizen of Britain and, far more importantly, safe. Shortly after, still spinning slightly from the whole experience, I fled to India to follow the trail to Kafiristan, while Amel stayed put in London. Where she still is. After our divorce came through she married a lovely Frenchman and they now have two beautiful daughters.

My story was still waiting for the happy ending.

Just before dusk we arrived in Bisham, where a granite sky hung low above the town. The rain had just stopped and the broken streets were muddy. Located on a natural junction between Dir and Gilgit, Bisham is a strategically important and conservative town. Hook-nosed men with sharp eyes and long beards wander the streets carrying guns. The shops sell locally made Kalashnikovs, shotguns, repeating pistols and pen guns. Women stay inside. As we alighted from the minibus, I advised Sarah to cover the *shalwar kameez* that she was wearing with a *dupatta*, or thin cotton modesty veil, that she'd bought in the capital. Most *shalwar kameez* are as sexy as potato sacks, which is precisely the point. Not Sarah's. She'd persuaded the Islamabad tailor to cut the mandarin-collared, knee-length shirt tight around her chest and rear, hugging her slender waist. It clung to her perfectly, showing off her shapely figure. I realised the purpose of the clothing had somewhat been lost but I didn't care; she looked fantastic.

We entered the hotel where the minibus had stopped. Behind a desk a middle-aged man and a young boy used greasy chapatis to scoop curry from a metal bowl. Chewing hard, they watched us approach.

'I'd like a room, please.'

The man grunted, nodded to the boy and indicated a key. 'Panj,' he said, his mouth still working like a cement mixer.

The young boy sucked his fingers, wiped his hands on his *shalwar* trousers and picked up the key to room number five. As he led the way down the hall and up a flight of stairs I noticed he had a crippled right leg and walked with a limp.

The room was shabby, with two single beds separated by a side table. Paint was peeling off the walls, cobwebs hung from the ceiling fan, a torn curtain had fallen to the floor. It was gloomy and damp, musty with the smell of stagnant water. The boy turned on the fluorescent strip light, and the room began to glow.

'Is this okay?' I asked Sarah anxiously. I knew there was nothing better in town. Tourists rarely stop in Bisham, and if they do it's only for a night.

'Of course. It's fine.' She threw her two small rucksacks onto the floor and sat down on the bed. It creaked in protest. She checked the sheets and turned up her nose. 'But I think I'll use my sleeping bag.'

Before the boy left I asked him if he knew what time a bus would leave for Gilgit in the morning.

'The buses come through around six o'clock,' he answered in excellent English. 'You will be getting a seat on one.'

We both lay down and read, but I found it hard to concentrate and watched Sarah out of the corner of my eye. Softly biting her lower lip, she now seemed far away, lost in whatever world to which her book had taken her; she couldn't have been thinking of me, but it hadn't seemed that way earlier in the day. Squashed onto the back seat of the minibus she'd been so tactile, holding my arm, resting her head on my shoulder, pushing her leg tight against my own. And the eager way she'd jumped in to inform the bus passengers that I was her husband, that we'd been married two years, that we had no kids but might do in the future . . . it was all way beyond what had been called for. Had she just been having fun, acting a part, playing a game, or was there something more?

Back in England, I had tried to do what Rob had suggested – treat the adventure as a business undertaking – and had pushed thoughts of romance to the back of my mind and concentrated on planning the journey. But what did I feel now? And how did she feel? Was I reading too much into Sarah's actions? Possibly, as a young woman setting out for the first time into the wilds of

Central Asia, she was simply seeking reassurance, resting her anxiety as well as her head on my shoulders. Perhaps being tactile and affectionate was purely an innocent part of a sweet and naïve character; conceivably she was just a very nervous passenger. But if not? If she was coming on to me in a romantic way, what then? I turned back to my book and smiled to myself. One thing I knew, I had plenty of time to find out.

6 Written in the Stars

Gilgit appeared just before dusk.

Having collected our belongings and struggled across the road, we checked into the Madina Hotel. Our small room looked stark, hollow and characterless. Beside the beds the mottled walls were peppered brown with squashed insects, the linoleum floor was cracked and turned up at the corners, and the window wouldn't open. It was not exactly cosy, and we soon set out to explore the town.

Surrounded by a dark and barren girdle of mountains, Gilgit bears a sense of oppression. As the population is multisecular – made up of Sunnis, Shias and Ismailis – there are often disturbances which occasionally escalate into full-scale street battles. Consequently, there is a large police presence which does nothing to improve the tense atmosphere. Added to that there's nothing much to see or do. The bazaar is simply a row of low wooden shacks stuffed with cheap and tacky Chinese goods; there are few decent hotels and even fewer good restaurants. For the traveller, it is now, as it has always been, simply a stopping-off point on the long road to China.

Walking down the main street we passed a low white bungalow. Constructed in the early 1870s, it was home to the first British political officer – Algenon Durrant – when Gilgit carried the title of the empire's furthest outpost.

'Can you imagine,' I asked Sarah, 'being stuck up here, on your own – nothing but a few wolves and bands of wild cut-throats for company – for three or four years at a time? The only way out is a six-week hike over the mountains to Srinagar, and from there another long journey to Delhi, Bombay and home. There was no telegraph either. All news of the outside world had to come by runner.'

'Bliss,' said Sarah, and defiantly raised her chin. Noticing my questioning expression, she continued a little more cautiously. 'Well, perhaps not bliss. I realise it would be hard, but wouldn't you like to have lived in a time when you could have really explored, when places like this, like Nepal and India, Thailand and Turkey, weren't spoilt by tourism? These days they're ruined, all those backpackers on their gap years filling the beaches, the mountains, the cities, their sole purpose being finding and trying the cheapest hash, and then showing off about it.'

'Still, I don't think it was much fun then either; poor old Durrant practically went crazy,' I countered, casually. 'After being stuck up here for a while he needed three years off in England to recover. I'll lend you a book about the history of the region if you like: *The Great Game*. It's an absolute must for anyone travelling in this part of the world. You said you wished you'd been born a hundred years ago, and with a penis. That'll tell you what it was really like.'

'Thanks.' I noticed she was blushing.

'And I wouldn't worry too much about any aversion you might have for backpackers,' I told her. 'I don't think many places we'll be going will have been ruined by them. Once we leave Kashgar it'll be a surprise if we see any.' Privately, I wondered what she thought we were.

The next morning we awoke to beautifully clear skies. Two of Gilgit's three daily planes had already landed. Sarah thought we were unlucky – if we'd stayed put in Islamabad for a couple more days we would have been able to take one. I wasn't bothered: the filming was going well, as was our relationship. There was no doubt in my mind that we were starting to break through each other's reserves, and beginning to figure out what made each other tick.

Having showered and dressed, we crossed the street to the hotel's modern annexe. Under a thatched roof, sitting at wooden tables, were the town's backpacking tourists. Some were reading guide-books, two were playing chess, another writing up a diary. Two more, with near identical hair – matted into long dreadlocks – were juggling in the corner. It was obvious Sarah did not approve of either the place or the people. We ordered breakfast – two poached eggs, coffee and toast – and found a table on our own.

'Listen,' I said, while we were waiting for our order to arrive, 'after breakfast I'm going to go off and do a few things. There are some people in town I have to see, to organise our transport and stuff. I'll be back here by eleven and then we'll leave for Hunza.' I was being deliberately evasive. I wanted to surprise her with a form of transport I knew she'd love. But I was also worried. 'Will you be OK on your own?'

I felt it was a delicate balance. The last thing I wanted to do was leave her feeling vulnerable and insecure. On the other hand I didn't wish to seem patronising and imply by my concern that she couldn't handle being alone. I knew it was safe enough in the hotel; I also knew she was going to have to get used to it sooner or later. I figured this was a good place and situation to start letting her find her own feet.

'Yes, of course,' she answered. 'I'll be fine.' But I could see that behind her glasses her eyes looked sharp and pensive. She pushed a hand through her hair and stared towards the kitchen. 'I'll do a video-diary piece somewhere. Sit in the garden or something.' She huffed. 'Where's our bloody breakfast?'

Video diaries were to be an integral part of the film we were making. We had been told by Lion TV that every day we should each find some quiet place, on our own, and do a ten-minute piece to camera about how things were going. Trying to use as many settings as possible – at the barber's, while doing one's teeth, watering the horses, collecting firewood, whatever – this was where our private feelings could come out. We were supposed to talk about how we were finding the trip in general – the horses, the guides, the problems of being away from home – and of course how we were finding each other. I was aware this posed some very surreal possibilities. What happened if Sarah and I did have an affair? Were we honour-bound to film it? And if so, how exactly? What about if things went in the opposite direction? That might leave us in the strange position of having to inform a camera, and therefore a potential television audience of millions, what we felt about the other person while quite possibly not telling each other. It was fine now while everything was going so well, but we were only four days into the trip; it was unlikely to stay this way for ever. Was it fair to go behind each other's back and sneak to the camera about each other's shortcomings? I hoped we wouldn't find out.

Eventually our breakfast came. We ate quickly and left. As I wandered off up the street I noticed Sarah taking out her camera. I wondered what she'd say. It was many months later when I found out.

This is brave. I mean there aren't any women. Where are they all? This is Islamic society and I feel very out of place. As far as they think, I should be behind closed doors, getting the food ready, washing the dishes, looking after the kids . . . I guess what all women were supposed to do sixty years ago before education, achievement, chance and ambition came along. Spotting two inquisitive boys giggling behind her, she smiles nervously at the camera and holds up our room key. *Anyway, I'm going to stop now because I think it's time I got back to my hotel.*

At Waljis, Gilgit's – and Pakistan's – leading tour operator, I sat down with Mr Shah. A dapper man of around fifty years of age, I'd dealt with him on many occasions over the previous couple of years. I told him we were on our way to Kashgar and wanted to hire a jeep and driver to take us up to Hunza. From there we'd travel by public bus. After agreeing to the first point he threw me some bad news.

'The road is down.' He sat back, hands cupped behind his head and smiled sympathetically.

'Down?'

'Yes, between Tashkurgan and Kashgar the road has been swept away. Some days ago there was some terrible flooding across the border in China – you may have heard about it on the radio – hundreds have been killed, whole villages washed away. There is now no way to get from here to Kashgar.'

'But there must be some way. What are you doing with your groups? You must have groups going to Kashgar. It's peak season.'

'We have. One Dutch and another English, but we can't go overland. We have had to fly them back to Islamabad, from there to Urumchi and then on to Kashgar. The road has already been closed a week. We don't know how much longer.'

This was a disaster. It was already very late in the year to attempt the journey; a major delay could prove fatal to all our plans.

Moreover, flying all the way to Kashgar was not an option for us now: the cost would be astronomic.

'Is there no other road?'

'No. Well, not really.' He leaned forward and picked up a pen. With both hands he began to spin it like a top. 'At least not for groups. But there is a track that you might be able to take.' Now grinning broadly, he pulled a map across his desk. 'I took it some years ago. Really one of the old Silk Roads, along here from Tashkurgan' – he pointed at the map – 'via Yarkand and Yingisar. Problem is, if the main road has gone, that one probably will have gone as well. You can try. Best you take the bus to Tashkurgan and find out there.'

Sarah gasped when she saw the jeep. Metallic blue with a canvas hood and knobbly tyres, it was an old American Willis made in the 1970s. Yussef, the driver – a fat and jolly man with clear eyes and shining head – opened the passenger door and simply uttered, 'Madam'.

All packed up, we drove out of town across a huge and high suspension bridge crossing the murky waters of the Gilgit River to join the Karakoram Highway. As soon as we were running smoothly down the open road, I began to explain to Sarah the problems with the road to Kashgar, the flooding, the villages, and that our road had been washed away . . . then I stopped mid-sentence. Suddenly it dawned on me that this was a good story, precisely the kind of spontaneous news that would give our television programme energy and life. Realising we must try to capture what was obviously the beginning of an important story on camera, I told her I'd tell her later. Sarah took it well, and agreed that her reaction must be caught on tape. But I knew we both felt frustrated. Already I could see how making the film was going to interfere with the smooth and natural running of the journey. For a while we sat in silence.

But soon I began to relax again. It was a stunning day, not a breath of wind or a cloud in the sky. We both sat on the back seat, side by side, enjoying the sensation of the warm breeze caressing our faces, and watching the world go sailing by. Driving through orchards of mulberry and apricot, where the sun, flitting through the leaves, left a dappled shade on the tarmac road, we passed mud-walled homes, small fields of maize, tethered cows grazing on fodder. School children in uniform-blue *shalwar kameez* ran out, and shrieked and waved as we passed. Then we rounded a corner on a steep cliff side and the vista exploded, stretching beyond the river to stark mountains that rose far away on the other side of the valley. I took pleasure in talking about the water channels, the terraced fields, the homes, the mosques, the mountains. Sarah was enthralled by the mountains, an enthusiasm we shared.

'I know it's nothing like this but I often go walking with my father in Scotland. There's nothing in the world I prefer than the feeling of all that space. Some people say it makes you feel small, dwarfed by the scale of the world. Not me, I feel free.'

'What's the highest mountain you've ever seen?' I asked.

'Oh, I don't know . . .' She thought for a few seconds. 'I suppose something in Europe, nothing that huge.'

'Well, prepare yourself. You're about to see your first seven-thousand-plus peak. And believe me, it's a buzz.'

Knowing where it was, I asked Yussef to slow down. This was a trick I'd played on unsuspecting tourists in the past. Sometimes it's ruined by an overcast day, or clouds shrouding the distant peak. Not today. The sky was pure azure and as we rounded the corner, there, erupting before us, from the side of the road to the top of the world, was the majestic form of Mount Rakaposhi: 7,788 metres of brilliant snow and ice framed against the deep-blue sky. We stopped and climbed out. Sarah, her mouth wide open and eyes stretched in wonder, glided towards it as though in a trance. Laughing with delight, I filmed her reaction.

'It's just . . . it's just . . . my God, the most beautiful thing I've ever seen.'

'Isn't it?'

'How high?'

'Nearly 8,000 metres. Just down there,' I said, pointing up the road, 'you can see all the way from the base of the mountain to the very summit. They say that the view stretches 9,900 metres, which makes it the longest continual mountain view anywhere in the world. Imagine that, say from Hammersmith to Tower Bridge, all visible, just climbing vertically towards the heavens; isn't that incredible?'

She turned towards me. 'Can we stay here a while?'

'As long as you want.'

She wandered off to sit on a rock, a little way from the road, her mind absorbed by what nature had placed before her.

We arrived in Karimabad soon after three. Having bought a shawl at one of the shops in the centre of the village's tiny bazaar – Sarah had forgotten to bring more than her knickers from England, for some reason, she'd failed to bring a coat as well – we took the jeep up to the Eagle's Nest Hotel. A small and comfortable guest-house situated on a ledge 3,000 metres above the Hunza Valley, it really has to be one of the most spectacularly positioned hotels in the world.

Ali, the owner, was amazed to see us. As I climbed out he rushed over, leaving two other tourists for dead, and, as is the custom, threw his arms around me. In his hand was a mobile phone.

'Oh no, Ali, what's this?' I took it from him.

'It is cell phone, Mr Jonny,' he answered, regarding me as though I must be slightly dim.

'I know what it is . . . I mean, what for? It can't reach too far, surely.'

'Karimabad, Altit, even Gilgit . . . it is very useful.'

'I don't believe it.' I turned to Sarah, 'That's it, you were right, the world has gone mad. Mobile phones in the Karakoram mountains. Whatever next . . . an Internet café?'

'Soon,' said Ali.

He led us down behind the accommodation. 'Is it two rooms or one, Mr Jonny?' Ali whispered with a glint in his eye. I gave him a wink and told him one. As we emerged from between two single-storey buildings, with the front of the rooms running right and left, we found ourselves on a ledge facing the most stunning view imaginable. From our little nest high on the sheer cliff face, the whole valley tumbled away beyond the tiny homes, the laden fruit trees and giant poplars, the old fort and mud-walled mosque, to where hanging valleys were concertinaed on one another, before crashing headlong into the colossal form of Mount Rakaposhi. Here, at the southern end of the valley, there appeared to be no opening, as if this was simply a world within a world with no way in and no way out. For the second time in a few short hours, Sarah sat down thunderstruck.

Night fell like a velvet curtain. We sat side by side above the ridge, staring out into inky darkness. Far below, lights from the village twinkled in clusters, seeming to reflect the starry sky above. There was no one else around. I poured us both a whisky.

Sarah lit herself a cigarette and calmly blew out the smoke.

Nonchalantly, I pushed my chair a little closer to hers so the arms were almost touching. The space between us felt heavy, pregnant, waiting for something to happen. I wondered if it felt that way to her. In the dim orange glow coming from the light beside our bedroom, her face looked soft, warm and content.

I turned towards the heavens. 'Can you see that formation there?' I asked, pointing almost straight above. 'The three stars in a line? That's Orion's belt.' Explaining the stars! Jesus, Jonny, how clichéd are you? I groaned to myself.

'Really?' She sounded interested and leant forward to catch a better view. As she did so our arms and shoulders touched. She didn't pull away.

'Yeah, and if you look above, the two bright ones, to the left and right, those are his arms, and below you can see his feet . . . there and there.'

'That's fantastic. What else?'

'Okay, well over here is the Plough – or Big Dipper as the Americans call it – probably the most well-known star formation.' This time I pointed to the west, just above the cliffs. 'But part of that's hidden by the mountains. Over there to the east, can you see that giant "W"? That's Cassiopeia, named after a mythical queen of vanity – don't ask me how but apparently she's looking in a mirror – and if you look straight down the valley, just above the mountain tops, you can make out Ursa Major, or the great bear.' Again I traced the formation with my finger. 'Two back legs, tail and snout, got it?'

'Yes . . . wow.' We were now so close I could smell her skin.

'That represents some mortal or other in Greek legend who was seduced by Zeus and consequently was turned into a bear by his jealous wife. Or something like that.'

'That's amazing,' said Sarah, smiling, still appearing genuinely impressed. 'How do you know about these formations, constellations and things?'

'I don't know many, just a few. When I was in Africa I had so many nights lying out under the sky I bought myself a book explaining the heavens and I tried to study them. Trouble was I was usually so knackered I fell asleep before I had a chance to learn many . . .' I wondered if I was sounding like a jerk and tailed off. A satellite came to the rescue. 'Ah, quick, can you see that one there . . . the one racing by?' I pointed directly overhead and tracked the movement of a bright light far away. In doing so our faces almost collided. I moved back but let my hand rest on her shoulder. 'You know what that is?'

'No.' She pushed her glasses further up her nose and squinted. 'It looks too far off to be a plane.'

'An American star.' I grinned. 'At least that's what most of the locals call them. It's a spy satellite. I imagine we'll see quite a few on this trip: American, Russian, Chinese. That one will be heading over Afghanistan. Probably looking out for Osama bin Laden or something.'

I turned towards her again and leaned forward. Our faces were only inches apart. But to my surprise I could see her expression had changed. She looked pale, uneasy, confused. She put down her glass and pressed her hand against her stomach. I withdrew mine from her shoulder and asked if she was OK.

'I'm not sure. I . . . No, I don't think I am. My stomach's been hurting for a while now. I hoped it would go away but . . . oh damn.' Suddenly her face contorted and she doubled up in pain. 'No,' she said again, 'I really don't think I am. Shit.' A moment later she was on her feet and charging for the bathroom, slamming the door shut behind her. It wasn't enough to prevent me hearing the sound of retching. Oh dear, I thought . . . so much for that. The six pack in my sponge bag would be staying put for now at least.

By mid-morning Sarah was over the worst of her illness. She still had pains in her stomach and was forced to spend a great deal of the time on the loo, but the fever had passed and she was now managing to hold down the rehydration drinks I made for her.

Unknown to me, while lying on her bed, she did a piece to camera.

Here I am in what must be one of the most beautiful places on earth and what have I got? Diarrhoea. Five days I've lasted from Islamabad to here and it feels like someone's poking a red-hot poker into my stomach and twisting my guts at the same time. I want to be running . . . jumping from rock to rock and doing this great two and a half hour climb up the side of a glacier, but I'm stuck here in bed, running to the loo every fifteen minutes.

Understandably, she was in a foul mood when she came outside to sit in the sun.

'I should think it's simply your stomach getting adjusted,' I said, trying to cheer her up as she slouched miserably into a chair. 'It happens to most people the first time they come out here.'

'But I'm never ill.' I could see it wasn't so much the illness that was the problem, it was the fact that her pride had been dented. She felt she'd failed the first great travelling test; becoming ill so early on, to her mind, simply wasn't cool.

'I wouldn't worry about it, you're bound to be fine in a day or two. I bet you picked it up in Gilgit. The place is notorious for filthy water; it's crippled stomachs a lot tougher than yours. Besides, it's probably no bad thing to get it out of the way early on.'

'I could easily pick something up again.'

'Yes, but you probably won't.'

'How can you possibly know whether I will or won't.'

It was a silly conversation. I didn't bother to answer.

'Look at this.' she pointed towards the valley. It was another fine day, just a few wispy clouds scratching their bellies on the mountains' highest peaks. 'This is what I've dreamed of all my life. To be somewhere like this. To go walking among the hills, to see the glacier' – I'd promised to take her to Ultar Glacier, a mighty ice flow that sweeps through a canyon beyond a ridge behind the hotel – 'I haven't even the energy to paint. It doesn't seem fair.' She ground her teeth and shook her head as another spasm cramped her stomach.

I found myself in something of a dilemma: the truth was I should have been filming. I knew it, Sarah probably knew it, but it was the last thing I wanted to do. Sarah being ill was a good story. Besides the broken road – a story we still had to capture on tape – it was the first real trial of the trip. Deciding that the film was more important than Sarah's brittle temper, I took out the camera and filmed a few shots: Sarah on the balcony, Sarah contorting her face when a cramp hit, a shot of the bathroom door while Sarah groaned in pain behind it. I also filmed myself making up a rehydration mixture while explaining the story. Generally she took the unwanted intrusion well, but as I was trying to cover one more angle she snapped at me. 'Do you have to keep bloody filming . . . haven't you got enough yet?' Sheepishly, I put the camera away.

I didn't know whether to stay or go, unsure if Sarah wanted privacy or if my departure would leave her feeling abandoned. In the end I compromised and took my book to the far end of the garden from where I was clearly visible but also out of her way.

And by five she was feeling better; well enough, she thought, to take a minibus 100 kilometres north to the Pakistani frontier town of Sust the following day and, from there, the government bus over the 4,700-metre Khunjerab Pass into China. It would be a long day, but armed with Imodium and plenty of water she felt she could handle it. Which was a relief. It was important we reached Tashkurgan as quickly as possible to make whatever arrangements were necessary to get to Kashgar. If the road was passable, we'd have a chance of making it to the famous Silk Road city in time for the Sunday Market.

That decided, we went for a short walk to a rocky knoll on a high ridge above the hotel and a magnificent 360-degree view of the sweeping valley below. As the sun slid behind the mountains, to the west the eastern peaks turned flamingo pink. A shepherd, minding his flock on a ledge just below, played a flute. The sound was rich and warm, light and free, drifting like a spirit on the warm evening air. Sarah took out her crayons and began to draw the golden peaks, while I found a rock and settled down to watch as the glorious day was lost to night.

7 The Evil Eye

The bus to China had just departed.

Standing by the roadside, dust and grit stinging our eyes, we watched dispirited as the tiny red NATCO bus, racing northwards, reached the end of the valley and disappeared behind a curtain of rock. It was Saturday morning, just past eleven. If the minibus we'd been travelling in hadn't had a puncture, we'd have been on board the NATCO bus with at least a chance of making Kashgar's Sunday Market. As it was, we were stuck for the day. Leaning from the minibus, the driver shrugged, grinned and waved farewell. Then he turned sharply on the gravel track and fled back towards Hunza.

The bewildering scale of the landscape engulfed us.

At an altitude of nearly 3,000 metres the air was thin and the light clear but, besides the mountains, the river and the long, thin road, there was little to be seen. Behind us crouched the farcically named Paradise Hotel, a single-storey, breeze-block structure painted a dismal shade of yellow, with a rusting iron roof and plastic sheeting that flapped at the broken windows. In front were two boarded-up wooden shacks and a rusting car. The frontier town of Sust was out of sight two kilometres up the valley.

'Isn't there another bus?' Sarah asked, looking around despondently, shielding her face from the mounting squall. 'There must be another minibus or coach . . . something we can take. We can't stay here.' She turned miserably towards the hotel.

'No, there is nothing,' replied the short hotelier happily. 'You stay here and leave tomorrow. Is best.' He flashed an ingratiating smile, displaying a row of small black teeth. 'Is no problem, I buy bus ticket for you. We have food, mineral water . . . Coca Cola. No one else stay, just leave all.'

'How many just left?' asked Sarah.

'Twenty-three. From French and Italy.'

'Shit.'

Though mildly concerned about my partner's disconsolate mood and the potential delay to the journey, in general I was buzzing. Never having travelled further north on the Karakoram Highway than Hunza, my eyes were at last feasting on something new. The nomad in me was leaning forward on the edge of his seat, eager to discover what was here, what was out of sight round the corner, what was hidden beyond the towering hills. From now on Sarah would know as much about what was to come as I would. Standing just a few metres above the swirling torrents of the Hunza River, surrounded on all sides by the Karakoram's stark yet colourful mountain peaks, on an unknown road to China, I could hardly have been more excited.

I glanced back at Sarah.

'There's nothing for it,' I said patiently. 'We'll have to wait here, then catch the bus tomorrow.' I began to pick up our bags. 'Besides, it's probably no bad thing; it'll give you a chance to rest. Take it easy for an extra day.' In an attempt to starve whatever bug had found a home in her gut, Sarah had barely eaten for thirty-six hours.

'Shit,' she sighed dejectedly. 'What a pain up the arse.' And she followed the man towards the hotel.

The room was small, just large enough to hold its two single beds and battered chest, but it was airy with a thin wire mesh covering an open glazed window which faced the mountains and wild river. Before us on its ashen banks a group of children were playing a game of cricket. Further away a woman in a scarlet shawl was collecting firewood.

Realising we still hadn't shot the piece to camera about the broken road to Kashgar – with Sarah's illness we'd both forgotten – I set up the camera, the mike, pulled the chest out between the two beds, placed the map on that, and asked Sarah to sit on the bed next to me. Having checked the sound level and made sure that everything was in the frame, I pressed record on the remote control.

'. . . so, that's about the size of it.' I went on, rubbing my chin. 'At the moment the road's closed. Maybe there's a way round here via Yarkand and Yingisar' – with my finger I traced the route – 'but if not we'll have to wait in Tashkurgan until the road to Kashgar opens.'

Sarah feigned surprise. 'My God. You mean we could be stuck in Tashkurgan? For how long? If bridges and roads have been washed away it could take ages. Jesus!' She slapped her forehead.

'Umm,' I groaned and, pushing a hand through my hair, scratched my head uncertainly. 'He said the floods have been terrible – especially around here – killed a lot of people. But the thing is, this is the only real road there is so they'll have to fix it fast. A great deal of traffic depends on it.' I sat up and looked out of the window. 'Anyway, there's nothing we can do, just hope for the best.'

Sarah turned and followed my gaze. 'I hope so,' she said, drawing inspiration for her performance from her current mood. 'I really bloody hope so.'

The scene finished, I turned the camera off.

'That was great,' I exclaimed happily, genuinely impressed. 'Quite the little actress.' At last she smiled. 'Now, we just need a couple of close-ups.'

Sarah lay on her bed and read. Not *The Great Game*, which I'd lent her, but some royal kiss-and-tell she'd picked up at a book exchange in Gilgit. Bored by my book of other travellers' tales of Central Asia, I left to play cricket and film the kids.

When I returned, Sarah had perked up considerably. She had drawn a wonderful picture of the surrounding hills, had drunk a pot of tea and eaten a bar of chocolate. 'Why don't we walk down into Sust, have a look around?' she suggested. 'It can't take long to walk.'

The narrow road cut a path parallel to the river. Here, muddied by snow melt, it appeared thick and grey, like crude oil or mushroom soup. Beyond the swirling waters a wide valley of silt and sand, punctuated by bleached glacial moraine, stretched towards low terraces of vivid green maize and onwards to the mountains. To the right, scarred and cratered mud-coloured cliffs climbed vertically from the road. From below they appeared like the crumbling walls of some long-forgotten fortress, ravaged by grapeshot and a thousand hostile armies. Now, late in the afternoon, the sun had gone, leaving the sky a dark and heavy leaden grey: a mountain squall was rising.

Sust appeared a paradox. A frontier town like so many others, it was a lively place, carrying with it an edge of danger, of transience, of cultures and creeds colliding, of people and their possessions for ever on the move. It also felt like a stark dead end. The giant cliffs that rose all around formed a natural barrier, a seemingly impregnable wall through which the world could not pass. Forced together with no way out, humanity sat and festered.

'The end of the world,' gasped Sarah.

The town itself was shabby and grim, a strange confusion of corrugated iron, breeze-blocks, polythene and canvas. Like a set from a futuristic, post-apocalyptic movie-set – *Blade Runner* or *Mad Max* – it appeared as ephemeral and temporary as the people who frequented it. On the only road, by neglected stalls, crowds of different races mingled. Animated Punjabi merchants shouted and cried at the Uyghur traders as they tried to extract the best prices for the newly imported, much-coveted goods. Han Chinese truck drivers swapped stories with their Pathan counterparts. Locals from Hunza, Gilgit and Kashmir muscled in, attempting to conduct business of their own. Flies swarmed, goats bleated and packs of stray dogs barked; generators thumped, truck engines whined and cheap cassette decks spewed out screeching Hindi film scores. There were money changers, clearing agents, commercial traders and cargo brokers; cheap and tatty hotels, *chaikhanas*, fruit, vegetable and fresh meat stalls. And through it all cut a biting wind, whistling through the valley.

There were no women and, walking beside Sarah through the busy throng, I could sense her apprehension growing. The men were a harder, rougher breed than the tourist-friendly folk of Islamabad and Hunza, and they stared her up and down with salacious eyes. She pulled her veil over her head. It made no difference. One man, a Pathan to guess by his appearance, pushed through the crowd towards us. He had a short beard, a long nose and an angry scar running down his cheek. His eyes were cold and as sharp as flint. They were trained on Sarah. It was an evil look of pure disdain, contempt, of a pious and self-righteous man reading the heart of a fallen woman. He didn't walk to our right or left but forced his way between us.

'I guess we should tie some black ribbons in your hair,' I said, watching her reaction anxiously.

'What . . . ?'

'To ward off the evil eye.'

Sarah tried to laugh, but the nervous whine became caught in her throat. Suddenly she looked pale and shocked, her confident edge shattered.

'Not a very pleasant man, hey?' I smirked foolishly, trying the lighten the situation.

'No.' She lowered her head and watched her moving feet. 'How are we going to get back to the hotel?'

'You want to go now?'

'Yes.' She stopped and looked at me like a lost dog.

Just for a moment I wondered whether I should tell her to relax, not to worry, to sit with me and have some *chai* . . . that there was really nothing to fear. But I could see she'd had enough. Her chin was jutting forward at a strange angle, wobbling slightly; it appeared she was close to tears.

'I'm not sure,' I answered, peering round rather helplessly. 'We can either walk or try to find a minibus or something.'

Just then, through the mayhem, I spotted a bright yellow taxi. It was a large Toyota Corolla, in fine condition, just as you'd find cruising Manhattan's lower eastside. The whole place was so strange, so surreal, neither of us questioned it. We simply pushed through the crowd, jumped in and asked the driver to take us back to the hotel.

This time, when Sarah started to read her Royal shag-buster I wasn't in the least disappointed. I realised she'd had such a cultural battering, such a giant sensory overload, she probably needed to escape to a more familiar world. Having made sure she was okay, I returned to town with the camera. To my mind such places are what trips like these are made of.

From Sust the road to China wound up through a narrow valley beside the tumbling river. The canyon walls were steep and dark, streaked with golden sulphur. Mighty chutes of gravel and loose rock hung between the canyon walls; as we drove beneath them pebbles scattered across the road. By the occasional waterfall, patches of green thorn, purple lilac and lavender grew. There was little else. As dry and desolate as these mountains were there were no crops and few animals.

We were the only tourists on the coach, the rest were local merchants. Sarah's aversion to dangerous roads and drivers seemed to have abated; she neither held my arm nor shut her eyes, and kept her head a long way from my shoulder. She stared silently out of the window while I talked to a man from Gilgit, who was on his way to Kashgar to sell leather jackets to the Chinese. He told me he'd heard the road from Tashkurgan to Kashgar was being worked on, and that if not open already would be very soon. 'In Pakistan,' he said resignedly, 'government are no working good. Too much corruption, too little money. Road goes, bridge falls down . . . many months to fix. No in China. Chinese men, working men.' I was pleased to hear it.

As we reached the top of the pass the valley levelled out. With immigration and customs dealt with at Sust and Tashkurgan, crossing the actual frontier was a formality. By a small stone hut a bored sentry raised a thin metal pole letting us out of Pakistan, and a few kilometres further on a young Chinese officer did the same, allowing us entry to his fabled land. Once again I felt a surge of excitement build in my chest. I moved to the front seat, next to the driver, took out the camera and filmed scenes from the window.

The road cut a path through a wide flat plain. Far away on either side low hills climbed; not the spectacular razor-tipped peaks of the Karakoram – we'd left those far behind – these were the rough and desolate High Pamirs. Here rough grass grew, feeding small herds of sheep and goats. Sarah spotted eagles spiralling high above. At this altitude there were no fixed dwellings, just yurts – cylindrical nomadic tents – which were moved to the high pastures for the summer grazing there. Close to the road, we passed an encampment of three such abodes. A group of men, women, two Bactrian camels and a small herd of horses gathered nearby. The horses were small, long-haired, scraggy-looking animals, mostly chestnut in colour with large heads and short legs. The men, dressed incongruously in tatty suits, round fur hats and black plastic boots, had weathered faces and slanted eyes. The women were wrapped in scarlet shawls and carried their young across their backs. It was a bleak land, harsh and severe. Though the sun still shone, it began to rain.

We arrived in Tashkurgan almost before we knew it. From the joyless plains we passed directly through a high steel gate, along-side a perimeter fence, and up to a large grey hangar. Uniformed sentries appeared as we disembarked, and they directed us towards the structure that obviously housed customs and immigration. As we were approaching the entrance an unctuous Pakistani sidled up to Sarah, held out a bag containing three cartons of Marlboro Lights, and an insipid smile broke across his face. 'Madam,' he said obsequiously, 'would you please be carrying these through the customs for me. I have six packets. We are only allowed to be taking three.'

Sarah looked confused but, not wishing to offend, agreed.

I was angry; not with Sarah but with the man. For a Muslim Pakistani to ask a woman for a favour, of this kind or any other, without first checking with the man accompanying her, is totally out of order. If the situation had been reversed all hell would have broken loose. But that was not all. To carry packages for unknown travellers across borders like this is not very smart. Afghan hashish, opium and refined heroin are constantly being moved this way and the sentence for smuggling drugs in China is death. I took the cigarettes from her and gave them back to the man.

Having passed easily through the formalities, we climbed into an old orange Lada with a broken windscreen and ripped plastic seats. The car had no ignition and it was only thanks to a push from the driver's mate that it spluttered into life. The driver spoke no English. Not that it mattered. We'd been told in Sust there was only one hotel in town, the Pamir, and we rolled out of the compound and onto a prefabricated concrete road towards it. Almost at once he turned right onto another wide avenue lined by pale poplars and shabby, two-storey concrete buildings. Telegraph poles carried loud speakers out of which metallic party rhetoric crackled. Red flags, faded and torn, fluttered on the breeze, and men in flat caps and Mao suits rode bicycles beside us, leaving us in no doubt that we were now in Communist China. Not that the men all looked Chinese. Far from it, they mainly had the appearance of Turks.

Xinjiang – meaning 'the new province' – is predominantly the home of the Uyghur people, a Turkic race that migrated from Central Siberia, and who populated Kashgar and the surrounding area during the early days of the Silk Road. Bar the odd sacking of their famous caravan city by the White Huns and Chinese, by virtue of being placed behind the protective shield of the Tian Shan mountains, compared to other races in the region, the Uyghuis of Kashgar enjoyed a relatively calm existence, managing to escape entirely from the mayhem caused by Genghis Khan, Tamerlane and a fistful of other Central Asian adventurers. They even managed to escape the murderous advances of the Imperial Russians in the nineteenth century during the Great Game as they swept across the continent in a supposed bid to wrest the Indian Raj from the British. It was only when the Bolsheviks started creating intrigue in the 1920s that Peking became seriously interested in the region and, worried as they were by the spread of communism, they annexed the region in 1935. Ironically, of course, only fourteen years later China itself turned to the doctrines of Marx. But it wasn't until the 1950s, during Mao's Great Leap Forward, that the face of Xinjiang changed for ever. Worried about this rebellious province on his empire's western flank, Chairman Mao flooded the region with loyal Han party workers from the east. At the turn of the nineteenth century the Han Chinese made up less than one per cent of the province's population. At the end of the twentieth it accounted for over thirty.

But it wasn't the men that I found so surprising: it was the women. Walking what appeared to be the town's main street in small groups, they were everywhere, both the indigenous Muslim Uyghurs and the Han Chinese. As befits their religion, most of the Uyghurs covered their heads in scarves, donned plain jackets, modest knee-length skirts, tights and knitted shawls. The Han Chinese didn't. Strutting their stuff like catwalk models, they proudly flaunted their pert and slender figures in tight, skimpy dresses. With their silky hair and pretty faces, they oozed sexual confidence. Having just travelled from an Islamic land, I was slightly shocked.

But I was also very excited. For the first time in three years I was experiencing an entirely new environment and a very different culture. I couldn't talk or understand any of the language, couldn't read the strange new script that hung above the various shops and civic buildings. I didn't yet know the correct exchange rates, had little clue of the customs, and I was largely ignorant of the political situation. I didn't know the laws, protocol, or even what to eat. Now north of the Karakoram I was a dry and brittle sponge ready to suck up all that I could; it was exactly how I liked it.

Nearing the end of the street the driver turned under an arch and into another compound. It looked nothing like a hotel – more a derelict institution for the criminally insane. Before us was a huge, grey, concrete structure, four storeys high and a block wide. The windows were painted black, the walls were cracked, the main door was locked and bolted. Above the entrance was a Chinese motif. One of the letters had fallen off. 'My God,' said Sarah, clearly unimpressed, 'we can't be staying here.'

We weren't. The car immediately swung sharply to the left, away from the crumbling warehouse, and carried us up to the hotel's entrance. It didn't look much better. We alighted and paid the driver 15 yuan, about $2.

Filming, we walked side by side up a flight of shallow steps and through the doorway. On the camera's monitor I could see a large rectangular hall, painted pale blue, with broad white pillars, a faded burgundy carpet and a long wooden reception desk running the length of the far wall. Behind it sat a young Turkish-looking man in a navy shirt and white tie. Next to him stood a thin woman with an angled face, wearing a sky-blue suit and what looked like a conical fez and nylon veil. Behind them, fixed to the wall, were four large clocks depicting the time in Islamabad, Paris, Kashgar and Beijing. Glancing up, I noticed Beijing was two hours ahead of Xinjiang. I wasn't surprised. Here, we were as close to Europe as we were to the Chinese capital. Having reached the desk, I propped the camera, pointing at the man, on the plastic surface and asked for a room.

Not in the least bit fazed by being filmed, he agreed and asked us to fill out two forms. His dark eyes were warm and friendly and darted between the two of us. In good English he also told us that although the road to Kashgar was still bad – closed to through traffic – if we were prepared to take a bus as far as we could, he felt certain we would then be able to walk a few kilo-metres along the damaged road, and find another form of trans-port on the other side to take us to Kashgar. Some other tourists had left that morning, he told us, and they had not returned. It was quite a relief. Having received our room receipt, we turned to leave.

But unfortunately, with our filmic travels, it was not quite so simple. To make the scene work, we needed more shots. First we left the camera on the desk, but this time had it pointing towards the entrance. Then, lugging our rucksacks over our shoulders, we rushed out and entered again. Having done that, just for good measure, we did it a third time while I held out the camera and pointed it at us looking open-eyed at the scene before us. The arrival scene shot, I then had to film the all important cut-aways: shots of the clocks, the telephone, the room rates, the girl's watch – which showed a picture of Leonardo Di Caprio and Kate Winslet and the doomed *Titanic* on its face. Finally, after ten rather embar-rassing minutes – a group of French tourists were watching us, thinking, I suspected, that we were either hugely vain or rather mad – we were finished. I was beginning to see what a bore filming was going to be.

Our room was in the cheap block on the other side of the concrete concourse. Again I felt that to tell the whole story prop-erly we must keep filming. 'To film half a story is to get no story at all': the words of Lion's cameraman rang in my ear.

We entered through two swing doors. Here there was no carpet, just cracked tiles leading down a dirty whitewashed corridor to where a frail-looking woman was sitting by a desk. In Western China, as in Russia and all the former Soviet states, you are not provided with your own room key. On every floor of each hotel a woman, known in Russia as a *dejournaya*, holds the keys to each room and allows you access whenever you want. I suppose it is simply a way of employing more people. Struggling under all our bags, we reached the woman and handed her the receipt. With an embarrassed smile she led us into the suite.

The first room was large and bare and in a terrible state. Flowery, flock wallpaper hung from the walls, bare light bulbs swung from exposed wires, and paint was splashed across the concrete floor like a Jackson Pollock canvas. To the left was a small bathroom. The basin had come away from the wall, the pale blue tub was stained and chipped. At reception the man had warned us there was no hot water in the cheaper rooms; he hadn't told us what water there was would be thick and brown. Through a bright-pink crushed-velvet curtain was the sleeping area. Two beds on opposite sides of the room; one under the only window, the other against the wall. Between was a desk with a large television sitting on it. I plugged it in – imagining perhaps BBC World, CNN? – it didn't work.

'Jesus,' said Sarah, sitting on the bed beside the window, disappearing in a cloud of dust. She began to laugh. It was so weird it was wonderful.

Worried the electricity might not last long, soon after six we hurried over to the main hall and into the dining room to eat. It was a quirky place, the size of a gymnasium, with large round tables that revolved on a central axis and shabby orange drapes. We sat down in the middle of the room by a central statue of a rearing dragon. The menu was huge and we understood none of it. It didn't matter. A young waitress made it perfectly clear that most of the dishes were unavailable. She told us to have rice, stir-fried vegetables and soup of some kind. We also ordered two beers, which she brought over at once.

In the far corner of the room the French group were finishing their meal and talking loudly. We understood from what we overheard that they'd been skiing on Mustang Ata, Xinjiang's highest mountain, and tomorrow were going home. One of them, a young man with a thick thatch of ginger hair, came over and asked what we'd been filming earlier. Sarah told him about the trip, the book and television programme we were making. 'Yes,' she repeated loudly, 'we're riding horses from Kashgar to the Caspian Sea.' It was hard to tell who was more impressed.

Sarah seemed to have perked up considerably. Gone was the quiet, rather long-faced reluctant traveller who had accompanied me for the past forty-eight hours. As she chatted happily to the French guy, it seemed she was returning to her old self. Hunza, I realised, had obviously taken its toll physically, maybe mentally as well, and the Pathan in Sust had really dented her confidence. Perhaps having faced the first real challenge of the trip, and come through it, she'd find things a little easier. It was going to be hard, she knew that now, but she also knew that she could handle it. I was delighted. We now had the chance to make up for lost time and become better acquainted and, I hoped, we'd soon be talking and laughing as we had done previously.

The Frenchman departed with the rest of his group, leaving us alone.

'So,' I said, stretching a little, smiling pleasantly in her direction. 'Strange place, huh?'

Sarah picked up her book. 'Would you mind if I read?'

I was thrown completely and was unsure how to respond. 'Would I mind?' I stuttered foolishly, feeling my face begin to burn. 'No, no . . . of course not. Go right ahead.' I looked away towards the ridiculous plastic dragon.

Did I mind? I tried to keep calm and told myself that if Sarah wanted to read, why shouldn't she? Just because I wanted to talk, so what? The trouble was, I did mind; I minded very much. Why did she want to read now, when only a moment ago she'd been happy to chat to the Frenchman? I found it hard not to take it personally.

I sat fiddling with my chopsticks. Once again the book she was reading started to irritate me. How could anyone from England be sitting here, in this strange restaurant, in this quirky town, on the edge of the Pamir mountains, deep in the heart of High Asia, and actually want to read about the sexual conquests of Major Ferguson? When the meal came we ate in silence.

Once I'd finished – with no one to talk to it didn't take long – I thought, to hell with this. Sarah was safe, still had half a beer left, and appeared content, so with few feelings of either worry or guilt I decided to leave. If she gained more enjoyment out of a crap book than she did from my company, she was welcome to it.

'If you're all right,' I said politely, 'I'm going to go and have a look around town. See what this place has to offer. I won't be long.'

'Sure . . .' she said, looking up from the book.

I threw my paper napkin onto the table and left.

There was no moon and the night was dark. On the town's only street a few people were milling around, sitting in shop doorways, standing by smouldering kebab stands, playing cards beneath the street lamps. There were a few civilian men – both Han Chinese and Uyghur – but most were young Han conscript soldiers. With its close proximity to the borders of five countries – Afghanistan, India, Pakistan, Tajikistan and Kyrgyzstan – Tashkurgan is a garrison town of huge importance. Many of the soldiers were little more than kids, appearing puny and weak, with spots on their chins and wispy hair on their top lips. Their uniforms seemed to match: thin, made of cheap material, they hung awkwardly over their gangly shoulders. Still, they were friendly enough; some even called out to me, 'Err-oh, M*iss*-ter.'

But it was the girls I couldn't take my eyes off. For the last four years the majority of my travels had been in Islamic countries with strict morals and conservative dress codes. In such places you seldom see women, never mind have the chance to enjoy their beauty. But the Han girls here were stunning. What's more it seemed they knew it and understood only too well the effect they were having on this sad foreigner. As I passed by two young girls – both in their late teens, wearing figure-hugging dresses and wedge shoes – they turned their eyes on me. Though I smiled at them, their expressions remained aloof and regal and they turned their heads away with mocking disdain. I didn't have too long to fret, however, for before me, standing in a doorway, silhouetted by a soft yellow light, was an apparition. A thin white dress hugged the exquisite curves of a delicious body. Dark hair fell to below the shoulders. Her hands rested with attitude on her slender hips. The light behind her clearly defined every nook and cranny of her frame; for all the modesty her clothes provided, she might just as well have been naked. What was more extraordinary was that she was beckoning to me. Just for a moment I found myself looking over my shoulder, checking it really was me to whom she was gesturing. I wondered what on earth she could want. Though this was a border town I thought it unlikely that she was a working girl; the scene just wasn't right. As I approached I could just make out her face; a small flat nose, rounded chin, skin that was clear and looked wonderfully soft. There was no hint of humour on her long, thin lips. She looked as cool and serious as a seasoned assassin. Her eyes were lost in the shadows.

'Come,' she said, and beckoned again with her finger.

Sliding back into the building she revealed a pool hall. The three tables, lined up in a row, were in a bad state of repair, the once green baize faded and stained, and the thick table legs dented and chipped. The concrete floor was uncovered, three of the walls unpainted. Propped against the fourth wall was a toothless Han with a cue in hand. A small boy – maybe four or five – was sitting in the corner on a plastic tractor. Was this her husband, and the boy their son? It seemed as though she was the manager. The toothless man racked them up.

It didn't take long; he didn't bother to hustle. Probably watching my roving eyes sliding up and down the woman's body he dispatched me with a modicum of fuss, and then charged me an extortionate twenty yuan, over two and a half dollars. Quite what for, I wasn't sure. Though I should very much have liked a rematch, just to hang around and enjoy the view a little longer, I realised I was in danger of blowing a sizeable chunk of our budget. I wandered outside again, sat by the doorway of a restaurant on a shallow stool and drank a beer. But before long I began to feel guilty about leaving Sarah and hurried back to the hotel.

I needn't have worried; she'd only just returned to the room herself and for the next ten minutes told me about having met this lovely Frenchman, one of the guys who'd skied Mustang Ata. He hadn't actually made it to the top and therefore hadn't skied all the way down. Halfway up he'd suffered an attack of altitude sickness and had had to return. Apparently he'd promised his wife he wouldn't risk his life more than was necessary and, though he'd been disappointed at first, he now felt that it was okay because he'd been true to his word, he'd tried and . . .

Jesus, I was thinking, do you think I give a fuck?

Once she'd finished I picked up my book and by candlelight read about other travellers' tales. One in particular caught my eye. In the early 1890s a young bride called Catherine Macartney described her journey with her new husband to Kashgar thus: 'If two people can go through such a journey without quarrelling seriously, they can get on under any circumstances. We just survived it, and it promised well for the long journey through life.' Good for her, I thought. That was more than a hundred years ago, on a journey a thousand times more arduous than ours. Perhaps, I pondered, we should have flown.

8 A Long Way from the Sea

The Chini Barg – or the Chinese Garden – Hotel in Kashgar was a huge disappointment. For one thing there was nothing that remotely resembled a garden and for another it was not, as I had been expecting, the quaint late-nineteenth century, converted residence of the first British Governor General to Xinjiang, George Macartney, and his irrepressible wife, Catherine. It was instead a semi-circular Soviet-style, concrete monstrosity, seven storeys high and a hundred metres long. A broken neon sign hung precariously above the entrance, faded flags dangled limply from paint-chipped poles and washing draped from innumerable open windows. As the van pulled up, a mangy dog was urinating contemptuously against the hotel wall.

On either side of the huge forecourt equally ugly concrete constructions slouched – two restaurants, a bus and truck stand, a tourist shop and Internet café – the sole attempt at elegance being a large round fountain, once again made of concrete, which rested incongruously before the hotel's main entrance. It didn't work, aesthetically or practically. The water in the basin was stagnant and green, a stud farm for mosquitoes. Having gleaned most of my knowledge of the region from nostalgic travel books of yester-year, I cursed myself for not reading a more up-to-date guide.

Our only consolation was that we were here at all; early that morning we'd almost been arrested. Told by the receptionist at the hotel in Tashkurgan that the road to Kashgar was now open to small vehicles, we'd agreed to his offer of having one of his friends drive us the 200 kilometres for the very reasonable price of $40. Unfortunately, however, just before we packed our luggage into the van the receptionist informed us that we couldn't leave after all. Someone – he didn't know who – had informed the police of our imminent departure, and as it was apparently prohibited in Communist China for foreigners to take anything other than state-run, or at least-licensed, transport, he told us we'd have to wait for the bus, which, in turn, meant waiting for the authorities to repair a bridge. It was either that or risk being arrested. Neither Sarah nor I particularly minded the latter option – a prison cell, a hotel room, we figured there might be little difference – but the van driver did. And Sarah had hit the roof.

'It's totally ridiculous,' she'd spat into the receptionist's face. 'You call the police and this informer now, and tell them to go to hell.' Through I doubted I'd have been quite so forthright, I felt equally irritated. The 'law' reeked of corruption, but whether on the part of the police or the hotel staff I really wasn't sure.

'Come on,' I said, leaning on the counter, trying a conciliatory approach, 'there must be something we can do.' I took a ten-dollar bill from my pocket and dangled it in front of his face. 'Perhaps if you call the police and ask them again.'

'I will do my best for you,' he said, picking up the phone and turning towards the wall. I looked at Sarah.

'This is crazy,' she hissed. 'Imagine if they won't let us go. We could be stuck here for days.'

'They'll let us,' I answered. 'There's probably no one at all on the phone. It's a con, that's all.'

'What?' Behind her glasses her sharp eyes narrowed.

The receptionist hung up and turned back to face us. 'It is OK.' He smiled lamely. 'You can go. But . . .' – he placed his hands face down on the counter; whatever the 'but' was it was obvious from his expression it was going to cost more than the $10 already offered – 'you must pay twenty dollars. They tell me there are some . . . administrative cost.'

'Administrative cost?' I asked incredulously. It was so absurd I began to laugh.

'Yes.'

'You mean a bribe.'

Grinning, he shrugged his shoulders.

'Ten dollars for you, and ten more for your friend, right?' I shook my head in amazed submission and gave him the extra money, regretting the fact that I hadn't been filming the episode.

Although we'd had to wait an hour while a team of bulldozers cleared a rockslide, most of the route had been fixed or diversions put in place, and we'd made the journey to Kashgar in under five hours.

Having heard me talk nostalgically about the Chini Barg Hotel, Sarah now appeared rather confused.

'It doesn't look much like an old British residence to me,' she said, peering upwards at the mid-seventies structure. 'Jesus . . . it's revolting.'

I climbed out of the van, concentrating on filming. 'It must be around the back or something. Unless they've knocked it down and built this in its place.'

We thanked our driver, picked up our bags and made towards the entrance. As we walked through the glass doors the scale of the place hit me. Stretching before us was a huge open lobby, which climbed through a vortex of seven storeys towards a perspex roof. At ground level, rows of low tables and plastic armchairs formed a wide waiting area, beyond which lay a snack bar, telephone exchange, computer centre and tourist boutique. Hung from the wall of the first-floor balcony were tacky gold-framed clocks, once again reminding us that the time in Kashgar was two hours behind the capital. An elderly tour group sat waiting for a guide. A female cleaner mopped the floor. A little bemused, we wandered over to reception to sign in.

''Ow long you stay?' asked the bespectacled Han woman behind the counter.

It was a good question. If we could have so much hassle simply hiring a van, I hardly dared wonder how long it might take to buy a couple of horses, find a guide, and secure all the necessary passes and permits to ride out of the country into Kyrgyzstan. 'Oh, about a week,' I answered, knowing the statement was ludicrously optimistic. If I'd said the two I now feared it might take, I was worried Sarah might break down on me. She'd been nagging hard during the drive, saying that we should move on as fast as we could . . . as though I didn't want to. I paid $40 for the first two nights, and the receptionist gave us our receipt.

'Is there someone who can help with the luggage?' I asked hopefully, looking for a porter. All eight pieces were scattered around our feet.

'I sorry. No.' The receptionist went back to her work.

We loaded ourselves up and battled manfully up the stairs. On the first-floor landing a young lad approached and offered to help. Much relieved, Sarah gave him two small bags while I off-loaded one. He looked at the room chit, nodded knowledgeably and marched off with confidence. Unfortunately, by the time we reached the fourth floor, with both Sarah and me panting like dogs, the conviction had drained from his face. He stopped, looked at the chit again, then at a door, then at another. 'Ah . . .' he muttered shyly, carefully avoiding my withering stare, and led us back down the way we'd come. Our room was on the first floor, near where we'd found him.

At least the room was fine: two beds, a fan, two armchairs, a flask full of boiling water, some cups and tea, and a bathroom. We were told by the jolly *dejournaya* – here dressed in an elegant black and white stripy blouse and black pencil skirt – that there was hot water all day long. Unconvinced, Sarah tested the bath tap and found a steaming jet of clear liquid. Once the *dejournaya* had gone and I'd finished filming, I threw myself onto the bed. So at last we were in Kashgar.

'Okay, so here's the plan,' I said, half an hour later, pushing a mountain of clobber up the bed. I sat down, clutching my notebook and pen. Sarah, having just showered, was rubbing her wet hair with a towel. Dressed in a T-shirt and trousers, she perched on the edge of her bed.

'It's Monday today, right, which means that because we missed the bus in Sust, and because of the problems with the road, we've also missed the Sunday Market.' I was talking as much to myself as I was to Sarah. 'That means we can't buy horses for a week, which leaves us the next five days to find out how we go about getting permission to ride out of here and into Kyrgyzstan once we do have them.'

'Yes, sounds good,' said Sarah, now cleaning the lenses of her glasses. Having rubbed them with a hanky, she held them to the light. Happy with the result, she pushed them back onto her face. 'In fact, thinking about it, it might work out better this way. After all, once we've got the horses we're going to want to leave here pretty quickly. Judging by what we saw coming into the city, it's going to be hard to find stabling for them.'

It was a good point. Kashgar is a bustling urban conurbation, surrounded by paddyfields and market gardens. I figured, if the worst came to the worst, we'd probably be able to find somewhere in the countryside to stable them, maybe with an owner of one of the many horse-drawn taxi trolleys we'd seen plying the streets. But Sarah was right: once we had the horses, the sooner we left town the better.

'Now,' I said, looking in my notebook, 'I have three ideas for getting the permits.' I was very aware that so far there had been precious few organised plans, which, as I've said, is usually how I like it, but I sensed Sarah was not overly impressed. I needed to show her that, at least to some degree, I had things under control. 'First we should find out what the official line is. I think I noticed the office of the Chinese Tourist Board just outside the hotel gates.' I waved a hand towards the door. 'If it's true that you're not allowed to travel on private transport in this country, I very much doubt the government will encourage us to ride horses, especially through a border region; still, it's worth a try.' Leaning backwards onto the bed, Sarah nodded. 'Then we can check with one of the new semi-independent travel companies. From what I understand there has been an easing in government policy towards small business, and I think there are now a few licensed tour operators who can help organise independent trips. And, failing that, there is one last place to try.' I flicked to the back of my notebook. 'It's a contact I was given in England. He runs a place called . . . here we are, John's Café, and apparently he can get you anything.'

'A regular Mr Fix-it.'

'Apparently so, though I expect at a crippling price.' I put down my book and glanced absently towards the window. 'Then, once we've got some firm guarantees that we can actually ride out of here and into Kyrgyzstan, I'll call Alex in Bishkek and confirm that he'll meet us on the Kyrgyz side of the Torugart Pass . . . and find out if Dom's around.'

This was one of the few things I had organised before leaving the UK. As soon as I knew that the journey was actually going to happen, I'd contacted a great friend, Dominico Mocchi, who'd recently moved his horse-trekking business from Pakistan to Kyrgyzstan. He'd given me the name of a tour operator he used in Kyrgyzstan, a guy called Alex, who he said could assist us securing visas, interpreters, provisions and further contacts in the region. If Dom was there himself, he'd help out personally by loaning us equipment, giving us advice, and, if he didn't need them, even loaning us some of his horses and guides. I did feel that this was a little naughty – few Silk Road travellers of yesteryear would have had it so easy – but I figured with our non-existent knowledge of horse travel it would be invaluable to have professionals around to show us the ropes until we became more learned. I'd spoken to Alex from England. He was now awaiting our call.

'OK,' said Sarah, standing up, 'that sounds fine.' She picked up her shoulder bag. 'So we won't be doing any more filming today?'

'No, I don't think so. We've got a week here at least to get the shots we need. Relax.'

'Okay, well I think I might go and see if I can send an e-mail. Let everyone back home know I'm fine.'

'Good idea,' I said, climbing to my feet. 'I think I'll go for a walk.'

As I straightened my back, I glanced out of the rear window and my vision fell on an ochre stone bungalow, twenty yards away, across a small patch of yellowing grass. Shallow steps climbed grace-fully to a wooden veranda, stained dark with age, and overhung by a tiled roof. A cluster of red plastic flowers, faded and bent, sprouted from terracotta pots at the entrance, where a sign hung in Chinese script. I realised immediately what I was looking at.

'Hey, Sarah,' I called over my shoulder. She was already by the door. 'At least they didn't pull it down. Come and have a look.' She wandered back across the room and peered out of the window. 'The first British Governor General's house.'

She smiled easily, and pointed to the far horizon. 'Never mind that,' she exclaimed, her expression a blend of surprise and wonder. 'Look over there, those must be the Tian Shan mountains.' Beyond the bungalow, the dusty poplars and city's iron rooftops, across the dry and pallid land, the Mountains of Heaven rose purple in the distance. 'I really can't wait to be up there.'

As I left the hotel gates, I was set upon by an army of money changers. Mostly Uyghurs, all were dark and weathered, wore cheap working clothes, cotton caps, and carried thick bundles of Chinese cash. 'Dollar change,' they said in unison, jostling around me. 'Rupee, rupee.' Still unsure of the best rate, I changed just $20 with the least pushy man and walked onto the street.

Once again I was in a fine mood. With Sarah happy at the computer and the camera safely locked in our room, I was free to explore the city alone and without distractions. Just the name of the place had long been enough to have the wanderer in me salivating with anticipation. Kashgar: it simply rings of adventure. During the heyday of the Silk Road, Kashgar was a vitally important oasis town, and had formed a sanctuary for the travellers heading to or from the terrifying lands of the Taklamakan Desert that lie immediately to the east. In those days the desert was a killer: lose your way and you'd die of thirst, but stick to the tracks and trails around its edge and the bandits and thieves that preyed on the loaded caravans would steal your goods and cut your throat. Crossing the Taklamakan Desert – roughly translated as 'Go in and never come out!' also known as The Sea of Death – was a perilous occupation. If you couldn't afford to pay local nomads to protect you, you were likely to vanish in the sands.

But it wasn't just from the east and west that the travellers came. As Sarah and I had discovered, Kashgar sits at a natural junction with the routes through the Karakoram mountains to India and the southern seas. From here the traders also journeyed, carrying fine cloth, cashmere, spices, jade, coral, pearls and precious gems. Hence a great market had sprung up. The geography hasn't changed and, though Kashgar's importance may have waned in recent times, the bazaars still thrive today.

It didn't take long, however, to realise that at the turn of the third millennium Kashgar is a tale of two cities: that of the modern Han and the ancient Uyghur. At first the road was wide and tree-lined, bordered by modern stores, hotels, dining rooms, a pool hall, a supermarket, and peopled by the two races with their differing creeds. But cutting down into a narrow alleyway I soon found myself lost in an exclusively Uyghur world, barely changed from the heady days of the old Silk Road, echoing that of *The Arabian Nights*.

Single-storey, terracotta brick buildings were squeezed close together. Under sun-bleached awnings, beside open sewers, cobblers, tailors and tinkers toiled. With cracked hands and broken nails, a tanner punched holes through an old leather harness; a knife merchant sharpened a blade against a spinning stone wheel; at an anvil a blacksmith beat a red-hot iron horseshoe. I stopped by a tatty wooden kiosk and bought a sheathed knife and a bone-handled horse whip from a young lad.

'Like Indiana Jones,' he cried with an impish grin.

'How on earth do you know about Indiana Jones?' I asked incredulously.

'We have video in China too, Mister.'

Laughing, I asked him if he could find me a sheepskin; I'd been told that, placed on a saddle, they stopped you getting saddle-sore. He disappeared only to return ten minutes later carrying a happy expression and what appeared to be a slimy, dripping blanket of wool. The blooded sheepskin had, I imaged, been removed from its owner only on demand. Thanking him, I declined and continued on my way.

I reached a junction where the street widened into a chaotic bazaar. To the right and left, manned by dark men with cheerful faces, rows of stalls stretched into the crowded distance. Calling loudly to the passers-by, they promoted their wares: brass tea pots and shining copper bowls, cheap metal cutlery and kitchen utensils, plastic plates and nylon blankets, leather whips and fox-fur hats. For ten yuan I bought the traditional, cotton, peaked Mao cap.

Local farmers had set up on the pavement. Since an easing of Communist regulations, farmers have been able to sell a percentage of their crops for their own profit. Some sold vegetables, sunflower seeds, eggs and corn, while others peddled fruit: apples, peaches, oranges and pears. An old cart pulled by a docile ass was piled high with watermelons. Behind it a crowd had formed, shouting their requirements to the flustered owner and his teenage son. Noticing a fig seller, I stopped and bought ten of his succulent-looking, enormous yellow fruits; they cost just a few cents each.

Pushing through the crowd, I felt my senses fill to a blissful overload. This was the world I'd come to see, the place of which I'd dreamed. Old men with wispy grey beards and faded skullcaps sat on stools, gossiping. Women, some veiled, others not – but all modestly dressed – scurried past, stopping to look, to haggle, to buy and to discard. Scruffy youths played pool on an outdoor table. Two pi-dogs copulated, and a forgotten donkey brayed. The aroma of kebabs cooking on charcoal fires, of discarded fruit and fresh-cut flowers, of shit, urine, diesel fumes, of humans, animals, heat and dust, rose to merge in an olfactory assault. And among the chaos a young man laid out his prayer mat, repositioned his skullcap and bowed in reverence towards Mecca. I found a two-storey *chaikhana*, ordered a pot of green tea and sat watching the confusion from the balcony.

It wasn't long, however, before a wind whipped up, pulling at the awnings like ships sails in a raging storm. I watched through half-closed eyes as the market traders hurried to secure their stalls and goods; as the women lowered their heads against the rising sand and dust and scurried home; as the shops shut and the street began to clear. The angry sky was soon a brilliant coral pink, weighed down by the sand of the Taklamakan, and I could barely see across the street. Unsure how long the storm would last, I picked up my bag and hurried back to the hotel.

'It is impossible.' The China International Tourist Services (CITS) office manager had no doubt whatsoever. 'No one has ever ridden horses over this frontier. The authorities will not allow it.' He spoke quietly, with calm control. 'You are not even allowed to ride a bicycle through this region – it is a very sensitive area, a military zone – if you can get the permits you must carry bicycle on jeep.'

It wasn't all bad news, at least he was letting us film the interview.

The office was long and thin, with a desk in the corner next to a glass cabinet full of books. Behind him hung a huge map of China and its neighbouring countries. We could see the route we wished to take. It looked a very long way. On the desk was a fifties Bakelite telephone. It rang. 'Excuse me,' said the young man, holding up his hand. He picked up the phone.

'That's not good,' said Sarah. Sitting side by side in front of the desk, we turned to face each other.

'No, but I think it's to be expected.' I lowered my voice.

'Remember this guy is the official voice of the government. It's not likely they'll actually encourage Westerners to go traipsing round in military zones, on horses, bikes, whatever. This country is still communist.'

'But he says no one's ever done it.'

'Then we will be the first.'

She forced a grin onto her face but seemed unconvinced. The official hung up the phone.

'You see,' he continued, 'we cannot issue the passes here. Firstly you have to get permission from the regional office in Kashgar. If you are just a backpacker this is now possible, there have been some reforms. But if you wanted to' – he held out his hands, palms up, as though he were a child ready to play catch – 'ride horses, the office here would have to refer it to the provincial capital in Urumchi, possibly even Beijing. That would take many weeks, months, and would in the end be turned down.' He sat back in his chair. 'No . . . you want to go to Kyrgyzstan, you take jeep.'

'And if we wanted to organise a private horse trip in Xinjiang,' I said, 'perhaps around Kashgar, towards the Taklamakan Desert or something, which tour operator would you suggest?'

He rattled his pen between his teeth and stared out of the door. 'Xinjiang Mountaineering.' He looked back at us. 'They organise many special trips for tourist these days – mountain climbing, camel safaris, jeep trips to the desert – perhaps you ask them. I will write down their address.'

We thanked him and left.

It was only a little after nine, but outside in the street the heat was already intense. The sky was white and oppressive, a stifling dust-laden haze and dazzlingly bright. I put on a pair of sunglasses. Standing by the gate, next to the noisy money changers, we waited for a taxi. When one arrived, swinging round off the road into the entrance, it was driven by a Chinese woman in her mid twenties. Sarah jumped in the front beside her. I climbed in the back behind a wire mesh screen.

'God, it's so cool to see all you women,' Sarah said, smiling at the driver. Unfortunately she didn't speak English, so instead Sarah turned her impressions towards me and the camera. 'No really, don't you think? And not only that, out and about and everything, but working properly, having a life of their own, doing what they want to do, wearing what they want to wear.' Turning back to the driver Sarah smiled and handed her the piece of paper upon which was written the address of the tour operator. A moment later we sped off into the traffic.

The road was wide, dual-laned, made of giant concrete slabs and shaded by wilting poplars and short, saggy acacias. In the centre of the road heavy motorised traffic pushed its way in both directions. At the avenue's edge, moving sedately, throngs of bicycles passed old men pushing carts piled high with produce. Some stopped to sell their wares, causing others to brake and curse. Beyond the walkways teeming with people rose an ugly mishmash of modern, high-rise, corporate office blocks and the older Communist proletariat buildings, an odd mix of old grey stone and new blue glass.

Here, the town's cultural contrasts were most vividly exposed. On the wide pavements, by the busy roads, Han girls in hotpants, miniskirts and tiny dresses sauntered happy and free beside skull-capped Muslims and their veiled wives. Mullahs, and imams, devout old Muslims with grey beards and dark robes, shuffled along the streets with their heads cast down, pushing hopelessly against the tide. Some clutched Korans like divine shields against the decadence that surrounded them, while others sought peace fiddling with their prayer beads. Most Uyghurs, in the restaurants and shops, on the buses and in their cars, seemed oblivious to the violent cultural collision that surrounded them. Like men the world over, they could be seen eyeing the pert bottoms and firm breasts with excitement and longing, and leered knowingly to one another. But beneath this apparent indifference a dangerous mood was growing. Over the last five years Kashgar, and Xinjiang in general, had seen a marked increase in Uyghur nationalism and Islamic fundamentalism with militant wings turning calm debate and peaceful protests into widespread violent clashes. Fanatics prepared and indoctrinated in the terrorist training-camps of Afghanistan had now returned home to cause havoc. Two years earlier, in one of the bloodiest episodes, a bomb had exploded at a Han hotel in central Kashgar, killing thirteen and injuring many more. Since then the Beijing authorities have clamped down on the dissidents with their customary ruthlessness. Thousands of Uyghurs have been arrested; many are still being held.

We turned left into a quiet back street and pulled up outside the entrance to Xinjiang Mountaineering Company. Following signs, we climbed a black iron fire ladder and emerged beside a shabby room. Inside, behind a desk, head down in paperwork, sat a young woman. She gestured to us to come in. Sarah was now filming.

'We would like to enquire about the possibility of riding horses out of China. We wondered whether you could help us with the permits.'

The woman looked at me blankly, then at Sarah and the camera. Unsure what to make of us, she turned her attention back to me. ''Orses . . .' she said, eyes wide, appearing confused, 'you wan' buy 'orses?'

'No, we are going to buy our own horses – at the Sunday Market – what we need is someone to help us arrange the permits and passes to get them, and us, out of China and into Kyrgyzstan.'

'Oh.' She studied me curiously again. 'Yoouuu, wan' buy 'orses?'

'Oh dear,' I said, turning to Sarah. She was trying hard not to laugh, biting her bottom lip. I looked back at the woman and smiled politely. 'Do you have a translator here . . . someone who speaks English?'

She looked nonplussed.

'We don't want to buy horses,' bellowed Sarah, going by the old British assumption that anything said loud enough in English will eventually be understood by foreigners. 'We need guides, permits . . . help! Do you understand?'

Amazingly, it seemed to work.

'Ah, OK.' She got up and walked towards the door.

A moment later the woman returned with a short, Uyghur man in tow. Somewhere in his mid-forties, he had thinning hair and a limp. His eyes were dark and kind. 'Hello,' he said. 'My name Oscar. Can I help you?'

'I hope so,' I said, and once again described what it was we were trying to do.

'Ah,' he said knowingly, once I'd finished, 'so, you wan' buy horses.'

I didn't panic. 'Well yes, but we will do that in the bazaar ourselves on Sunday. What we need are the permits to ride them over the Torugart Pass; to export them from China.'

'Yes, I see . . . but thees no possible. No problem for you ride horses in Kashgar.' He stood up and pointed to a large map that hung on the plastered wall. 'You ride horses to here, is no problem. Thees sixty kilometres from here. But after thees soldier . . . is military zone. No bicycle, no motorbike, no private jeep . . . no horses. You take company jeep, I organise for you and wife. Is better.'

He glanced at Sarah in an ingratiating manner. She turned away and placed the camera on the desk in an attempt, I imagined, to capture the whole scene.

'But Oscar, we don't want to go by jeep.' I tried to keep the exasperation out of my voice. 'We want to ride. You know, a big journey by horse from Kashgar along the Silk Road, all the way to Turkmenistan.' I gestured flamboyantly out of the door, towards the distant hills. To emphasise the point Sarah traced a line from the existing map onwards across the blotchy wall.

'I went you horses?'

'Went?' asked Sarah.

'He means rent.'

'We don't want to rent, or went, anything,' she stormed, starting to lose her cool. 'We are going to buy them ourselves. Do you have a boss?'

'Boss no here.' He looked up. 'Boss no speak English. Where you stay?'

'Chini Barg,' I answered.

'Okay, I ask boss if we help then I come an' tell you. No one ride horses from China, tourist take company jeep.' He grinned hopefully. 'But I try, OK?'

'OK,' we said and left.

On the way out, across the courtyard, I turned anxiously to Sarah. 'This looks like being harder that I had expected.'

'Yes.' she frowned. 'Just why did you pick Kashgar as the starting point?'

I was beginning to wonder.

John's Café, as a neon sign by the road declared, was 'a piece of home on the Old Silk Road'. It was the only travellers' restaurant in Kashgar and served the same menu available to travellers the world over: banana pancakes, French toast, milkshakes, burgers and chips. We sat down at one of the many plastic tables under a draped awning and, feeling a little like frauds – it had been less than ten days since we had eaten home cooking – we decided what to have.

The waitress came over. Sarah ordered a cheese and tomato omelette and orange juice; I asked for ham and eggs and a cup of real coffee.

'Is John here?' I asked.

The girl pointed to a tall Han Chinese man chatting to two Uyghurs at the bar. Wearing a cream, multipocketed 'journalist' waistcoat over a blue and white pinstriped shirt, he looked smart and well-heeled. His hair was fine, falling forward in a sweeping fringe towards a pair of pear-drop shades. I guessed his age to be somewhere around mid-forty.

'Could you tell him we'd like to see him, please . . . when he's free.'

She nodded and walked away.

Most of the other tables were empty. On the far side, reading a guidebook, sat a Japanese tourist, and behind him two locals were playing chess. Tuesday is not a day for Western travellers. Most spend a maximum of three days in Kashgar, largely for the famous market. There's little other reason to hang around.

Immediately John came over to join us. Having trained the camera on his seat, I turned it on and stood up.

'Herro,' he said, flashing a grin that showed two gold teeth. Around his wrist hung a chunky metal-strapped watch, and a thick gold ring, diamond studded, resided on a finger. Business must be good, I pondered. I shook his hand and introduced him to Sarah. The niceties over, we sat down. I was eager to explain our business.

'John, we have both heard many things about you,' I said, sounding rather more sycophantic than I had intended.

'You 'ave?' As he laughed his slanted eyes disappeared. It was rather endearing, like a cheeky child. He took a cigarette from his packet and, having tapped it on the table, popped it in his mouth.

'Sure; that if you want something doing in Kashgar you must first see John.'

'I do my bes'.' He flicked open his silver lighter, sparked the flint and brought the flame to the cigarette. After inhaling deeply, he blew out the smoke and snapped the lighter shut. 'So,' he said, 'Wha' can I do for you?'

I leaned forward, and nervously rapped my fingers on the table. I knew that this was it, make or break. Having been turned down by the government tour operators, with little or no confidence in Oscar and his agency, John was our last hope. If he thought it possible, then it probably was, but if he said no, that with things in China the way they were there was no chance of riding across this border, then that would be that. We would be left with no alternative but to slide, tails very much between our legs, into Kyrgyzstan on foot. And how humiliating would that be? All along I'd pitched the journey, both to the camera and the paymasters at Lion TV, as a trip by horse from Kashgar to the Caspian Sea; to buy our horses in the famous bazaar and ride over the Torugart Pass. How could I change that now? And what would Sarah think? To a certain degree she was trusting her life on my judgement. If I was capable of making such a howling gaffe as not finding out that the very first border we planned to cross would be closed to our passage, she'd have every right to feel rather concerned about my competence. We simply had to ride out of China, whatever the cost, whatever the problems. I breathed in deeply.

'OK, John,' I said, bringing my hands together, 'in short we want to buy two, maybe three, horses in the Sunday Market and ride them over the Torugart Pass into Kyrgyzstan. From there we want to ride all the way along the Silk Road, through Uzbekistan, Tajikistan and Turkmenistan to the Caspian Sea. As you can see,' I pointed to the camera and microphone that were trained on him, 'we're making a television programme about the journey and I am writing a book.' I stopped and looked at him, almost unable to ask the question. 'Do you think it's possible?'

'Hah!' he threw back his head, laughing. It was an infectious cackle, making both Sarah and I laugh, albeit rather uncertainly. 'You wan' to buy 'orses in the Sunday Market and wide 'em to Europe?' He slammed his hands down hard on the table – making the camera shudder – incredulity stamped across his face. The way he said it, it did sound rather ridiculous. I smiled apologetically.

Then, in an instant, he stopped laughing, his smile dulled and he pulled thoughtfully on his cigarette. I could see his mind working, both on the possibility of such an endeavour and on how much he could earn for his part in it. Television, books, horses . . . all depending on him. He must have known he could charge a fortune.

'Well?' I asked again. 'Do you think it's possible? We have money and, hey, you might even be on television.'

'Huh . . .' He grinned. 'I no know for sure. But yes, maybe. No one 'as ever done this before. Three year ago Frenchman buy 'orse in the Sunday Market, but he wide to Urumchi. That easy. But you way Soviet Union, big difference. Chinese gowenment no like tourist cross this border, even now. Five year ago no one cross, no locals, no foreigner . . . no one. Is problem.'

That much I did know. At the beginning of the sixties Sino–Soviet relations nose-dived with the two differing forms of the same ideology falling out and turning their backs on one another. For thirty years China's western border with the USSR had been sealed as tightly as the iron curtain. Though it had opened up since the demise of the Soviet Union and the birth of the independent Central Asian republics, relations were still tetchy. For any tourist wishing to travel this way permits were needed as was a licensed tour operator to escort you on both sides of the border; we hoped John would accompany us to the Chinese frontier, where Alex would be waiting to lead us into Kyrgyzstan. I wasn't surprised no one had ever done it on horse, but I saw no reason why it should make a difference.

John took a long last drag on his cigarette and stubbed it out. 'But maybe. I know big man in military . . . he General . . . three star.' He tapped his shoulder. 'He work in this area. We see. If I get 'old of 'im, maybe.' He then sat back and smiled broadly. 'You know, I like thees plan . . . is good plan. Always tourist ask John to get jeep, take to desert, to Khunjerab Pass, buy plane ticket to Beijing, Islamabad, Delhi. No one wide 'orse to Europe, hah.' He shook his head again. 'I try my bes'.'

The rest of the week lumbered on but things went far from smoothly. Returning to John's Café twice a day to glean whatever information we could, sent us from euphoria to despair. At first

John told us yes, he'd had a word with his friend 'the Big Man' in the army, who'd seen no reason why we could not fulfil our plan. We'd got drunk in celebration. Then, the next day, he said no, that there was another 'Big Man', even bigger it seemed, in the same unit, on the same post, who had refused us permission to go. The day after that he explained that once again it might be possible if a compromise could be worked out – driving the horses part of the way in a truck – and then, once again, that he really wasn't sure. His military friend, he told us, had now gone to Urumchi on business and wouldn't be back until Friday. He promised us an answer by Saturday evening.

Kashgar itself did little to relieve our anxious moods: the heavy skies and muggy air, the stifling heat and billowing dust, were always oppressive and gave little respite. The frustrations got to us both. Sarah became angry, aggressive towards the invisible men that were scuppering our plans. 'Jesus, what's their problem?' she'd demand rhetorically. 'Why can't they just let us bloody go? What harm are we going to be?' I tried my best to reassure her, to explain that such setbacks, such highs and lows, were all part of the travelling game, but she remained taciturn and unconvinced. Clearly pissed off, walking through the streets alone, Sarah expressed her views to camera . . .

> *I'm fed up with waiting. All we ever seem to do is wait for buses and things. Most people only stay in Kashgar for three days, we've been here nearly a week. I just can't wait for the next phase of this journey to start. All this Chinese bureaucracy is really starting to take the wind out of my sails. This was supposed to be a riding trip, not a test of my –* she pauses and scowls – *patience!*

Living cheek by jowl in a small hotel room it was inevitable that we'd begin to get on each other's nerves.

'Jesus Christ, Jonny,' swore Sarah, when entering the bathroom one time, 'do you really have to turn this place into a swimming pool every time you take a shower? Can't you sit down and keep the water in the bath?'

Sensing space was needed, most days I didn't see that much of her. I wandered the bazaar, leaving her to paint, do her own pieces to camera, read her book (*The Great Game*, at last!) and send and receive e-mails.

At first I wasn't too bothered by this. It was natural, I felt, for the disappointments to affect her and for her to want to be in contact with home. But as the week wore on, and Sarah's time lost in cyberspace increased to two to three hours a day, I began to feel resentful. Not only did it feel like I was being forced to battle on two fronts – trying to organise the journey and keep her spirits up – I was also feeling more and more alienated.

She had told me that her boyfriend was away on holiday and that the e-mail contact was with her mother and sister. I found that bizarre. She was, after all, a twenty-five-year-old girl, used – at least so she'd told me – to travelling on her own; surely her umbilical cord had been severed long ago. It irked me that by being denied knowledge of what was in the marathon correspondence I was deprived of a large part of her feelings, removed from her inner thoughts, distanced from her problems, and therefore unable to get to know her. As a consequence, there were now few jokes and laughs between us, little camaraderie and certainly no flirting. For reasons I really couldn't fathom, it seemed to me that since her illness in Hunza we'd slipped from close friends and potential lovers to a relationship more akin to a boss and PA on a business trip.

So why not talk about it? But what to say? For all I knew it was her normal daily routine to spend three hours a day at the computer and another two reading? What right did I have to tell her to leave the e-mail alone and talk to me about whatever it was she was writing home? Besides, I've always found the most scary six words in the English language to be 'I think we need to talk.'

In the evenings we'd go back to John's Café, but this seldom really improved the situation. For a while we'd chat, play a game or two of backgammon, but it was never long before Sarah retreated to the safety of her book. If John came over or we met other tourists she'd stop reading and become her old self, bursting back into life as though kick-started by the strangers. She was charming, animated, exuberant and full of life – the girl I'd met in London – but as soon as they left she'd close up, turn off and once again fall silent.

At times this irritated me so much I'd find myself making petty arguments with her. 'Do you have to order the most expensive drink on the menu, Sarah? What do you think, that we're here to have a holiday?'

'No, of course I don't,' she replied with a look of steel. 'You have beer. What's the difference?'

'Nearly two dollars,' I retorted.

'Well, I'll buy them with my own money then.'

'Good, then do.'

It was pathetic; I knew it, but I was angry with her. I knew she was bored, frustrated by the problems Kashgar was throwing up, but little of that was my fault. Her actions were making me feel small and insecure and, unsure how to handle the situation, I resorted to trying to make her feel the same. But five minutes later I'd be overcome with a sense of guilt and shame and, hating the tension that now hung between us, say something complementary. 'By the way, that picture you painted this morning was excellent.' And Sarah, equally uneasy with the fiction would catch the bait and reply, 'Oh, that's nice, did you think so?' It was a weird way to live. Not with a lover, nor even a friend – simply a person I really didn't know. And neither of us had any way out. On Friday I e-mailed Bishkek in Kyrgyzstan, primarily to check that Alex was ready to meet us on the pass, whenever it was that we'd arrive, but also to ask if Dom was around. To see a real friend would be a very welcome relief.

Finally Saturday came. Unfortunately, John's verdict hardly gave cause for great delight.

'My friend, the General, he no return,' he said, sitting at our table.

'Still in Urumchi?' I asked gloomily.

'Yes, he still there.'

'So what about tomorrow? At the market?'

'I thing you mus' buy 'orses tomorrow,' he said.

'Really, you think it's going to be OK, in the end?'

'No for sure, but I think.' Seeing the frustration in my face, he continued in an almost pleading tone. 'You know is very 'ard. No one ever do this. I try. I try my bes'. Really.'

'I know . . . thank you.' We both understood none of the problems were his fault.

'I also arrange for you to put 'orses in garden at Seiman 'otel' – he pointed across the street to Kashgar's other main hotel – 'and I arrange for 'orseman to 'elp look after them. He name, Abdul Karim, Uyghur man, good man, he 'elp you nice.'

'Thank you,' said Sarah, 'that's very kind.'

'Then I speak with big man Monday soon as office open. But tomorrow I think you buy your 'orses. But I think only two, in case problem. If no can go you jus' sell them back.' At that John started to laugh, imagining, I assumed, a hilarious scene we could only guess at.

We returned to the hotel where, thinking of the day ahead, I prepared the camera gear and studied my Uyghur phrase book.

9 A Fistful of Dollars

The sun was high, the sky bright blue. Sweat glistened on my face, stung my eyes, stained my shirt. Rising dust dried my throat. Dodging the defecating rear of a reversing mule, I began my piece to camera. 'The Yakshanbe Bazaar, the Kashgar Sunday Market, same today as it has been for a thousand years or more, since the heyday of the Silk Road.' Holding the camera at arm's length, the lens pointing at myself, I forced my way through a throng of humans and animals that was suggestive of biblical times. 'Every week the town's population swells by thousands as people from all over the region come to buy and sell their wares. And here you can buy anything and everything from fruit and vegetables, clothes and hats, ironware, woodwork, ropes and carpets to sheep, goats, donkeys, cattle, camels and, of course, horses.' I paused to sidestep an albino Uyghur pushing a trolley, upon which three sheep were fastened with ropes. One of the beasts bleated maniacally, sensing perhaps that his number was up. 'And that's why we're here today: to buy two horses to carry us over the Torugart Pass, out of China and into Kyrgyzstan.' Having reached the far end of the animal bazaar, I turned and stopped to allow the camera to capture the scene behind, where wild-faced locals, flailing whips and spurs, were charging furiously at horses in order to drive them on. 'But it isn't any old nags we're after . . .' I paused and stared directly into the lens. 'We want horses descended from heaven.' Then I turned to face the action.

'What do you think . . . was that all right?' Sarah was standing just in front of me, out of shot, smiling anxiously.

'Yeah, well done, it was great.' She took the camera. 'But I think that was the easy bit. I don't envy you this.'

Before us was a frenzy. On a dusty stretch of level ground, the size of a narrow football pitch, gold-toothed Uyghurs and ethnic Uzbeks in embroidered skullcaps, three-quarter-length cloaks and high leather boots joined Kazaks and Mongolions test-riding potential acquisitions. Sweat dripping from their Turkic faces and the necks of their raging steeds, they tore up and down, raising a wall of orange dust. Some used stirrups and saddles – rounded supports made of leather and wood with large phallic pommels – others did not. They all carried whips of plaited leather and beat the horses aggressively across the rear and around the face and eyes. On either side four-wheeled trolley carts were lined up, front to back, forming impromptu stands on which young kids stood to wave and shout and old men sat and gossiped. It could not have looked very different two thousand years earlier when Zhang Qian had wandered through the bazaar searching for his horses from heaven.

In 128 BC Zhang Qian, a Chinese emissary and Silk Road pioneer, wrote, 'The region has many fine horses which sweat blood; their forebears are supposed to have been foaled from heavenly horses.' The term stuck and though the blood had more to do with angry parasites living under the animals' skin than anything celestial, soon these remarkable steeds, renowned for their size, speed and incredible endurance, had captured the imagination of emperors, soldiers and poets. Desperate to obtain some of the divine beasts to revive the flagging fortunes of a failing Chinese army, Zhang Qian's emperor and sponsor, Han Wadi, dispatched missions to the courts of Central Asia, which in turn blasted open the trade routes between East and West, carrying, among other things, silk to Europe and wine to China.

A thousand years later they were coveted by Genghis Khan and his Mongol hordes. Using the animals' remarkable stamina the 'yellow peril' or 'horsemen of the apocalypse' were able to conquer one third of the earth's surface in less that fifty years. By means of a relay system, it was said, a message could be sent 3,000 miles, from one end of the empire to the other, in under three weeks. The Heavenly Horses of Central Asia could be said not only to have played a major part in the formation of the Silk Road, but to have helped shape the political boundaries of Asia itself.

As soon as Rachel suggested riding horses home, I knew in an instant what an interesting and important part they could play in the adventure. Were they still around today, another millennium on? And, if so, what did they look like and where could they be found? Could we, like warriors from the past, ride Heavenly Horses across the Mountains of Heaven? Some say the Heavenly Horses originated in the Ferghana Valley, but others maintain that they were in fact the famous Akhal Teke breed from the southern deserts of Turkmenistan. Though I realised the chances of us actually being able to buy two heavenly steeds were almost nil, as both regions lay unavoidably on our path I could not ignore the challenge. In these celestial animals I saw a fascinating quest and an exhilarating blend of history, adventure and romance: the very essence of the trip. Zhang Qian had begun his search for the blood-sweating beasts in Kashgar. So would we.

Having explained this to camera, I gulped and wiped the dirt from my face. 'Right then,' I said, shuffling uneasily on my feet. 'I guess I'd better go and try one. You OK with the camera?'

'I'll be a lot better with this than I would be buying horses.'

'And the radio mike's working OK?'

'Yes, it's fine.'

'Try to cover all the angles, and be careful of the dust.'

'I'll be OK, Jonny.' She failed to keep the impatience out of her voice. 'Just get me a decent horse.'

'I'll try.'

Realising there was nothing else to be done to delay the inevitable, I pulled on my gloves, readjusted my cap and, trying to show a confidence I most certainly did not feel, strode towards the nearest horse.

It was a bay gelding, with a dark mane and tail, a rounded head and well-proportioned body, around fourteen hands high: he certainly wasn't descended from any heavenly breed – he was too short and squat for that – but he did look honest and strong. Saddled up, he was ready to go. Standing beside him was a short, plump man in an elegant, deep-blue velvet cloak that in accordance with the local style reached down to his knees. On his bald head was a matching skullcap. He had thick stubble and fat lips.

I asked him how much he wanted for the horse.

Surprised, but evidently delighted by my interest, the man grinned, revealing a row of metal teeth. 'You buying?' His voice rasped, metallic, like an alien's.

'*Ha*,' I said nodding. 'Maybe.'

I could see the old dog weighing up the situation. A Westerner who wanted to buy a horse? Allah was at last smiling on him. He mumbled a prayer and fiddled with his beads. How could this stranger possibly know the correct price? Maybe he doesn't know a thing about horses. Perhaps the price could be doubled, tripled even. Another man, a Mongolian by appearance, overheard our conversation.

'You buying?'

Again I said maybe.

'*Ha?*' He looked confused.

'*Ha. Asp*, big journey, Torugart Pass, Kyrgyzstan . . . big journey, Soviet Union, Caspian Sea.' Almost the entire extent of my Uyghur used up, I fell silent.

'Soviet Union?'

'*Ha.*'

Now the Mongolian appeared amazed and delighted, and began to laugh uproariously. He stamped his foot and slapped his thigh incredulously, and then disappeared into the throng to disperse the news.

'*Tort ming*,' said the fat-lipped man.

'Tort ming . . .' I started to go through my Uyghur numbers, '*bir, ikki, uch* . . .' When I looked back the man was holding up four fingers. Four thousand yuan. I made a quick mental calculation. About $300. As we'd budgeted $500 for two – including equipment – it was more than we could afford, but only just . . . I had to start somewhere, and I made it clear I wanted to test the horse. He agreed, and I climbed astride.

The moment I was in the saddle my nerves disappeared. It was just a horse like any other. I turned it onto the dusty track and set it to a canter. It responded at once, throwing its head back, prancing like a Lippizaner. The neck was short, the withers thin. I could easily reach forward and touch his ears. Though the stirrups were far too short, the saddle was comfortable and with the leather reins I could feel its mouth; as I took a pull, it actually responded.

'*Yakshi, yakshi* . . .' I shouted to the owner over my shoulder, telling him his horse was good. I never could play poker. '*Yashqa kirdingiz?*' How old is it? I asked.

'Seven, eight . . .' I was aware he could tell me anything.

'What's its name?'

'Torugart,' he replied.

'Did you hear that, Sarah?' I shouted above the raucous din. 'This horse is called Torugart. It must be destiny.' Noticing her standing on a wall, I reined the horse round to face her. 'It's expensive, top end of our budget, but I reckon it might do for you.' But she was concentrating too hard on the filming to respond with words, and simply nodded.

By this time the news was out, and a great crowd had gathered round the edge of the track. There was no one else riding now. I was alone, at the centre of this feral stage. Just for a moment the world beyond disappeared. The problems of the trip, the permits and permissions, my relationship with Sarah, the film, the book, which horses to buy and how much to pay, all faded from my mind. Sitting on that horse, in the middle of the arena, with the timeless faces all around, I could have been a man from any century. Just for a moment my Silk Road fantasy stood before me, alive and kicking. I was Marco Polo, I was Zhang Qian, I was Genghis Khan, taking to the saddle on a horse sired and bred in heaven. Digging my heels in the horse's flanks, I raised an arm and exploded into a cloud of dust.

The horse was lovely. Still, I hadn't a clue how much I should pay. As Fat Lips took the bridle, another man approached. He was leading a muscular black stallion.

With confidence growing, I now found myself leaping from one animal to another, some with saddles, others without, riding them among the inquisitive crowd of onlookers. Each time, the price of the horse was shouted out, as well as the specific region it came from and how old it was. At fifteen hands one was relatively large, with a thick neck, strong hindquarters and an elegant head, but it proved far too expensive; another two were slightly lame. There was a gorgeous grey, and it fell within our budget. At first I thought, this is it: Clint Eastwood in *Pale Rider*. But when I dismounted I noticed two strange lumps, the size and texture of ripe mangoes, under the stomach, where the girth would go. I jumped astride another.

Every so often I became aware of Sarah – on a cart, crouching low by a wall, at one point even up on a roof – doing a valiant job filming. Out of the corner of my eye I could see she was having problems keeping grubby children behind her field of vision and the fine dust from the microphone and lens.

Fat Lips led Torugart out again. Not only was he a fine-looking horse, he also had a very mild manner. To emphasise this, Fat Lips squatted down and crawled beneath his belly. Once there he threw his arms this way and that, kicked out with his feet like a Cossack dancer, and screamed and shouted; the animal remained totally placid. I checked his hooves, which appeared fine, and, without any idea what I was doing, pushed up his lips to check his teeth and gums.

'What do you think, Sarah?' I asked, hopefully. She was now standing just before me. 'Will he do for you?'

'Is he calm enough?'

'For sure, very. And out here I'm surprised such an animal exists. Do you want to try him?'

'Christ, no . . . I'll take your word for it.' Lowering the camera, she moved forward and patted the horse's flank. 'Can we afford him?'

'Maybe.'

I asked Fat Lips again how much money he wanted. '*Tort ming*,' he said defiantly – about three hundred dollars.

Just then another man appeared, leading a horse. It was black with a white streak running down its nose, and a long and tangled mane. He was a scrawny beast, with ribs protruding from his side and surely the most enormous set of teeth a horse has ever owned. Yellowing, like a heavy smoker's, they forced their way through tightly stretched lips, giving the horse the appearance of permanently holding a lunatic grin, and I fell for him at once. There was something rather mad about his eyes as well. They weren't smiling but appeared fed up, pissed off, as if he knew he'd been the butt of many jokes and was bored by the whole event. I wasn't too concerned. Like Torogart, he seemed docile enough, allowing me to stroke his head and neck. His name was Kara, which meant 'black'.

'*Letch pour*?' I asked for his price.

'*Ikki ming, yatta yuz.*' Around $200 or 2,600 yuan. Perfect.

'How old?'

'Twelve.'

Kara had no saddle, so I jumped on him bare back. My feet

could easily touch underneath his belly, and again I could hold his ears. At first he wouldn't canter, preferring to trot double-speed instead. It was an uncomfortable gait, especially without a saddle, sending me bouncing this way and that like a sack of grain. But once he did break into a canter, he was a very easy ride. When I dismounted and tried to check his feet he lashed out violently, causing the excited crowd to leap back, laughing nervously, but surrounded as we were by so many people, I figured it was fair enough. Away from the market I felt sure he would be fine.

'So what do you think then, Sarah?' I asked, brightly. 'Torugart for you, Kara for me.'

Sarah wasn't quite so sure. 'I thought you were looking for a Heavenly Horse,' she said, regarding Kara with a dubious expression. 'He looks like he's come straight from hell to me.'

I laughed. 'Well, looks can be deceiving.'

'But do you really think he'll make it? You look very big on him.'

'Well, he'll make it out of China, if we get permission, and, if the worst comes to the worst and he struggles in Kyrgyzstan, we can always sell him and buy another. As we don't know yet what's going to happen we don't want to waste money unnecessarily, buying one of these really good horses. After all, as John said, we might have to sell them again here or even give them away.' I turned and looked at Torugart. 'Besides, it's more important at this stage that you have the better horse; I'll get by, I'm sure.'

Sarah smiled. 'OK then, let's have them.'

The money paid, we proudly walked our new acquisitions from the bazaar. It was a wonderful feeling. Though Sarah was right, and neither of the horses even remotely resembled anything celestial, they were horses that appeared sound and strong, and we'd purchased them more or less on budget. Until that moment, I hadn't even been sure we'd get that far.

Our euphoria was short-lived. Leading the horses through town, we soon realised we'd been ripped off badly. On hearing how much we'd paid for the animals, most of Kashgar's inquisitive townsfolk made no attempt to hide their mirth and simply fell about laughing. After ten minutes of questioning I decided it was better to save face and lie.

This fear was confirmed soon after we arrived at the Seiman Hotel and found Abdul Karim, a stocky, scruffy Uyghur horseman with a shaven head and sparkling eyes who'd been asked by John to look after us. As there was no space to tie the horses in the orchard – the trees were either too low to the ground or packed too tightly together – we were told to walk them through a pair of broken wooden gates and into a walled area that at one time had accommodated the hotel's swimming pool. Not any longer. A few years earlier the city's party bigwigs had decided it was far too bourgeois to have a pool in town, so it was destroyed; it now resembled a bombsite. Piles of rubble, wooden stakes, smashed paving stones, twisted rods of rusting iron and, of course, the thoroughly hazardous empty pool itself presented themselves before us. I could hardly imagine a less suitable place to stable two newly acquired horses. Abdul Karim told us it was all right – living just across the road, he would be able to keep an eye on them – and tied Torugart to the flimsy wall and Kara to an iron stake. Though Abdul's shoes were split and trousers zipless and held up by a bind of rope, we believed him. He was the horseman after all.

Once secure, Abdul checked the horses out. Torugart he pronounced young and fit, with a strong rump and good feet, but reckoned $200 should have been enough to buy him. With Kara he was disgusted. Having taken one look at his scrawny sides and some hairless patches on his narrow back – something I hadn't noticed in the bazaar – he told me Kara wasn't worth a hundred. Shaking his head and tutting loudly, he reckoned $80 max, and that was for the butcher! Not even Kara's endearing smile could appease him. Pointing at his mouth, Abdul explained through mime and his smattering of English that with teeth that size he must be at least twenty years old and would have problems eating; this, he thought, might account for Kara's anorexic figure. As if to contradict this theory, while Abdul bent to check Kara's feet, Kara swung sharply round and snatched a lump from Abdul's arse. This did nothing to improve relations between the two and, as Abdul Karim leapt aside, rubbing his behind, cursing in Uyghur expletives, Kara started snorting wildly, pounding the earth and spinning round the iron post.

I was a little embarrassed by my choice of animal, and blamed Kara's aggression on the iron post. 'Why did you tie him to this?' I asked Abdul. Forced into the ground next to a shattered path, it left Kara stomping angrily on sharp, uneven concrete. 'This bad, Abdul. No *yakshi*. We must tie him to the wall.' I pointed towards the entrance where Torugart stood as docile as a milking cow.

'Okay,' Abdul said, looking round through narrowing eyes. Spotting what he needed, he strode over to a large peepul tree that rose majestically in the corner and picked up a fallen eight-foot branch lying just beneath. Then, while Sarah and I looked on in frozen disbelief, he charged at Kara with a bloodcurdling scream, 'WOOORRRRR!' This, unsurprisingly, did not have the desired effect of calming Kara down, but simply sent him into a new frenzied spasm of flying hooves and snapping jaw. I turned to Sarah and shook my head.

'What the hell have I bought?' I asked dejectedly. 'It's not a horse, it's a bloody rottweiler.'

'It's not the horse that's the problem, it's this maniac!' She jumped forward towards Abdul, and held the branch back in mid-attack. 'Stop that, stop that at once,' she bellowed. 'It's a horse not a wild animal, you idiot.' She stared at him with utter contempt. 'Can't you see you're just making him more angry?'

Abdul reluctantly threw down the weapon and cursed. 'Ah, thees 'orse crazy.' He stepped back, slapping the side of his head, and pulled up his trousers defiantly. Still pounding the earth like a fighting bull, Kara held Abdul warily in his sights.

'Abdul, we leave now.' There was obviously nothing to be gained by staying. In fact, we seemed to be making things worse. Besides, I'd seen enough and with many things still to do, wanted to get away. 'Can you give them some hay and water? We have to go back to the bazaar to do more filming, buy saddles and equipment. We'll come back later and check that they're okay. Tomorrow morning we'll go riding.'

Abdul grunted approval, but did not look best pleased. And with one last unconvinced look at the first horse I had ever owned, I turned and walked away. I couldn't help but think that I'd just made another howling gaffe.

Back at the bazaar we struggled once more through the masses, the stifling heat and rising dust to gain some extra shots of Sarah and close-ups of the fray, That done we turned our attention to equipment. Finding bridles, ropes, and felt mats for beneath the saddles – known here as *numnahs* – was easy, but saddles themselves proved a problem. Asking didn't help. Once we managed to make people understand what it was we were looking for, we were simply led on a merry chase through almost every quarter of the heaving market. This did give Sarah the chance to buy a sheepskin jerkin, me a black wool jacket and both of us a warm fur hat, but proved a fruitless search for what we really needed. Eventually, returning to the animal section, we persuaded two horsemen to sell us their own saddles. I'd tried out one of them earlier – a black leather cushion connected to a metal frame, it was one of the most comfortable saddles I'd ever sat on. With plenty of padding and leather thongs from which to tie sleeping mats, coats and water bottles, it was ideal for riding long distances. But the haggle was a nightmare.

Surrounded by an aggressive crowd, one man agreed 300 yuan for his saddle, but, on hearing that his mate was holding out for 400 for the second, he upped his price accordingly.

You can't do that,' declared Sarah, dumbfounded. 'What kind of businessman are you? You make a deal then break it?'

I agreed and, raising my voice, called his bluff. 'OK, so we don't take your saddle, only his one.'

But the saddle seller was a great deal better versed at this game of bluff and counter-bluff than I was, and simply shrugged and said OK. Rather shamefaced, I began to haggle again. Just then I noticed an ugly, pockmarked Uyghur youth had his hand in my trouser-leg pocket, the pocket where I kept my cash.

'What the fuck are you doing?' I shouted, grabbing his wrist. After all the pent-up frustration of squabbling for the saddles, it was a joy to let rip at someone uninvolved. 'You stealing from me? Huh . . . huh, you a thief, a thief?' Gripping him tightly, I held up his arm. Everyone's attention switched from the saddles to the pickpocket, who, sensing himself in on awkward corner, began to chuckle nervously. Suspecting the locals would turn on him rather than me – in Islam stealing, particularly from travellers, is a cardinal sin, and under Chinese law a crime punishable with many years hard labour – I felt my confidence growing. 'You get the fuck away from me,' I yelled into his hideous face. 'Or I'll go and get the police. *Police*. You understand? *Police*, you stinking little thief.' Still, not wanting to see the scene turn nasty, or involve the authorities, I pushed him away and, with a helpful kick up his bony arse, watched him scurry off into the crowd. A few minutes later we'd agreed a price of 700 yuan for both saddles and a leather whip for Sarah. Struggling under their heavy load, we wandered from the maul.

By five, both thoroughly exhausted, we were back at the swimming pool.

Much to my relief I found that Kara had been moved and was now tied like Torugart to the thin brick wall. There was no sign of Abdul Karim, but we could tell they'd been fed and watered. Feeling more confident and wanting to make friends, I approached Kara with an outstretched hand. It wasn't a good move. The moment I was within kicking range, he pinned his ears back, spun his arse round and his two rear hooves come flying towards my face.

'Shiiiit!' I yelped, jumping clear.

'Come on,' said Sarah, in a small and tired voice. 'Best leave him be tonight. He'll have calmed down by the morning.'

I was only too happy to agree.

After a shower and rest at Chini Barg Hotel we returned to John's Café and drank until we were both very drunk. We decided we'd earned it.

At eight the following morning, a little thickheaded, we returned to the Seiman Hotel. The sight that greeted us was not a pretty one. At some point during the night Kara had had a fight with a small thorn bush, now destroyed, that had been positioned just behind his arse. With his tail caught in the spiky shrub, he'd evidently yanked on his head collar, demolished a large section of the flimsy brick wall and had broken free. His tail was now thick with prickly burrs and appeared like a matted dreadlock. With that lunatic grin still smeared across his face, he regarded us contemptuously from the far side of the enclosure, beneath the peepul tree, ready for the morning's duels. A tail full of burrs? I shook my head. That was all we needed.

Abdul arrived a few minutes later. With raised arms and a few harsh words he caught Kara easily enough and tied him to another part of the wall where the bricks were two layers thick. He then went to help Sarah tack up Torugart.

Feeling that I should handle the preparations of my own horse – I was after all about to undertake a 2,500 kilometre journey – I picked up my saddle and approached Kara. One hand outstretched before me in a gesture designed to alleviate fear and build up trust, I whispered, 'OK boy, whoa, whoa. That's a good boy, whoa . . .' Once again Kara spun round and let fly with his two rear hooves. This time one of them caught my arm.

'Fuuuuckk!' I shouted, shocked, dropping the saddle in a heap at my feet. 'You little bastard, I'm trying to be your friend. Jesus Christ.' I felt like punching him. Instead I stood back, shaking, and watched as Kara once again began to paw the earth beneath him.

This was not what I'd expected and I was at a total loss what to do. Having ridden since early childhood, I knew and understood that the best way to be master of a horse, to gain its respect and its subservience, is to act like you're the boss, whether you think you are or not. It was drilled into me early on: never, under any circumstances, show that you're scared. If you do, they'll know in an instant and treat you with contempt. As a consequence I have never really been afraid of horses; after all, as in most situations in life, if you go in pretending you're in charge in all probability you very soon will be. Over the past fifteen years I had ridden a variety of horses on four of the five main continents, and this theory had always stood me in good stead. Until now. I have to say that Kara scared the shit out of me. And there was little I could do to make the brute think otherwise. Feeling rather inept, I waited for Abdul.

Once Torugart was ready – tacked up with consummate ease – Abdul came striding over. Without breaking step, he just bellowed his now trademark. 'WOOORRRRR!', stepped up to Kara, forcing him back, untied the rope and led him through the wooden gates and up to a small apple tree. Once there, he wrapped the rope round the tree's trunk and pulled it tight, thus forcing the left side of Kara's head hard against the bark. He then threw the end of the rope over Kara's neck, looped it underneath and told me to hold on tight. So long as I held a firm grip on the rope, Kara was going nowhere; at last he was under my control.

"Orse crazy, crazy,' muttered Abdul, angrily placing the saddle on Kara's back. As he began to fasten the girths – it didn't help that these Chinese saddles had three leather straps – Kara again tried to pull free. But leaning back, using the tree for support and extra purchase, I could hold him in place quite easily. What worried me was that I was the only one in Kara's field of vision. And his deep moist eyes did not appear too kindly.

Mission accomplished, Abdul disappeared to fetch his own horse. 'Shit.' I stood back and wiped my brow. I could feel my heart pounding behind my rib cage. What a way to start the day – I felt exhausted already – and now I had to ride him. I looked back at Sarah.

'You OK?' I asked, thanking the Lord that at least Torugart was calm. This would be the first time Sarah had ridden since we'd undertaken a horseback camera trial in England. There she'd seemed far from natural in the saddle, and from holding a bad position had ended up with a very sore, and blistered, rear.

'Yeah, I'm fine,' she said, standing at Torugart's side, holding his head. 'What about you? What are we going to do if Kara does this every morning? Now we've got Abdul, but what about in the mountains, in Kyrgyzstan? If you can't even get close enough to saddle him up, we won't get far.'

I didn't need to hear this; I knew it well enough. 'It's probably just teething problems' – I tried to sound convincing – 'you know, he doesn't know us yet, he doesn't know this place. Maybe when he does, when he trusts me, he'll calm down. He was fine in the bazaar.' I turned and looked at Kara. 'If not, I guess we'll just have to find another Abdul Karim.'

'Or another Kara . . .'

'Or another Kara.'

'I think he's been ill-treated,' she said, viewing him pityingly. She was probably right.

When Abdul returned, perched sideways on a mangy chestnut brute, I gave Sarah a leg-up onto Torugart. Once in the saddle she appeared terrified, sat awkward and tense, and clung white-knuckled to the reins.

'Don't worry,' I told her, looking up. 'You'll be fine. And remember if things get too tough you can always swap with me.' She tried to laugh but found the effort too great. Her concentration now lay elsewhere.

Standing back, I suddenly found myself sighing ironically and shaking my head once again. Not for the first time the lunacy of the situation struck me like a physical blow. The scene that now unfolded before me – Kara and his snarling face, Abdul Karim and his flyless trousers and toe-split shoes, the shattered swimming pool and the broken wall – could hardly have been less similar to the one screened in my brain back home in England. Sarah didn't help. Not only was her face a ridged mask of terror, but to my eye her riding gear appeared ridiculous. Though no doubt sensibly attired for a morning ride, in beige jodhpurs, brown half-chaps rising to the knee, a tight black T-shirt, white, suede gloves and a purple plastic motorcycle helmet she'd bought in the bazaar, she appeared more Chelsea girl meets Pony Club eventer than a Central Asian horsewoman. In my opinion part of the fun in undertaking trips like these is dressing up for the role. When I rode my motorcycle round Africa, I didn't wear a smart blue Gore-Tex biking outfit; in my mind I was playing Mad Max and fucked-up leather and tired jeans were more the order of the day. Similarly in Afghanistan, while traipsing across the Hindu Kush in search of Kafiristan I wore no warming ski jackets or shiny red kagools; I dressed as the Afghans did. And here we were in Kashgar for goodness sake, about to launch ourselves off on a journey back in time to follow Zhang Qian along the old Silk Road! My suede chaps were discreetly tucked away under my khaki combats; my much-used Afghan waistcoat I wore over a pale long-sleeved T-shirt; around my neck was tied an old bandanna; and on my head a local cap was squarely placed. Purple plastic crash helmet indeed!

'Wouldn't you be more comfortable in your combat trousers?' I ventured innocently. 'And do you really have to wear that hat?'

'Jodhpurs are far more practical,' she replied, her jawbone clenching tightly. 'And I'll wear the helmet until I feel more confident.'

Smiling wryly to myself, I united Kara and pulled him from the tree. To my immense relief he let me mount him.

Following Abdul Karim we walked beneath the arched entrance of the old hotel and out onto the street. Turning left away from the city centre we passed small fruit stalls, nut stands, barber's shops and butcher's. At the taxi trolley park, one of Abdul's mates waved a cheery greeting before cracking his whip above his horse's head and moving off towards town. At first the traffic was dense: noisy tractors, diesel trucks and whining two-stroke bikes, some tooting their horns in merry recognition as they passed by. As nervous as she was, Sarah saw little humour in their noisy antics.

'Shut up,' she shouted at the smiling drivers. 'Jesus, can't you fuckers just shut up . . . shut up and slow down.' She was expecting English manners, respect for horses and their riders. Amazingly, neither of our mounts batted an eyelid; they strolled along as casually as mules.

Most people we passed looked our way. Often they waved and laughed and shouted greetings to us and Abdul, who was enjoying himself enormously. Suddenly the focus of attention, he sat proudly in the saddle, acknowledging all, answering their questions with swollen self-importance.

'Jaw-ni, and Soo-rra.' Smiling broadly, he repeated our names.

Soon we crossed a bridge over a mud-brown river and were out of town, into an area covered by market gardens. The motorised traffic died away to leave just bicycles and donkey carts. Carrying produce from the fields to sell in the town, the drivers appeared in high spirits. Some carried watermelons, others onions, chillies, sacks of potatoes and clusters of maize. Just before an army checkpoint we turned off the main road. Here the tarmac disappeared to leave a pleasant track of hard-baked mud, dappled in the morning shade. On either side, tall silver poplars climbed towards the brilliant sky. Behind them were low brown homes, with thatched roofs and mottled walls, where children played in the dust. At last it was quiet, save for the gentle sound of birds singing and workers talking and laughing in the fields.

'This is more like it, hey?' I asked Sarah, who was riding a short distance behind me and had now visibly relaxed.

'God, not half. I hate that traffic . . . what a beautiful day.'

'How's Torugart?'

'Fine. What about Kara?'

'Great.'

He was, too. To my profound relief he was behaving impeccably. From this position, where he could not see me, he was easy to control. Not only that, he was actually a very pleasant ride; he walked out athletically, could shuffle easily in the half-walk-half-trot manner of the East, and was particularly adept at a trim, collected canter. No faster than a trot – but very much more comfortable – he seemed to enjoy the bouncy, languorous movement and could keep it going indefinitely. Abdul informed me it was the stride favoured by the taxi carts, leading him to believe that that was what Kara used to do; it might also have explained his aversion to the saddle. I liked riding him and found myself running a hand through his mane, talking to him, stroking his flanks; I hoped my choice was not so dire after all. Perhaps we would be friends.

After a couple of hours the track ended. Abdul Karim led us right, along a small ridge dividing two fields. On either side men and women, girls and boys, were squatting close to the ground, harvesting chillies. At the end of the ridge where the fields finished was the wide and dirty Tumar River; unfortunately the bridge was down. Unknown to Abdul the centre section – some twenty metres of one hundred – had been completely knocked out by the recent floods. The high mudbanks sprouted plastic bags, bits of sacking, broken poles and torn clothing. They made a sad testament to the twenty-seven villages now washed away and the seventy-odd villagers killed by the flood.

Save turning back, there was nothing for it but to cross the river. Abdul pushed on first into the flat brown torrent. Both Torugart and Kara followed without fuss. At first the water was shallow, barely reaching the animals' knees, but the further we traversed the deeper it became. Soon it was up to their bellies, splashing fiercely with the exaggerated movement of their rising hooves. I had to lift my legs, jockey style, to try to prevent my boots being filled with water. I didn't succeed. As Kara stumbled on an unseen trench, I had the choice of either dropping my legs or taking a bath.

On the far bank villagers were searching through debris for anything they could salvage. Noticing us, some stood and waved.

At first we thought they were merely being friendly and waved back, but then we saw our problem. The bank on the far side was now so steep – an impenetrable wall fifteen-feet high – there was no way for the horses to scramble up it. Though we were almost across the river, if we continued in the direction we were heading we'd be stuck. Two men pointed frantically up the river towards the broken bridge. Following the direction of their outstretched arms, we turned and continued directly upstream. We passed a group of men diverting a channel with sandbags. Some more were pumping water from a flooded field. We rode between the bare concrete pillars and twisted steel rods that once carried cars and trucks between Kashgar and the south. Just beyond, the bank had been levelled to form a track which lead out of the river. Halfway up the bank, hidden beneath the surface, was a sheet of rusting iron. As the unsuspecting horses clattered over it, it vibrated and boomed like rolling thunder, sending Torugart leaping terrified into the air. Sarah did well to stay astride.

Unfortunately the track led us onto another noisy highway. Once again the drivers, spotting us as foreigners, smiled and waved and tooted their horns in friendly camaraderie. Again the spirit was lost on Sarah, who futilely berated them. Fortunately she had more effect a moment later when she decided to cross the road to take a quieter side street. Paying no heed to a forty-ton truck that was screaming down the road, she urged her horse across the highway and, with a determined jaw, held up a hand, policeman-style, commanding the truck to stop. Her purple plastic crash hat could have been a solar topi. I couldn't help thinking she'd have made a marvellous Victorian *memsahib*.

Twenty minutes later we were back at the hotel.

With Kara now calm, I decided I might risk trying to remove some of the burrs from his tail. He'd drunk a bucket of water and was happily eating hay; I'd ridden him, I'd fed him – I hoped we might have bonded. Sneaking surreptitiously round his rear, I cautiously took hold of his tail. It was thick with burrs, stiff as a piece of wood. Standing well to the side, I began to remove them one by one. But they were sharp and dry and clung tenaciously to the rough horsehair. Some crumbled in my hands, making the job far harder, others pricked my fingers, drawing blood. I was lucky they were the only injuries I sustained. Having barely made an impression on the burrs, a huge kick sent me reeling backwards across the yard.

The second week dragged slowly on, much the same as the first. Because of the horses we had a new focus, something to do, something to look after, worry about and enjoy. But beyond them, life in Kashgar remained pretty much the same. During the day, once we'd ridden, and the horses had been taken care of, we still spent a great deal of time doing our own thing, and in the evenings returned to John's Café. Since Sarah sat there and read, it gave me little option but to read myself. Though a part of me longed to move tables to sit with other travellers, I was reluctant to do so. We were supposed to be a team, and if reading was her preferred escape then I felt that I should join her.

And as time wore on I began to worry less. I realised that in the greater scheme of things these were still very early days. I told myself that for Sarah things must be very strange and that I had to let her find her feet, both in her travels and her relationship with me. Things would be better once we were away from the stifling town – and the e-mail – and into the mountains. I felt confident that we'd then start to settle down. Forced together, day and night, we'd simply have to form a closer bond.

On Thursday evening, John came and sat at our table.

'OK,' he said, lighting a cigarette, 'It's like this. I 'ave good news and bad news. Good news I find way for you to take 'orses out of China, but really this big problem.' He leant back and laughed. 'As I say, no one done this before, but for me is OK. You ride from 'ere, Kashgar, to military zone – this seventy kilometres away – then you 'ave put 'orses in truck and you travel in special jeep like tourist. Army man, big man, he say impossible to wide 'orses to pass.'

'Can't we bribe him?' I asked hopefully. 'Slip him a hundred bucks, for "administrative costs"?'

'Oh no,' said John, shaking his head vehemently. 'Theese Chinese Army very strick man, hard, no take money. Impossible. Before soldiers take money, now no. Big problem: government kill you.' With a hand above his head he mimed being hanged. 'You must take truck and jeep to near the top of the pass and then ride down to Kyrgyzstan. Is only way.'

'OK.' I looked at Sarah with a hopeful smile. 'At least that way we get to cross the border with our horses. If necessary we can always fake the military zone for the film . . . we don't have to show the truck.'

'Yep, it's fine . . . good news.' She took a cigarette. 'So what's the bad news?'

John grinned at her. 'But thees only 'alf news. Bad news is we 'ave to get vet's certificate and export licence for 'orses; otherwise no pass customs 'ere and no allow into Kyrgyzstan.' He flicked his ash. 'Even with this we no know if you allowed into Kyrgyzstan. Thees you muss find out.'

I already knew the answer to that. That very morning I'd received an e-mail from Alex in Bishkek, telling me there was no way of discovering whether or not we'd be granted permission to import horses into Kyrgyzstan. No government department he'd spoken to had had the slightest idea about such rules . . . no one had ever asked before. He'd explained we would simply have to risk it and hope for the best. Alex also confirmed that he would be on the Torugart Pass to help us cross the frontier – all he was waiting for was the date – and, though he'd made no direct mention of Dom, he added that as per our request two of my friend's trusted horse guides and four of his horses would also be there to help us on our way.

'And can you organise the vet's certificate and export licence?' I asked.

'I do, no problem; take blood test, fill form . . . but they mus' pass. Thees very important in China. Some years ago, big earth-quake happen in the east, Yunan province. They bring many horse from Xinjiang to help out. Some horse have disease, kill all local horses. Big problem. And the test cost money.'

I didn't doubt that. Until now we hadn't really discussed the cost of John's services. As we both knew he was our only chance of succeeding in our mission, there seemed little point. Though both Sarah and I found him charming, it was obvious where his flash watch and diamond-studded ring came from – people like us. His smile was suddenly a little unctuous. I expected the worst.

'How much money?' I asked warily. 'Trucks, permits, jeeps and guides . . .'

'I do my bes' . . .' He stared past us to the road. 'Since like this . . . maybe thousand dollar. Everything.'

I nearly choked on my beer. We had about $7,000 for the entire trip. To blow such a huge portion early on – and for such a short fraction of the journey – would put a major strain on later stages. I wasn't sure how Lion TV would respond to being asked for more money. Though things were still looking promising, they were yet to secure a broadcast deal. On the other hand, what options did we have? The only alternative would be to wait in Kashgar until the following Sunday, try to sell the horses in the bazaar – no doubt losing a fortune in the process – and then travel by foot over the border and start again. It was not the beginning to the film I had in mind. No, we had to do it and worry about the expense later; maybe tighten our belts in Kyrgyzstan.

Seeing my concern, John took my notebook, opened it up and began to scribble. 'I write down for you . . . truck three hundred dollars, jeep and permits . . .'

'Don't worry, John, I believe you.' I smiled tentatively and took a sip of beer. 'At least this way we are able to go. At least this way the film will be what we said it would be.' I looked at Sarah and she was nodding. 'No, it's OK really . . . thank you.'

I slouched back in my chair.

Then, quite without warning, Sarah shook her head and began to laugh.

'What's so funny?' I asked. John looked on, intrigued.

'I'm trying to imagine a vet taking blood from Kara. I hope the poor man has a good insurance policy.'

When we returned to the horses the following morning, all dressed up for another ride, Abdul was looking very smug. Kara's tail was burr-free. Late the previous evening, unbeknown to us, Abdul had taken it on himself to have the horses shod, and in the process dealt with the tail. When I asked whether the blacksmith was still alive, he explained that, far from a trial, it had been a doddle. Kara had simply been roped, thrown onto his side, and dealt with from an incarcerated horizontal position. While Kara lay there helplessly, they had pulled out all the burrs and washed his tail. I was impressed. What was even more amazing was that apparently the vet had already been and taken the horses' blood. So long as Kara wasn't suffering from any hideous disease – not out of the question, considering his maniacal countenance – we'd be on our way. Sadly, though, it wasn't a sign that Kara's behaviour would improve. He still had to be strapped to the tree before we could saddle him up.

The three of us set off on our daily trek. This time we stayed clear of the main roads, sticking instead to narrow lanes and farm tracks. Both horses continued to behave well, shying at nothing, quickening their pace on demand, and they seemed to be fit and strong. Abdul had a new jovial demeanour. He tried to tell us stories about horses and his life, and when he tired of this he shouted out words of Uyghur which neither of us understood but dutifully repeated. However, as we rode on, my mind drifted from the streets around Kashgar to beyond the mellow hills. On the western horizon, almost floating above us, the Mountains of Heaven shimmered, tantalising me with dreams of the journey to come.

PART THREE
High Plain Drifters

'Castles made of sand / Fall into the sea'

Jimi Hendrix

10 Into the Hills

As far as triumphal arches go it wasn't very grand. Stuck high in the Tian Shan mountains, battered by winds that swarm relentlessly over the lonely pass dividing the People's Republic of China from Kyrgyzstan and the former Soviet Union, the surprising structure stood forgotten and forlorn. Splintered and cracked, faded and worn, it rose a bleak remnant of a past era and a strange gateway to a far from certain future.

There were no sentries guarding the entrance and exit to these eastern lands, no customs and immigration, no barracks and no mess – on the Chinese side they had been taken care of twenty kilometres back down the road in Atush; in Kyrgyzstan they were apparently situated at the foot of the pass. All that remained on the frontier itself was a dilapidated, unmanned shed, two flagless flagpoles and a low-slung metal fence. Yet, as I turned Kara beneath the arch's ochre belly, a wide grin creased my weathered face. It was unlikely anyone would have passed this way by horse in forty years, perhaps forty more for an Englishman. After all the worries and uncertainties Kashgar had thrown up I now felt proud, exhilarated and deeply relieved. My impulsive plan to ride horses west from the famous Silk Road caravan town – a plan hatched spontaneously in the saddle while riding with Rachel – hadn't proved so fanciful after all. It had cost money, it had taken time, but ultimately it had also been possible; now all that remained was officially to enter Kyrgyzstan and the small matter of 2,000 miles to the Caspian Sea.

With a smile as wide as my own, one of Dom's Kyrgyz horse guides, Murat, rode Torugart beside me. It was a four-mile hack down to the Kyrgyz border post where Sarah would be waiting. Cold and nervous, she had opted for a lift in the minibus in which Alex had travelled up to the head of the pass to meet us.

Murat was friendly and warm, and I took to him at once. A

thickset man of Mongolian stock, all his features were oversized – a long round nose, wide puffy lips, a thick jaw and ears with long fleshy lobes, he appeared like a caricature. His jet-black hair was thick and straight, cut in the dubious 'mullet' style favoured by footballers of the eighties – long at the back and short at the sides – and a bandit's moustache framed his mouth. But his most startling feature flashed in his smile: half his teeth were made of solid gold. Perhaps feeling an affinity with my horse, he pointed at Kara's yellowing teeth and roared with unbridled pleasure. In Russian, broken English, mime and laughter, he explained that with such a perfect set of dentures my horse should advertise a dentist's practice. It was immediately obvious Murat's character matched his giant frame and, though his red jeans, white trainers and bright green kagool failed entirely to marry with my image of a Kyrgyz horse guide, I was happy he'd be with us for the next stage of the journey through the heart of the Tian Shan, the Mountains of Heaven, on the spectacular 500-kilometre mountain trail to Osh.

I gave Kara a pat on the neck and explained he'd just made history. He seemed an unlikely beast for such an honour.

The journey up from Kashgar to the border had gone smoothly enough. A long straight road, bordered by giant poplars and telegraph poles, had climbed steadily towards the hills. The trucks returning from the border post at Atush had thrown up a few awkward moments. Their loads had been covered by bright-blue plastic tarpaulins which flapped wildly as they sped past. This scared the hell out of Torugart, sending him charging off the road and onto the surrounding plains, with an equally terrified Sarah clinging desperately to his mane and reins. I dropped back and rode Kara at Torugart's side, shielding him and Sarah from the oncoming trucks, and soon both horse and rider calmed down and we rode on until dusk without further mishap. That evening we camped by a small lake. Abdul Karim took care of the horses, feeding them hay and oats that he'd brought in the jeep from Kashgar, and we set up our tent. To my surprise, however, Sarah opted to sleep outside on the dirt, citing the beautiful evening and the limited size of the tent; I felt absurdly rejected.

In the morning we'd ridden another twenty kilometres to a

prearranged spot and waited for John, Mr Fix-it from the café, to arrive. The truck he eventually turned up in could hardly have been less practical for carrying horses. It was a high-axled, flat-backed, steel-floored, low-sided lorry, used, I imagined, for transporting bricks. The only way to get the horses on board was to back it up to a large mound of rubble, lower the tailgate onto the dirt to form a kind of gangway, then lead the horses up the rocks – blindfolded in Kara's case – and coax them onto the back of the truck. None of this proved easy. While stumbling up the rock, Kara fell over backwards, rolled ungraciously to the ground, and then set off at a good lick back towards Kashgar. Once we'd caught him and finally led him successfully up the rock, he decided to jump over the tailgate into the truck. Landing on the slippery steel floor, his feet splayed like Bambi on ice and he skidded forward out of control, crashing headlong into the unsuspecting Torugart, who promptly collapsed as though shot through the head. With John's help, customs and immigration were dealt with easily enough in Atush and, having said farewell to him and Abdul Karim, we continued on to meet Alex and Murat as planned on the top of the Torugart Pass at two o'clock.

Rounding a corner where the track plunged steeply 100 metres to the left, Murat and I were now greeted by what looked like a set from a James Bond movie. A high barbed-wire fence, two layers thick, stretched before us left and right, cutting in two the plateau that lay below us. Where the metal wall and road collided a wire-mesh gate barred the way to a huge compound of hangars, sheds and offices. Beside the gate was a sentry tower and two threatening tanks. Behind them three commercial trucks were parked. From our vantage point above the complex I could make out soldiers – Russian and Kyrgyz, so Murat informed me – loitering by the fence and gate where the minibus was parked. Sarah was standing beside it.

Any anxiety we might have harboured about crossing officially into Kyrgyzstan with our horses was quickly dispelled, however. The five guards who manned the post, here dressed in Soviet camouflage fatigues – the hammer and sickle insignia still fixed to the centre of their caps – listened patiently as Alex explained our plight. They then called for an elderly man – evidently some kind of animal import official – who checked our vet's certificates and import licences and, finding nothing wrong, allowed us entry.

We were then directed towards a large grey hangar to the left of the compound where our own papers would be examined. The wind had picked up and rattled the frame of the building, causing the giant doors to bang and crash with eerie echoes. The horses seemed totally unconcerned and both stood calmly. Over a mechanics' pit a large articulated truck – used to run goods between the Kyrgyz capital, Bishkek and Kashgar – was being searched by guards. As we secured the animals they stopped their work to stare at the strange new consignment passing across their frontier and discussed us in whispers.

We passed through immigration and customs without any problems. Through Alex, the officer in charge – a Russian from Murmansk – asked a lot of questions about what we were doing, where we had been and where we were going, but there was nothing sinister to the interrogation. It seemed to me that he was simply trying to relieve a little of the boredom built up by a humdrum, regimented life on the edge of this dismembered empire.

The formalities over, we moved through into a stark canteen. Faded wallpaper covered the walls, a long strip light hung from the ceiling, and beyond a cracked window stretched the mountain plains. Sitting on the bench before a trestle table, talking to another Kyrgyz man and a young Russian lad, was someone I was very pleased to see.

'Dom!'

'Hey, Jonny –' was all he could say before I smothered him. Having released my friend, I stood back and looked at him.

'Shit,' I laughed, still holding his arms, 'this is an odd place to meet.' We were as near to Moscow as we were to Beijing, as far from the Arctic Ocean as we were from the Arabian Sea. In short we were dead centre in the very heart of the Asian land-mass and in an ex-Soviet customs canteen; it could hardly have been more surreal. With a broad smile he agreed.

I introduced him to Sarah, and he in turn presented the two men he was with. The Kyrgyz man, who had a kind face and soft brown eyes, was Akylbek, the second horseman that would accompany us on our journey through the mountains, while the young guy was a translator called Nicolai. Unable to ride, Nicolai unfortunately would not. Dom explained that as his season had just finished he was happy for us to use his staff and some of his animals. He was also pleased that given the timing of our arrival in Kyrgyzstan he'd been able to join Alex on the trip up from Bishkek to meet us.

'Strange thing though,' said Dom, once we were all seated. 'I thought I saw you last week.'

'Where?'

'Up at Lake Izzi Kul, in the east of Kyrgyzstan. I saw these two Europeans riding over towards me. I knew you were coming this way, over the Torugart from China, and I just thought, Jesus Christ, you're already through and have come up here . . . maybe looking for me.'

'So who was it?' I asked, surprised. There couldn't be many Westerners riding round Central Asia.

'They were a French couple,' he replied. 'They're doing almost the same journey as you. They started in Almaty, Kazakhstan, nearly a month ago now and are heading to Khiva . . . or the Caspian Sea, I can't remember which exactly. He's a geologist, she – his wife – speaks fluent Russian, is an artist and . . .' – he dropped his chin and whispered – 'oh my god, was she gorgeous.'

'Oh yeah.' ribbed Sarah.

'No, really unbelievable.'

'What were their names?' I asked.

'Sylvian and . . . Prescilla.'

'Queen of the steppes.'

'Exactly,' replied Dom smiling. 'You never know, you might bump into them.'

Just for a moment my happy bubble deflated. I didn't want to hear of anyone else living my dream, especially someone who sounded as if he was doing it a whole lot more successfully than I was. Sylvian's companion was not someone he'd picked randomly from a newspaper advertisement. His companion was his wife, who was beautiful and spoke fluent Russian to boot. But I quickly realised that if they were travelling three weeks in front of us it was unlikely we'd ever meet or even hear about them again; there must be a thousand different trails across Central Asia. Why should we choose the same one?

A moment later Alex appeared with two old women carrying bowls of rice, salad and mutton stew and, far more importantly, a large bottle of vodka. He opened it, squashed the lid flat – as local custom dictates: an open bottle has to be finished – filled six shot glasses and introduced us to the ways of Kyrgyz toasting.

Standing, holding the small glass before him, he said, 'I would like to welcome Sarah and Jonny to Kyrgyzstan and wish them luck on their forthcoming journey.' We all stood, he translated it for the others, and we then crashed our glasses together and downed the drink in one.

'So,' continued Alex, sitting down, turning to me, 'now you must make a toast.' He began to pour more vodka into the glasses. 'It is our tradition.'

'Okay.' I stood, thought for a moment, then raised my refilled glass. 'I should like to thank all of you for coming to collect us, for helping us across this border and especially to Dom for introducing us to you all.' Again we drank the liquid in a single shot.

'Right,' said Sarah, pulling me down and standing up, 'my turn. I know it's strange but I want us all to toast the mountains. I'm just so happy finally to be here.'

We drank to the Soviet times and Communism, to free trade and the West, the Kyrgyz soldiers for letting us in and the Chinese army for allowing us out. We raised our glasses to the film we were making and the book I was writing. Murat even toasted Kara's teeth. The first horse, he said, he had ever seen that was so happy it smiled all day. 'You wait,' I told him, 'tomorrow you can have the job of saddling him up.'

With the vodka gone and the meal finished, a glazed-eyed Alex took to the floor again. 'Please,' he said looking at me, swaying slightly on his feet. 'Now you and Sarah can ride across the plain to where we are going to camp tonight. It is only a short ride, maybe one hour. Then tomorrow, with Murat, you can ride over the pass to Tash Rabat. This is a beautiful Silk Road caravanserai.'

'Seriously,' interrupted Dom, 'Tash Rabat is a fantastic stone staging post, ancient. It'll be a wonderful place to sort things out.'

We staggered outside. The horses had been moved from the

hangar and were now tied to a pole by the entrance to the restaurant. They both seemed calm. Dom took one look at Kara and almost choked. 'Jesus Christ, Jonny, what the fuck have you bought? He'll never make it.'

'Course he will,' I answered drunkenly and, with an exaggerated swagger, climbed astride.

Sarah, who was more drunk than I, found mounting a good deal harder. Placing her foot in the stirrup she managed to pull herself up to the saddle but, try as she might, could get no further. After three aborted attempts, with Dom and I crying with laughter, Alex gave her behind a push and over she went.

After a few minutes the minibus with Dom, Alex and the others had disappeared in a cloud of dust. Before us all that remained was a stark, flat plain bordered by a low trail of snowy peaks and a telegraph line directing our path towards the setting sun. There were no trees, bushes or shrubs – save the coarse grass, no vegetation of any kind – just the wild and silent mountain steppes, stretching away endlessly before us. Smiling broadly, I held the camera out at arm's length, trying hard to catch both of us in the shot, and cried joyously towards the lens, 'We did it! We crossed the border and now we're wild and free in Kyrgyzstan . . . heading off into the wild blue yonder without so much as a care in the world!' To be riding here, slap bang in the centre of Asia, should have carried with it a daunting feeling of distance and space, of miles to be ridden and problems to be solved. As it was I felt euphoric; happy and free and very much alive.

'Wow,' said Sarah, her face the image of delight, 'we did it, we really bloody did it.'

'Yep, from now on we're heading home, thousands of miles towards that sun.'

'It's just totally unbelievable.' She breathed in deeply, savouring the moment while she looked around. 'Mountains everywhere . . . what an incredible sight.' She then turned her head and looked at me. 'Thank you,' she said, surprising me by her sincerity, 'thank you for bringing me here and showing me all this. This is what I left England to see, not bloody Kashgar, Islamabad and all that shit. This is my dream, this is what I've longed to do: to ride a horse across land like this.' She stood in her stirrups, waved an arm theatrically above her head and screamed, 'YEE-HAARRRR!' to the mellowing sky. Then, turning her heels into her horse's sides, she sped off at a canter.

As I watched her go I couldn't help hoping that perhaps things would now begin to settle down between us; that all the teething problems we'd experienced on the journey so far had simply been a manifestation of our coming to terms with the trip, the filming and each other. As Sarah had said, this was what she had come here for, to ride wild and free across the mountain steppes, not to lumber through the bureaucratic quagmire Kashgar had thrown up. Amen, to that! Most of the practical problems were now behind us, I hoped. We'd crossed the border into the former Soviet Union and had therefore entered the Commonwealth of Independent States – a free trade area with shared language, common customs, culture and border agreements. In Akylbek and Murat it looked as if we had a small team we could trust, and horses, with one probable exception, that could manage a sizeable chunk of the journey. Added to that the filming, though intrusive and at times hard work, was going well and I was accumulating plenty of good material for a book. As I watched Sarah ride away happily towards the vast and untamed wilderness, across the plain to the snow-capped mountains and the setting sun, I was filled with an optimism I hadn't felt in weeks. With the warm vodka coursing through my veins I felt certain that this new, exciting phase in the journey would bring us closer together, that riding to Osh through the Mountains of Heaven would be the start of something new.

Dom and the others had set up camp on the edge of a nomads' small encampment. Ten yards from the minibus and our four tents squatted two pale canvas yurts. Rising from the grassy plain they appeared like giant toadstools in the fading light. Next to them was a rusting railway carriage, bearing rubber tyres. Dragged up here for the summer months, the strange contraption provided alternative accommodation while the owners grazed their herds. Smoke trailed from a central flue only to be dispatched on the gentle evening breeze. At its entrance, by makeshift steps, two wild-looking children sat cross-legged, drawing with sticks in the dirt. Beside them lay a mangy dog. As we approached, the children stood and ran inside.

To the left of the yurts stood a wire corral holding fifteen foals and two mares. By one – a short and shaggy chestnut – a woman sat on a tiny stool, easing milk from the animal's udders into a plastic bucket. Behind her stood a man. He was older, her father perhaps, with a portly belly, wearing a worn and grubby pinstriped suit and knee-length leather boots. On his head rested one of the most bizarre hats I've ever seen: tall and conical, made of white felt and embroidered with black cotton, it resembled a bishop's mitre or funky lampshade. With their round faces, slanted eyes and small flat noses, the family appeared Mongolian. Their cheeks were cracked, their lips split and their hands looked coarse and hard; even in summer the windswept steppes of Kyrgyzstan was a hostile world for humans. Across the lonely moor herds of wild horses roamed.

With the sun gone the air turned bitter, stinging my cheeks and turning my breath to smoky vapour. Not that this bothered me as I reined in and dismounted; on the contrary, as I looked west towards the flamingo skies my heart surged. As Alex had said, eight hours' ride in that direction across a range of distant hills lay Tash Rabat, an important Silk Road caravanserai and staging post. How many others over the centuries, I fancied, must have passed by here on their way from China to the West? How many others must have set up camp where we were camping, slept where we would sleep, stood where I now stood, holding their horses, the same raw air biting their cheeks, contemplating the journey ahead? Suddenly the thought of travelling the ancient road filled me with wonder: what trials, what adventures, what dangers and rewards would cross our path? Standing there, facing the mountains, the sky and the complete unknown, I felt exhilarated. At that moment I wouldn't have wished to be anywhere else on the planet.

Sarah, who was standing beside the railway carriage, was evidently charged by similar emotions . . .

This is like nothing I've ever experienced before. Standing here with this Kyrgyz family, the horses nearby, camp set up, we're in the middle of nowhere and I can't tell you how happy I am. She smiles broadly, her face positively glowing. *It's all been worth it, this long wait.*

I untacked Kara and, as Abdul Karim had taught me, hobbled him with the rope that extended from his head collar. Worryingly, he didn't try to bite or kick me but allowed me to tie his front feet up without any fuss at all. I tried to shoo him the ten yards to the watering hole and to eat the grass as the other horses were doing, but he just stood there, head down, looking as sad and dejected as a circus clown. I brought him some water in a plastic bucket; he barely touched it.

Dom came over.

'My God,' he said, 'I don't know where you found this horse but he's in some state. Those teeth are a nightmare for him, and look here,' – he pointed at the bare patches on his back – 'this is probably where a harness or something has rubbed.' With his hand he felt along Kara's withers. Kara immediately spun round, his normal angry self, and tried to bite us both. 'There . . . you see,' said Dom, jumping back, 'you said you've been having problems saddling him, well that's why. There's something wrong with his back.' He pushed his hands deep into his pockets. 'Maybe it's just a sore, maybe it's something more serious. One thing's for sure, he'll never make it to the Caspian Sea . . . or even Osh.'

'I know.' I smiled resignedly. 'Got any ideas?'

'If I were you I'd swap him at Tash Rabat. There are many horses there.'

It sounded like a promising plan.

'You won't get much for him but at least he'll be OK and you can pick up a local horse more used to the terrain. If you try to take this horse over the mountains I think you'll probably kill him.' He dropped his neck into his shoulders and shuddered. It was starting to get cold.

'And I tell you another thing,' said Dom, looking out across the misty plain, 'you're very late in the year to be trying this . . . riding all the way to the Caspian.'

'Huh, tell me something I don't know.'

'What will you do if you get held up?'

'Deal with it.' I shrugged and stamped my feet against the cold. 'I mean we can only do our best. The important thing is that we do actually make it to the Caspian Sea. If we have to put the horses on a truck for a few miles to make up time, so be it.'

'Won't that matter . . . for the film?'

'I don't know, Dom. I guess not really. It's supposed to be about real life.' I smiled. 'Besides, if we need to we can always fake it.'

We turned and headed back towards the camp. The deep red glow was fading fast; darkness was falling as a sickle moon rose above the lonely hills. Beneath it horsemen in thick black shawls were rounding up a herd of horses and driving them towards a shallow lake. Mist licked at the animals' hooves; steam rose from their flanks. Silhouetted by the blood-red sky, they appeared like ghosts.

'So what about Sarah?' asked Dom with a grin. He knew Rachel from his time running horse trips in Pakistan. He knew about our breakup and something of the story; it was natural he should ask. 'She seems like a nice girl.'

'Yeah, it's OK.' I pulled my collar close round my neck, then blew warm air into my hands. 'Fine, really. It could be better, but you know . . .' I looked over to the minibus where Sarah was laughing with Alex and Murat. They'd opened another bottle of vodka and were drinking from plastic cups. 'There were a whole heap of problems in Kashgar – nothing serious, just a struggle to communicate properly – but I think things will improve from now on. She got very bored there, frustrated. Now we're on the road I expect the excitement to take over. I hope so anyway.'

'Well, if it doesn't here, it never will,' said Dom, his eyes widening. 'This country is fucking beautiful. Really, you should think about bringing tourist trips here. It's a lot easier than Pakistan, believe me.' He nodded towards the group. 'Talk to Alex about it . . . he's great to work with.'

'Tourist trips?' I chuckled. 'To be honest, Wild Frontiers is about the last thing I'm thinking about right now. I think I've got my hands full with this journey for the time being.'

A wild dog that looked something like a cross between a husky and an Alsation came bounding over. 'Ah, Yalki Palki,' cried Dom, crouching to welcome the animal. It immediately fell to the ground and rolled over to have its belly rubbed.

'Whose dog?'

'We found him a couple of weeks ago near Lake Issi Kul, same day we met the French' – he pointed vaguely behind us – 'he's been with us ever since. You guys should take him with you. It's fun to have a dog like him around and he's good at spotting trouble. There are horse thieves and bandits in these hills. A dog can be useful.'

I stroked Yalki Palki's head, and he immediately twisted round and licked my hand. 'It's a strange name, Yalki Palki. Does it mean anything?'

'"Bloody Hell", I think.'

In camp I was pleased to see that Alex had supplied a large modern two-man tent for Sarah and me. Of khaki green, with fly sheet and insect shield, it would give us a fine and cosy shelter. Our tent was small; this would be much better.

We had dinner, cooked by Sarah on a small kerosene stove, drank more vodka, talked and laughed. I found the group fascinating: each member carried the imprint of the region's history. Alex, a slight man of Slavic descent, with fine fair hair and brilliant blue eyes, was of noble blood. His great-great-great grandfather had been a Russian prime minister under Tsar Alexander I. The grandfather of Slava, the minibus driver, had been a German prisoner of the First World War, imprisoned near Tashkent in 1916. He was currently in the process of trying to gain German citizenship to take his small family back to the land of his ancestor. Nicolai's grandparents had been deported from Moscow to Siberia during Stalin's purges; his parents had then moved south into Kyrgyzstan. And Murat informed us that his wife was a Dunga, one of Kashgar's Chinese middle classes, and was forced to flee across the frontier during the unstable times of Mao's Great Leap Forward. I was enthralled by this encounter with living history.

As the only woman, Sarah was the main focus of attention. Matching the men drink for drink, it seemed as much for the challenge as any desire, between their stories she had them roaring with laughter at her toasts and comments. It was good to see her having so much fun. It was almost midnight by the time we prepared to turn in.

Murat and Nicolai said goodnight and headed to their tents. Akylbek followed.

'Alex,' said Sarah, pulling her shawl close around her shoulders, 'do you mind if I sleep in the minibus? It's bloody cold out here tonight. I'll freeze.'

'You don't want to sleep in the tent?' he asked, glancing first at her and then at me. I sensed Dom's eyes throw a quizzical look my way. As I had in front of Abdul Karim, I felt embarrassed, even slightly humiliated, and turned my eyes to the ground. They had obviously been expecting Sarah to sleep in the same tent as me, as had I. The cold was all too clearly a thinly veiled excuse, for Alex had provided us with two wonderful ex-army sleeping bags that would have kept us warm in an arctic blizzard. I couldn't help but feel small. Head turned down, I skulked away.

'No, not tonight, I'm freezing,' said Sarah, placatingly. 'If I sleep in the van, Slava can turn the engine on during the night and keep the heating going.'

'Oh . . . OK, sure, whatever you like. But you'll have to get used to it soon, the minibus will leave the day after tomorrow.'

'I know, it's only for tonight.' I heard her say.

I found my torch and struggled inside my tent alone.

A horse's scream killed the silence of the plains.

Struggling from my tent just after dawn, I found Kara snorting viciously, pounding the ground with his hobbled front feet. Before him stood Torugart. With a sudden swing of the head my angry brute lunged at Sarah's horse, sinking his teeth into Torugart's neck. A moment later they were both tumbling to the ground, scrapping like a couple of drunken youths. My heart sank. What, I wondered, had pissed off Kara this time? Whatever had Torugart done? Nothing, most likely. I had to face it, my horse was simply mad.

Murat couldn't catch him; neither could Akylbek. Every time they tried to grab Kara's head collar the horse swung violently round and aimed a well-directed pair of hooves in the direction of their heads. Murat laughed and joked, pretending the horse was funny, mimicking his unusual smile, but I could see in his eyes, by his agitated manner, that he was also worried. Dealing with Kara for the next three weeks was not something that he'd had in mind when accepting the job. Unable to catch him they had no alternative but to shoo him into camp. With his front ankles still hobbled together he looked comical, jumping forward like a circus seal.

As usual, tacking Kara was a nightmare; without the incomparable Abdul Karim or a suitable tree to strap him to, this morning was worse than ever. Having finally caught him using a bag of oats, an anxious Murat refused to do more than hold his head, leaving me to do the rest. Having the explosive fury of a half-ton animal directed at you before breakfast is a very tiring and unnerving business. Despite the fact that a harsh frost encased the ground, by the time Kara was saddled and ready for the off I was exhausted and soaked in sweat.

After a short breakfast we prepared to mount. Like a movie star emerging from her heated Winnebago, Sarah opened the minibus door and strode towards her saddled horse. We said farewell to Alex and Dom, who would drive round with Akylbek, Slava and Nicolai and meet us at Tash Rabat, and thanked the nomads. They'd been kind to us, giving us butter, cheese and yoghurt. The young mother in a scarlet shawl and black cotton scarf who'd been milking the mare the previous evening hurried over and as a parting gift offered each of us a china bowl of *kumis*, Kyrgyzstan's national drink. Warm and frothy, the horse's milk was thin, bitter and slightly fizzy – tasting like bitter yoghurt or liquid goat's cheese – but seemed strangely uplifting; they told us it was slightly alcoholic. Her husband, Bazaar Bek, was a short man dressed, like the soldiers at the frontier, from head to toe in ex-Soviet army camouflage fatigues. He carried an old rifle slung across his shoulder and binoculars round his neck. He'd been a conscript soldier with the former Union's army and had fought in the Afghan war. As Murat was unsure of the exact route over the pass and down to Tash Rabat, Bazaar Bek agreed to show us the way. Accompanied by Yalki Palki and two more yelping dogs, we rode from camp, north-west towards a range of distant hills.

Beside the lake the ground was damp and marshy. Reeds and wild flowers grew at its edge. White birds with wiry legs and pointed beaks paddled in the shallows. Further away the earth turned red, became dry and brittle, covered in rough green weeds, and cracked under the horses' hooves. Dens of marmots – a mountain animal resembling a beaver – blighted our route and forced us to travel slowly: a hoof down one of their deep holes and a horse's leg would snap as easily as a brittle twig.

Within an hour we were out of sight of the camp on a plateau, closing in on the low green hills. No trees or bushes punctuated the rough grasslands, only cold grey rocks, veined with granite, rising at random from the wild earth. Without a breath of wind it was calm and quiet, the only sounds the jangling stirrup irons, the panting dogs and the horses' hooves as they shuffled across the dirt. Our voices were magnified by the space and silence.

We were now on the mountain trail between Kashgar and Osh, one of the main arteries of the old Silk Road. Nearly 2,000 years earlier Zhang Qian himself had come this way, like us, travelling to Ferghana in search of the Heavenly Horses. How good it felt to be on his trail. Once again the excitement of riding the ancient trading route – the Jobek Joli, as the locals call it – churned within me. Hypnotised by the lazy rhythm of the horses' hooves, my mind began to wander. I imagined caravans of old, laden with fine fabrics, spices, precious stones and jewels bound for the markets of Byzantium and Rome; I pictured the hired escorts armed with swords and spears, bows and arrows; the merchants and the bandits; I saw the evening camp and heard the stories round the fires. For a long time I'd wanted to ride the old Silk Road, and now at last I was.

It wasn't long before my romantic reverie was broken by more immediate concerns: I was lagging a long way behind. Using my legs and heels I tried to inject some life into Kara's stride, but with little success. I flicked his neck and rear with my leather whip, uttered words of encouragement, cursed and swore, but nothing made a difference. At first I wasn't overly worried, simply surprised. Though certainly an arrogant and ill-mannered brute, he had at least shown himself to be fit and strong in Kashgar; I'd had no problem riding there for four to five hours at a time. But Kashgar was considerably lower, maybe as much as 2,000 metres. As he stumbled listlessly on, head down, snorting and wheezing like an old asthmatic, I wondered if he could be suffering from altitude sickness. I felt sure all he really needed was a good drink of water but, as if to prove the old adage, when I led him to a shallow brook he simply wouldn't oblige. It was unbelievably frustrating. I'd been under the misguided impression that horses were bright animals. Not Kara. I scooped some water into my hands and drank, as if to remind him what to do. He just gazed at me through vacant eyes, that ludicrous grin still smeared across his face. Pulling his head down I pushed the salubrious liquid against his nostrils. Still he wouldn't drink. 'Arrgh, you stupid fucking ass,' I shouted in frustration. 'Can't you just take a bloody sip?' He shied back, a look of abject fear in his rheumy eyes, shaking his head as though I'd offered poison.

Having remounted, I removed the camera from my saddlebag, attached the microphone and tried to record something of my feelings on video tape. My attention diverted, Kara immediately veered drunkenly right, then left, and ground to an exhausted halt. Utterly frustrated, I replaced the camera in the saddlebag and continued to drive him forward using my hands and heels; there was nothing else to do. A long way ahead I could see Sarah, laughing and chatting gregariously with Murat. It was quite an achievement since they spoke barely ten words of the same language. Her evident good humour did nothing to improve my spirits.

'Why don't you stop?' a voice inside my head was screaming at Sarah. 'Jesus Christ! Can't you see I'm in trouble? We're supposed to be a team, helping one another . . . at the very least take out your camera and film!' I felt my temper rising. All the problems, uncertainties and annoyances of the past weeks came flooding back. The mountain steppes that had felt so magical a little while earlier now rose around me like prison walls.

At last they came to a halt by a rapid-flowing river. They were searching for a suitable place to ford. I saw my chance to catch them up and once more dug my heels into Kara's sides. I also removed the camera, sensing another dramatic shot, but to my utter chagrin before I was close enough to film the scene effectively they'd moved onwards, crashing headlong into the icy water.

'Fuck,' I spat under my breath and tried again to hurry Kara along. But by the time I'd reached the near bank they were climbing out the far side, leaving me nothing to do but follow.

'Are you OK?' Sarah asked nonchalantly as I emerged from the glassy torrent.

Once more a voice raged in my head. 'Do I fucking look OK? For the last two hours you've not cast so much as a look over your shoulder to check I'm all right. My horse won't drink, can barely walk, is about to drop dead under me; I can't film because all my energy is going into making the bastard move, and here you are swanning off into the distance, fluttering your eyelids at the bloody guide. No I'm not O-fucking-K, I'm fucking ANGRY!' But the girl that stood before me now appeared like a stranger. I felt I didn't know her at all, and I was unsure how to tell her to pull her finger out, to help with the filming – that this wasn't just a holiday – that at the very least it would be kind to show some concern for me.

'Kara's in a bad way,' I mumbled darkly, feeling my eyes narrow under heavy brows, annoyed with myself for not saying what I was really feeling.

'Yes, my horse too,' replied Sarah with a shrug. 'It's hard work for them up here.' She then turned and trotted off to catch up with Murat.

I urged Kara to follow them up the steep bank which lead back to the mountain path. As I struggled up its grassy surface my saddle slipped backwards and as I dismounted to tighten the girths around Kara's puny sides, my trouser leg caught on one of the three sharp buckles, tearing it from knee to crotch. If I had had a gun I would have shot someone.

Soon we reached a steep ridge of shale and rock that led to the windswept mountain pass. The climb was terrible. Cutting a route along a narrow shelf of splintered slate, the perilous path zigzagged towards the distant summit. Bringing up the rear I had to dismount and literally drag Kara after me. When that didn't work, I had to stand at his side and whip his bony arse. It was the only way to move him forward.

With the sun gone, snuffed out by a thick black cloud, the wind picked up and snow began to fall. Within moments we were climbing into a mounting blizzard. At 3,500 metres the air was thin and raw and I found myself struggling on the loose rocks, gulping desperately for oxygen. My legs became weak, my arms went limp, my mouth as dry as paper. Alone, it would have been hard enough; with Kara it was a nightmare. With freezing hands I checked my pockets for my leather gloves and discovered that I'd lost them.

Up ahead, almost at the top, I saw Sarah sitting on Murat's horse, being led by the gallant guide. She appeared to be laughing. In my head I pleaded with her to take advantage of her freedom and position to film some dramatic shots, but she just rode on.

Then Kara was down on his knees, his belly, labouring haplessly. Having veered from the narrow path onto crumbling shale, he'd slipped and fallen; for one dreadful moment it appeared he might lose his balance all together and be lost down the craggy slope into the abyss below. But hanging on to the reins, taking the strain, I just managed to hold him steady while he found his balance. His lungs were heaving, pushing his frail ribcage in and out, his quivering nose streaming. He looked up, and the eyes that regarded me were tragic and lonely. He seemed to be telling me he'd had enough.

I tried to encourage him up, pulling at his bridle, whispering, shouting, stroking, hitting; he didn't try to bite me, just lay on the broken slate, pathetic and confused. Struggling myself on the loose rocks I managed to clamber round behind his rear and flog his scrawny flanks. I hated it. I despised whipping him so hard – no matter that he'd tried to kick me to hell and back every day for the last fortnight – he was a sad animal, down and out, and the violent action made me shake. But at last it worked. Drawing on one massive effort, Kara suddenly scrambled to his feet again and lurched pathetically forward. I looked up to see that Bazaar Bek, having safely delivered his horse to the top, had returned to help me. He took the reins and pulled Kara forward while I encouraged him from behind. And eventually we reached the crest of the pass.

There, tumbling away before us, range after range of mellow smoky-green valleys and blue-tinged peaks cascaded into a pastel distance. Crystal waterfalls crashed from dark ravines to emerge as silver ribbons far below. Wreaths of mist slipped between the folds of neighbouring cliffs before falling into a dark abyss. And high above a lonely ridge an eagle hung in the vast expanse of sky, his wings motionless, as if made of rock. The snow stopped falling, the storm clouds parted and the sun burst through to strike the hills with golden rays. It truly was a perfect spot. Sarah stood awestruck. Murat was grinning broadly, proudly displaying his golden teeth. Even Bazaar Bek, a man who'd seen the sight a hundred times, appeared impressed as he silently smoked a cheap cigarette. All of them were happy, satisfied in their work, enjoying where they were and what they were doing. I wanted to feel the same. I wanted to share the exhilaration, the sheer wonder of being swept up in the spirit of adventure on the ancient pass. I wanted to feel the same rush of excitement I'd experienced the previous evening and on the morning ride earlier. But somehow I could not. Clawing away at the pit of my stomach was a nagging feeling that somehow things were intrinsically wrong. Not simply with my partner, with my horse or the journey that I was making – however hard, they'd work themselves out – no, it was something more deep-rooted that I couldn't quite put my finger on. A sense that here, on the old Silk Road, high in the fabled Mountains of Heaven, I'd finally bitten off more than I could chew. I shook my head and cursed darkly. The journey, it seemed, was once again turning into another painful voyage of self-discovery I'd neither planned on nor subscribed to.

Three hours later, tired but relieved, we crested another low ridge and found Tash Rabat below us. It lay at the edge of a flat maidan of lush green grass, beside six nomadic yurts, and was an impressive sight. Sheltering in the lee of a black granite cliff, constructed of dark stone with a huge arched entrance, domed roof and corner turrets, the caravanserai appeared like some ancient eastern castle, a mythical outpost from some long forgotten legend. Before it, sweeping out of sight behind a sheer ridge, was a wide green valley. Dotted upon it were hundreds of animals: horses, cattle, yaks and sheep. We sat for a moment in a row and watched in silence.

As we rode down into the valley, a little while later, a horseman approached. I heard him ask Sarah if I was her husband. 'No,' she replied forcefully, 'he's just a friend.' It appeared I'd been divorced.

11 Calling a Truce

'What are you looking so serious about?' asked Sarah.

Having watched the minibus carrying Dom, Alex and Slava back to Bishkek disappear down the dusty track, Sarah turned towards me. We were both sorry to see them depart – knowing we'd probably not see them again – but that wasn't the reason for my anxiety.

'Sarah, come and sit down,' I said, pointing towards a low stone wall to the side of the old caravanserai. 'I think we need to talk.' Now that the others had gone I had no more excuses. Though I hate such confrontations – and cowardly avoid them wherever possible – I knew we could not continue travelling in this way. Propping myself on the smooth pale rock, I began nervously to rub my hands together. Sarah sat down next to me, astride the wall as though it were a horse, and set about lighting a cigarette. In the back of my mind was the thought that we should be filming the scene – from a docu-soap point of view confrontations like this are riveting – but it all seemed too intrusive.

'Listen,' I said, looking at my hands, 'it's nothing too intense, I'm just not altogether happy with how things are going at the moment – I can't really believe you are either – and I figured it's probably better to say why and try and solve the problems than keep stumbling on with them all bottled up.'

'Really?' she said, appearing surprised, 'what's wrong?'

'Well, the main problem we seem to have is one of togetherness, or rather lack of it . . . I mean, for much of the time we seem to be on different trips.' I took one of her cigarettes and lit up as well. 'Yesterday on the pass I was really quite upset by your behaviour. It was obvious Kara was in a bad way, that I couldn't keep up, and yet you barely bothered to even look over your shoulder to see if I was still there. I felt you should have slowed down, stopped and tried to find out what the matter was, shown a bit of concern.' I threw the used match to the ground, worrying that I sounded rather lame.

'Huh,' she scoffed defensively, 'but you became totally unapproachable. You closed up, got this big black face and dark demeanour . . . and . . . and I just didn't know what to say to you. You're frightening when you get like that.' She pulled determinedly on her cigarette. 'Really you are . . . frightening.'

'OK, but hang on' – I could feel my pulse quicken – 'I know what you're talking about, I know that I can get like that, but the point is at what stage did I become like that? I was perfectly happy in the morning. I was fine when Kara was going OK and we were riding across the plain. Didn't it occur to you that something must have been pissing me off pretty bad to make me react like that? Have you seen me that way before?'

'No, but it doesn't make it any easier to penetrate.'

'But had you shown some concern I wouldn't have got like that in the first place. Rather than it being *my* problem, it would have been a problem we'd both have had, one we'd have shared, and therefore I wouldn't have got pissed off and wouldn't have needed penetrating. I . . .'

'Chicken and egg, Jonny,' she said defiantly.

'What?' I asked, somewhat confused.

'Anyway, yesterday I was nervous myself. It was the first big mountain ride. I didn't know how it would be. You know my riding isn't so good . . . I had my own things to worry about.'

'That isn't how it looked from where I was sitting.'

'Meaning?'

'Meaning that it seemed to me you were having a fine old time. Which is great, I'm glad. But I wasn't and as a team I expect a little more, I don't know, camaraderie. Look at what happened on the road back in China where those trucks were screaming past, scaring Torugart, where you were having a bad time.'

She nodded.

'Well, I didn't just leave you to fend for yourself, did I? I came back and helped. But yesterday when the tables were turned and I needed support I got nothing. It shouldn't be a one-way street.'

'I'm sorry,' she said, but without a great amount of conviction, and took another long drag on her cigarette.

'And there's another problem, Sarah: the filming. It is what we're here for.' I looked across, eyebrows raised, and saw that her face was beginning to mellow. 'With Kara the way he was, it must have been obvious that I couldn't shoot much. Therefore you should have instead. Yesterday was a really good story, just the kind of thing that will make this film work, exactly what Lion told us to look out for . . . a high pass with a horse falling over, nearly dying, me having a miserable time, the weather turning foul, snow and hail. It would have made a brilliant opening sequence to the horse journey. As it is, we really have nothing.'

'There'll be other passes, other stories, it doesn't matter that we missed one.' Her voice had softened, lacking conviction. 'It was the *first* pass, after all; I needed to think about riding.'

'But it's precisely because it was the first pass that it was so important. And the fact it was so fucking dramatic. Of course there'll be others but the reason why we're having this chat now is so we don't have to have it again. You've got a camera which you said you're accustomed to using . . . so use it.' I turned my head down and studied the end of my cigarette. 'It was one of the main reasons I picked you – because you said you were keen to be involved in the filming.'

She was quiet for a moment, weighing up the situation, and pulled a last drag on her smoke. 'Yes, OK,' she said at last. 'I'm sorry.' She smiled in what I took to be a genuine apology and squashed her cigarette against the wall. 'But, like I say, however it looked I was nervous.'

'OK . . . it doesn't matter.'

We both sat in silence for a while. Before us at the edge of the flat maidan, surrounded by the rough green hills flecked with purple heather, was a babbling brook and whitewashed cottage. The humble dwelling had a black corrugated iron roof with a square brick chimney, out of which pale smoke climbed. Had it not been for the yurts, and the yaks that grazed nearby, I would have sworn we were in Scotland. By the entrance to the building Murat and Akylbek were busily checking the provisions, chatting to Nicolai who'd stayed for an extra day to help with translation. Beyond them, a warm, rich evening sun was sliding behind the mountains.

I flicked my cigarette away. 'While we're talking, perhaps there's a bigger issue we should discuss.'

'Uh-huh,' said Sarah, regarding me cautiously.

'I don't know, Sarah,' I said, kicking the dirt with my feet, 'everything seemed to start so well. Back in England, on the way up through Pakistan, we were always nattering, having a laugh' – I picked a small stone from a crack in the wall and passed it from one hand to the other – 'and then, well, it all just seemed to stop. In Kashgar or just before.'

'I found that period very hard.'

'Why?'

'Oh, I don't know . . .'

'You talk about my cutting you out yesterday. For me it felt you did the same back then. Reading your books at dinner, practically living for the e-mail. Did I do something to offend you?'

'No, no,' she exclaimed quickly. 'I was having a very hard time. That was all.'

'How? Why?' I asked again.

She was silent for a moment and studied her feet. 'I was homesick.' She sighed quietly, embarrassed, as though it were a mortal sin.

'Homesick!' I gasped. 'Why on earth didn't you say something?'

'I don't know.' She shrugged. 'It's hard to tell a virtual stranger that you've suddenly been overcome with the homesickness of a thirteen-year-old. Especially someone like you. Drawing, reading, writing home on the e-mail were my ways of escaping.' She paused and dragged reflectively on her cigarette. 'But it wasn't just that. I was missing my boyfriend as well.'

Boyfriend? Of course. Though I'd conveniently managed almost to forget that a boyfriend existed, it seemed Sarah had not. Perhaps she wasn't quite as finished with him as I'd supposed. I sighed. 'Sarah, I had no knowledge of what was going on in your head. If you were missing home and things, you could have talked to me about it. Shared it. I'm actually quite a good listener.'

'Could I?' She was not convinced.

I wasn't either, but I ploughed on just the same. 'Yes, of course . . . it's what I mean about us being a team, helping each other through whatever happens. It goes for emotional problems every bit as much as it does practical ones.'

'Maybe,' she replied. 'Even so you could have said something, you know. Asked me what the problem was or tried to convey something of what was going on inside your head. If you were feeling so cut out, why not tell me? After all, it's hardly surprising that in such a situation I was homesick. It's a bloody weird experience you know.'

I laughed, recognising that she was probably right. I should have made more of an effort to get inside her head, to find out what her problems were. To talk. 'It's not easy,' she went on, 'to come out and say things like, I'm bored, or I'm really missing my boyfriend, or my sister or mother, to someone like you,' she continued calmly. 'You're used to being away, travelling alone, used to such a life and everything. I didn't want you to think me a wimp.'

'A wimp?' I cried, and threw the stone at a distant yak. 'I'll be very surprised if that's a word I ever use to describe you, Sarah.' She smiled back, evidently pleased that as a hardy traveller she hadn't been found wanting. I wondered about mentioning the tent situation. It seemed to me that sharing one might give us the space and time in which to form a real bond. But the reference to her boyfriend stopped me. I worried it just wouldn't sound right. Besides, the issue would come up again naturally soon enough once we were way up in the mountains. Instead I said, 'The one thing we must try to do is be more together. The biggest problem, I'm now realising, is that with no past friendship, shared acquaintances, relationship, history of any kind, when things go wrong it seems they can do so very quickly indeed. We've got a long way to go. Let's at least try to be friends . . . OK?'

'Yes.' she replied with a grin. 'I'm sorry about yesterday.'

'And I'm sorry I became so bolshy.' I stood up. 'Come on, let's get the boys and crack open a bottle of vodka, and toast . . . I don't know' – I threw up my hands – 'a new direction.'

'Excellent idea,' she said, jumping from the wall. 'After that little talk I could do with a drink.'

The following day was Sarah's birthday. From the Kashgar bazaar I'd bought her an embroidered shoulder bag for her paints and pads, a small knife and a bandanna; the latter largely so she would stop nicking mine. She appeared genuinely touched when I handed them to her in the yurt the two of us were now sharing, and kissed me affectionately on each cheek. I was very relieved we'd had our chat. At last the air between us felt light and clear, no longer so confused. I felt sure she'd now take a more active role in the filming and planning, and I resolved to be more aware of her feelings and, when she looked sad, to try to help her through it. With luck we'd become more of a team. Mention of her boyfriend had also made me realise that whatever thoughts I may have harboured back in England and at the beginning of the trip, Sarah was not a single girl and any romantic notions would definitely have to be shelved. And that was fine.

Most of the day was spent in preparation for the mountain ride to Osh. The four horses Dom was lending us – two as pack animals and two to be ridden by Murat and Akylbek – had to be re-shod, equipment had to be packed up neatly and the food that Alex had brought from Bishkek checked. Once we left Tash Rabat, bar one or two tiny villages, we wouldn't see civilisation again for at least two weeks. Everything we needed we would have to carry with us.

The final obstacle to our departure was the matter of my horse. To my relief the solution proved easier than I had thought it might. Horses in Kyrgyzstan were a good deal more numerous than across the border in China – especially here at Tash Rabat – and cheaper than their Chinese counterparts; either that or with Murat and Akylbek we weren't taken so blatantly to the cleaners.

Jergil, the watchman of the old fort, who wore the strange conical felt hat I now knew to be a known as a *kalpac* – the traditional headgear of Kyrgyzstan – soon provided me with a new animal. A jet-black stallion, around fifteen hands high, he was twelve years old, with a long tasselled mane and tail. He was also as fat as butter. For Kara I had had to skewer new holes in my saddle's girths because he was so thin, for the new horse I had to do the same only at the opposite ends. It seemed ironic in one deal to go from an anorexic cripple to a fat-bellied slouch. In exchange for Kara and another $100 I wondered how much of a good deal he would prove to be. Still, I was at least able to saddle him up without the risk of losing my teeth.

'What's his name?' I asked Jergil once the deal had been completed.

'Nima?' He looked at me blankly.

'No name,' said Murat. 'Is 'orse, that all.'

'People seldom name their horses in Kyrgyzstan,' explained Nicolai. 'Here horses are used all the time – as transport, food, for their milk, even as agricultural vehicles – they have no need to name them. It would be too sentimental, like a farmer in your country naming his tractor.'

Sarah stroked the horse's face. 'Then you'll have to name him, Jonny.'

I stood back and looked at him, but as nothing immediately sprang to mind I declined the offer. 'I think I'll wait and see how he goes first.'

As it happened I wasn't the only one who wanted a new horse. Sarah had her eye on one of Dom's animals, a beautiful black gelding, around fourteen hands, with long slim legs and an elegant head. On three of his fetlocks he carried long white socks, and a small white star burst between his eyes. Even though he stood proudly, holding a similar shape to English Thoroughbreds, he was far too small and dainty to be one of the strong, speedy Heavenly Horses of local legend. However, one thing was for sure, the closer we were getting to the Ferghana Valley, the more princely the horses were becoming.

'Murat,' said Sarah, gently touching his arm, 'can I ride this horse, and use Torugart for the baggage?' At first the guide seemed unsure, alternating his vision quickly from her to the horse and back again. The horse, which they called Younger, was only four and had therefore not fully developed. He seemed to be wondering about it carrying her weight.

'Oh, go on,' she purred sweetly, holding his arm and smiling prettily. 'It is my birthday, Murat.' Murat nervously returned her grin and said OK. I felt a little sorry for Torugart's being demoted in this way. He had hardly put a foot out of place.

In the shade of the ancient building, like countless travellers before us, we shoed the five horses. My new acquisition was as calm and placid as a beach donkey, taking the freshly forged thick iron footwear with nonchalant good manners, as did three of the others. But a small chestnut they called the Kyrgyz Express was a different matter altogether. Like Kara, the fiery beast kicked and bit and spun around as though possessed by the devil himself. There was no way to shoe him standing up. We had to rope his ankles, throw him over onto his side and, while three of us sat on his head and rump, let Akylbek do the business. Not that that went altogether smoothly; twice Kyrgyz Express managed to burst free from our tenacious grasp, once slicing a nail through Akylbek's hand.

I rushed off to get my first aid kit. When I came back Murat was laughing, running round in a circle making the noise of a siren and twisting a hand, like a light, above his head. 'Nine, nine, nine,' he happily cried as Sarah dressed a surface wound, 'Sarah, Jonny, emergency.'

'Oh shut up, you big brute,' chided Sarah, and as she stood up thumped him playfully on the arm. Feigning agony, Murat fell over onto the dirt.

'This is a bad horse,' I said, turning my attention back to Akylbek.

Through Nicolai, the horseman explained that the horse simply hated being shod. It was, in his opinion, the strongest horse of the group and the best by far on the narrow highland paths. Before Dom had bought it for his horse treks it had been owned by a hunter and was as sure-footed as a mountain goat.

Once they were all shod, I saddled my horse and rode him directly up the hill behind the caravanserai. Just as I'd thought, the fat-bellied hog was woefully unfit and within minutes was huffing and puffing just as Kara had been the previous day. Murat came galloping up behind on his larger grey. Solid and muscular, it looked like an old English charger.

'This horse is nearly dead as well, Murat,' I said, as he reined in beside me. 'What have you got me? He's no better than Kara.'

As usual he roared with infectious laughter. 'Eating, sleeping, no walking,' he said and dismounted. I jumped down and climbed astride the grey while Murat took mine. And as Murat kicked and whipped some life into my reluctant nag, I continued at pace up the hill. Strong and fit, the graceful animal ate up the ground, delivering me to the end of a ridge high above the valley in only a few minutes. From there the views were stunning. To the east I could see the pass we'd climbed the previous day and behind that, shimmering like glass in the hazy distance, the Torugart Pass and the Chinese frontier. Below, the valley was bathed in a golden sun, flowing like a river towards the north where the mountains rose and fell once more.

On the way down some young children came rushing from a yurt to meet us. One little girl, with a beautiful Mongolian face, dressed in a scarlet jacket, held up her arms as my horse passed by. Feeling like a cowboy I leant down, scooped her up and deposited her on the front of my saddle. Her name was Zarina and, as I held her tight, she began to sing.

That evening we had dinner in a yurt at the end of the maidan. It was owned by Zarina's father and mother. They were a kind couple who invited us into their summer residence so that we could film a traditional Kyrgyz family scene.

The home was surprisingly cluttered. There was an iron stove towards the rear with a thin flue expelling the smoke through a retractable hole at the centre of the roof. Around the edges were bound reeds and on the floor a thick felt matting. A dark wooden table, around which we all sat, was knee high and badly chipped, and stood in front of the stove. There were boxes, cushions, pictures on the walls; a giant plastic clock was propped on a ledge; there were saddles bridles, ropes and pails and behind a screen a baby slept. Again we were given *kumis*, followed by *laghmann* – spaghetti in a meaty broth. Until this trip I'd thought pasta came from Italy but, Nicolai explained, in fact it's just another example of the trade between East and West on the old Silk Road and it was European travellers who took it home from China.

Eager to continue exploring the myth of the Heavenly Horses, I asked our host if he'd heard of such a legend.

'Only in my dreams,' he said, with a wry grin. 'But they say the horses of Ferghana, especially around Osh, are famed for their size and strength and speed. I don't know, I have never been there.'

'Yes,' agreed Murat, excitedly. 'Horses of Osh are said to be magnificent. Apparently there is a famous mountain just outside the town. Big and steep' – with arms and hands he made an expansive gesture – 'coloured orange. Somewhere there they say there are hoof prints, giant hoof prints, cast in the rock, which were made by a horse who came from heaven.'

'Hoof prints?' I laughed, 'In the rock?'

'Certainly,' cried Murat indignantly. 'Long ago there was a king who was chased by his enemies up to the summit of some nearby hills. Completely surrounded, facing death, the horse took a giant leap over the rocks, the trees, the whole town, to this mountain on the other side. The spot where the horse landed the hoof prints remain.'

'Sounds like you've been dreaming,' said Sarah. 'Either that or drinking too much vodka.'

'And there are paintings too,' continued our horse guide stubbornly. 'Ancient paintings of the Heavenly Horses, high up on cliff walls.'

'Have you ever seen them?' I asked.

'No,' he answered. 'I have been told.'

'Then we shall try to find them.' I chuckled contentedly.

What our host said next was not such pleasing news. He had heard that day from a herder further down the valley that four Japanese nationals had been kidnapped by Islamic rebels holding out in the Batkent region, close to the Tajik border. As a consequence, soldiers from both the Kyrgyz and Uzbek armies had converged on the area in an attempt to rout them out. Batkent lay no more than thirty kilometres from our intended path.

Still, the news did little to disrupt another merry evening; it was after all Sarah's birthday. Again we drank vodka and toasted her and the days ahead. As we headed back towards our yurt and sleeping bags the sky above was inky black, sparkling with stars. Just outside the cottage we stopped to say goodnight to the others. Sarah took Murat's arm. 'Hey Murat, why're you sleeping in the house and not in the yurt with us?' Mumbling an incomprehensible answer, he shuffled nervously on his feet. 'I'm very offended you chose to sleep in there,' she continued, smiling cheekily. Murat seemed as nonplussed by this as I was.

We didn't leave early the following morning. Sensing a grand filmic moment – departing from the famous Silk Road staging post – I decided that we should spend some time getting the scene shot right. Done well, it could make for an epic moment in the programme: four cowboys, six horses and a dog moving down the valley, possibly the opening sequence to an episode. However, having scanned the valley with my David Lean hat on, I realised that the direction we would be travelling was nothing like as dramatic as the view the other way, towards the higher hills. We would also be shooting straight into the sun. Therefore, after a brief consultation with my partner, we decided to fake it. Having set up the cameras – mine at the southern end of the valley looking back towards camp, hers in camp to catch our departing rears – we climbed onto the loaded horses and rode casually up the valley. Then, having passed the far camera, much to the confusion of all who watched, we turned and rode back into camp, whereupon we turned once more and did it again. And again. And then, just to make sure we had every angle covered, we did it one more time while I took hand-held shots from the saddle. And by the time we'd done all that, taken the close-ups and stocked and marked the tapes, it was time for lunch.

Having eaten and packed up properly we prepared to leave again. With all the filming and general confusion I'd pretty much forgotten about Kara. In fact, to be perfectly honest, I hadn't given him a second thought since swapping him the previous day with Jergil. Now, just as we were about to leave, I caught him watching us from a grassy ridge just behind the cottage. Standing there, front feet slightly splayed, his head held low and mouth still fixed in that pathetic grin, he made a tragic figure. I wandered over, holding in view those ridiculous teeth and lugubrious eyes, and I couldn't help feeling a little sorry for him. I gave him an apple, which he promptly dropped, and stroked his dismal head. He didn't try to bite me, but just stood there, still, staring to the front. Feeling obscurely treacherous I mounted my newly acquired round-bellied beast, and led the way from camp.

Riding south down the valley, the narrow track took us between two sheer canyon walls. The rocks were dark and harsh, standing firm against the soft green valleys that hung suspended to the left and right. Gliding on the thermals thrown up by the cliffs, eagles soared high above. It was a beautiful afternoon: cotton-wool clouds dangled in a clear blue sky and a strong sun warmed our backs. With only had a ten-mile ride to the first night's camp, we were all relaxed and happy to be underway.

After a mile we came to a gate, the official entrance to the historical sight of Tash Rabat. A fat babushka in a dirty cotton throw came waddling from an adjacent cottage, screaming something in her native tongue. She refused to let us pass without payment. This was slightly ridiculous as there was no way of stopping us simply riding round the gate, across a shallow ditch and up the other side, but Murat decided it was more prudent to assuage her anger and cough up.

Soon we were out of the canyon, off the track, and making a trail of our own across a vast plateau, where the dry grass had been burnt to yellow by the summer sun. For the first time in a long while the horizon appeared far away, leaving a giant sky to dome above us. At the edge of the world another range of low green mountains caressed the skyline. There were no sharp peaks among them, no harsh angles or jagged cusps as there had been in China; here the distant hills were as smooth as sand dunes, as if they too had been sculpted by prevailing winds.

Some distance away I watched Sarah take out her camera and do a short video diary.

> *We're not on a road or even a track any more . . . just following Murat, our excellent guide . . . and it's fabulous. At last every evening will herald a beautiful new day, every pass a stunning new view, after every mountain there will be more beyond.* She looks wistfully into the distance. *I'm this far away from heaven.*

I too was filled with an electric feeling, a sense of wonder and joy at the world around me and of how lucky I was to be moving through it. Now, at last, we were riding the Central Asian Steppes. And beyond us beckoned weeks of this. I felt so happy I began to sing. Murat, obviously equally overcome by the moment, dug his heels into his horse's side and exploded into a gallop. Unfortunately in doing so he dropped the rope of his pack horse – the very excitable Kyrgyz Express – who took off at lightning speed in the opposite direction. Eager to join the fun, Yalki Palki took chase behind the bolting animal and before Murat could even change direction the loose horse was a long way off, heading back to camp. An embarrassed Murat had little option but to follow suit.

It was two hours before a sheepish-looking Murat returned and we were able to head on towards the hills. Once again I found myself lagging behind. My horse was fine, just lethargic and unfit.

This time Sarah stopped and asked if I was OK. I thanked her for her concern and said that though the horse was slow he was fine and that she should carry on; she rode up front with Murat.

Soon after six we crested a low pass and found a mighty wall of rock climbing vertically 500 metres out of the hills before us, stretching for miles into the distance. The top was flat, forming a rocky plateau, the sides sheer and smooth. Burnished by the setting sun, framed by the grass and the deep-blue evening sky, it glowed orange and red, amber and gold, pulsing, shimmering, as if alive. Surrounded by the mountain wilderness, it seemed like another world, like a set from *Star Wars* or *The Land That Time Forgot*. Then, in a moment, the sun was gone and the rock turned deathly grey.

'Kalkada,' bellowed Murat against the swirling wind that licked the mountain pass. 'White Rock.' He then pointed into the distance to where four jagged peaks rose above the plain, stabbing at the sky like fingers. 'This name MELS. Marx, Engels, Lenin, Stalin.' As he uttered the names he pointed to each peak in turn.

An hour later we made camp by a small stream on a ridge beneath the giant rock.

12 Out in the Cold

Making camp didn't take long. Each of us quickly found a job to do and accepted it without fuss. Having unloaded the pack animals, Akylbek and I loosened their girths – the horseman thought it would be better to leave the saddles on until the animals had cooled – removed their bridles and hobbled their feet while Murat and Sarah started setting out the tents: a pair of modern dome-shaped two-sleepers and a large, floorless canvas monstrosity, orange and green, to use for storage and cooking should it rain. Murat and Sarah seemed to derive considerably more fun from their job than we did from ours. While we struggled with frayed ropes and dangerous hooves, I noticed Murat sneak up behind an unsuspecting Sarah with a rope of his own. As she knelt down, concentrating on plastic poles and a nylon fly-sheet, Murat whipped the rope round her ankles and in a matter of seconds had her hobbled. Shrieking with laughter, he danced away like a naughty child.

'Oh yeah, very funny, Murat,' groaned Sarah, feigning annoyance. 'Why don't you grow up and act your age . . . now come here and untie me.' As she regarded her feet she smiled lightly and bit her bottom lip.

By the time they were ready to hoist the main tent I was finished with the horses and able to help Sarah hold it up while Murat secured the corners and sides by bashing steel pegs through the black rubber eyes that protruded from its edge. That done, Sarah started to pull supper out onto a plastic sheet placed in front of the tent, and to chop onions and potatoes while Murat assembled his paraffin cooker. Akylbek collected wood and set about making a fire, and I carefully labelled, logged and stashed away the video tapes we'd shot that day. Within the hour we were all sitting round a roaring fire, a cup of vodka in our hands.

It was a blissful moment; or should have been had I been able to forget my preconceived idea of a Silk Road mountain camp and enjoy the reality that lay before me. Once again I found myself questioning the validity of the scene; the tents were either too modern and neat, or ugly and old, and the food, spread across the large plastic sheeting, was positively embarrassing. Organised and bought by Alex and Murat, and laid out by Sarah, were pots of jam, butter, pickles, slices of smoked cheese, ham, sausage – known here as *kolbasa* – and bowls of dried apricots, sultanas and prunes. There was bread and biscuits, even chocolate and double cream. And that was just for starters. A fine pork stew – pre-prepared and carried in sealed glass jars – simmered on the cooker. It was a feast, such as is normally provided for well-healed tourists on a six-day trek, not a spartan meal for the hardy Silk Road traveller. Part of me felt like a fraud, but I was also very hungry, and after only a moment's hesitation was munching eagerly on a slice of soft, fresh bread, piled high with jam and cream. I wondered how to film the scene convincingly, to keep it in line with my nostalgic image of the past. In the end I didn't bother.

Darkness fell quickly. Within minutes it was jet black beside the cliff with just a faint line of amber light hanging above the western hills. Unable to use torches for fear of scaring the horses, Akylbek and I had to rely on our ears to catch and unsaddle the grazing beasts. When we returned, Murat was trying his best to tell Sarah a story. With his lack of English and her lack of Kyrgyz or Russian, they were evidently having problems.

'Hey, Jonny!' shrieked Murat, for some reason more optimistic about my powers of translation. 'This joke. Chuchka joke.'

'OK,' I said, sitting down with a grin on my face. I'd already heard a couple of Murat's Chuchka jokes. They were similar to jokes the English tell about the Irish, the Russians about the Poles and the Aussies the Kiwis, but these were about the Eskimos of northern Siberia.

The joke had Murat in fits of giggles but, even once we'd managed to translate it, left Sarah and I at a loss. All of Murat's anecdotes required a drawn out game of charades for Sarah and I to gain even a rudimentary understanding of them. I imagine in Russian they were very entertaining – Murat's whole manner was so enthusiastic and endearing – but with so little shared language it was an extraordinarily frustrating and tiring situation. I began to realise just how much of a handicap the language barrier was going to be and I found myself wishing we'd been able to bring Nicolai or another translator along. How many stories would we miss on the trip because we couldn't understand those telling them? Still, eager to discover as much as we could, we battled on, and from what we did manage to garner Murat was a very interesting character. Like everyone else he had been a conscript soldier in the Soviet Union's mammoth army and had served as a quartermaster at a large base near Tashkent, in charge of supplies for the Afghan war. By his own immodest admission he was an expert skier, parascender and parachutist, and had been the Kyrgyz national climbing champion two years running. He loved his country with a passion, but was very sad to have seen the Soviet Union disintegrate and many of his tales were sad lamentations, prefixed with the nostalgic expression, 'In Soviet times . . .' In those days, he said, there had been money, jobs, housing, general prosperity, but now, because of Moscow's financial withdrawal from the newly independent Central Asian states, there was mass unemployment, a crumbling infrastructure and rising crime. I wanted to learn in his own words about the world from which he came, but it was an exhausting process and after a while my brain could take no more. I lay back on the roll mat and let his words wash over me. By the flickering light of the mellow fire his golden teeth flashed like jewels.

When Murat eventually fell silent I sat up and yawned. 'Right then,' I said, smiling sweetly at Sarah, 'I guess it's time for bed.' I climbed to my feet and began to gather our possessions together.

'What time up?' asked Murat.

I told him six o'clock. He groaned. I smiled. Sarah didn't move.

'Murat,' she said, sheepishly smiling at the gold-toothed guide, 'do you mind if *I* sleep in the store tent?' My jaw dropped. For a moment I couldn't believe my ears. I stood looking down at her, quite at a loss to know what to do or say. For security reasons Akylbek had decided to sleep in the cold, damp, floorless tent – for Sarah to say she *wanted* to sleep there could only be read as an ill-disguised way of saying, 'I'd rather swim through sewage than climb into a tent with you, Jonny Bealby.' I felt as though I'd been slapped across the face. I turned to Murat who was regarding her strangely. He shrugged.

'You don't mind, do you?' asked Sarah, glancing momentarily at me.

'No, Sarah, you're right,' I growled, turning quickly away. 'Why should I care? You can sleep where you like.' Having dropped her water bottle back down beside her, I trudged towards what was now unequivocally *my* tent.

Once inside I pulled off my trousers and top and, without brushing my teeth, climbed into my sleeping bag. As I lay there in the darkness, heart thumping, listening to the three of them preparing for the night, my mind began to spin in a frenzy of confusion. No matter how hard I tried to calm down and tell myself it didn't matter, I could not. It just did. Was I really so repulsive to her that she'd rather sleep with the horseman in a cold and draughty, floorless shelter than in a modern tent with me? What did that say about the state of our relationship? It seemed to me that Sarah was throwing all the hard-found words we'd had the previous day contemptuously back in my face.

Outside I heard Yalki Palki whimper. Sitting up, I unzipped the door of the tent. Pleased not to have to spend the night alone and in the freezing cold, he happily clambered in and licked me on the face. Having settled him down, I lay back and stared into the darkness. A volley of thunder rolled across a range of distant hills and light rain began to fall. However I looked at it, I couldn't help feeling that my worst fears were coming true. My romantic, idealistic Silk Road odyssey was turning into a nightmare and there was nothing, it seemed, that I could do about it.

Just after dawn I unzipped the tent and struggled outside. During the night the skies had cleared, allowing a frozen mist to creep down the valley and cover the fly sheet with a thin layer of ice. Though the mist had now gone, a hard frost smothered the grass. It cracked and splintered underfoot.

I climbed high above the camp, passed where the horses were grazing, by the stream's rocky bed, and washed and shaved in a pool of clear and icy water. I knew it was important to record something of my feelings on tape, but when I turned the camera on words failed me. I felt humiliated again and was unsure how to express myself. After a while, staring into the lens, I mumbled something unconvincing about our talk, that it obviously hadn't done much good because things were still tense between us and that she refused to sleep in the double tent with me, preferring instead the store tent and Akylbek. I switched it off and returned to camp. Grimly, I stoked the fire, lit the paraffin stove and made a mug of coffee. As if sensing my loneliness, Yalki Palki came bounding up, wagging his tail and began to lick my hand.

When Akylbek emerged from the store tent, some fifteen minutes later, it was with cheery good humour. When Sarah surfaced she was equally bright. What surprised me was Murat bursting bare-chested like some mountain Tarzan from the same canvas shelter. Had no one used the other two-man tent?

No doubt sensing my anger, over breakfast Sarah kept up a constant stream of chatter. It did nothing to improve my demeanour. It was a frustrating business striking camp. We had to wait an extra hour for the sun to climb above the cliffs to dry the tents before we could begin to pack them away. During this time I kept myself busy – checking equipment, numbering tapes – trying hopelessly to hide the dark mood which held me in its grip. But it did no good. I knew I was behaving badly, irrationally, and that my mood was casting a shadow over the whole group, but this only made me more angry with myself.

Finally the tents were deemed dry enough to pack, we loaded the horses and prepared to mount. Frustrated that my horse – still without a name – had been so slow the previous day, I decided to try a new one out. Akylbek suggested Kyrgyz Express. He was small, barely fourteen hands, but having seen the speed and strength with which he had taken off the previous day I had few doubts he could carry me and so agreed at once. With Akylbek's help, I loaded my horse up with the baggage and we prepared to leave.

'Shall we get a parting shot?' suggested Sarah, still trying valiantly to break my frozen mood. 'It would be great filming that way as we depart.' She pointed down the valley. 'If I set the camera up here, and we all walk past . . .'

'Sure,' I said, 'whatever.'

Once in the saddle and out upon the twisting trail, much to my relief the problems in my head began to dissipate. Surrounded by such exquisite beauty it was hard to wallow in my own self-obsessed misery for long, and soon I was again enjoying the sense of liberty the environment imparted. I began to ponder whether I'd been all together fair to Sarah. After all, it was only my idea that we should sleep in the same tent. In London she'd said that we should, and it had been her idea to buy a tent, but perhaps she'd just changed her mind, and if she didn't want to now, why should she? It was embarrassing in front of the others, it was even a little hurtful, but when all was said and done, did it really make a difference? Looking across the valley to where she and Murat rode side by side, I resolved to try again to make things work. Still, when I saw her do another piece to camera, I found I was a little nervous about what she might be saying.

> *I'm finding it quite a struggle with Jonny . . . when we're camping, getting up in the morning requires a lot of effort. You really have to be full of beans, energy . . . and I find Jonny just hangs around like a big black shadow, not contributing much.*

My new horse was wonderful, as strong as an ox, yet pleasant and calm as well. Akylbek had been right: Kyrgyz Express evidently had some problem in the past while being shoed, for in every other regard he was as good-natured as a lamb. Not only that but he was also a joy to film from; it was as though he had been trained for the job. Part of the brief was to gain as many long shots of us riding through the hills as we could; not from the saddle but from a stationary point on the ground. Such dramatic, sweeping shots of us passing through valleys, across rivers and over passes would prove invaluable while editing, to link more focused, static bits of action. The only way to do this was for one of us to ride ahead of the group, set the camera up on the tripod, place the tripod on a rock, a ridge or small hill, turn the camera on, gallop back to where the others were waiting, turn and then walk casually though the shot, looking for all the world like we were simply continuing on our way. Kyrgyz Express was a master at it. Used to the solitary life of a hunter's steed, he'd canter away from the others without any fuss at all. Once at a suitable location he'd stand, unchecked, while I arranged the shot. He was small enough for me to leap back onto without any difficulty and, as fit as he was, could gallop around all day. Compared to Kara and my recently acquired lump of lard, Kyrgyz Express was magic.

Soon after eleven we came across a flock of sheep being herded down the valley by two cowboys. Akylbek and I helped drive them through a narrow ravine and onto a plain of grass. Light on the bit, quick on the stirrups, it was fantastic fun to twist and turn among the throng of animals, and it felt wonderful to be working.

At the end of the plain were two yurts and a canvas tent. Before one of the yurts, seven mares and five young foals were secured by ropes to a long metal pole driven into the ground. Beside that was a platform, six foot square, covered in small white spheres. From a distance they looked like golf balls.

As we were passing, an old man pulled back the canvas door and emerged from the dwelling. Uncommonly short, with rounded shoulders, he was dressed in a white smock, secured round the middle with a thick leather belt, baggy grey trousers and knee-high leather boots. His face was not Mongolian but Slavic, lined and pale with a wispy beard and sunken eyes. On his head he wore a peaked cap and pinned to his breast pocket were a row of tarnished medals. He invited us in for *kumis*.

Inside, the yurt was unusually spartan: a low table was positioned at the centre with a small iron stove against the far wall and, by the door, a wooden keg used for storing the *kumis*. Felt carpets covered the floor and reed mats lined the walls. Once we were all seated his wife appeared through the entrance. As short as her husband but twice the width, wearing a long baggy dress, holey woollen shawl and red silk scarf wrapped around her head, she scooped the mares' milk from the barrel with a ladle made from a vegetable gourd and deposited it in china bowls. Eager to record the interesting encounter on film, I turned the camera on the old soldier and asked him what the medals were for.

He straightened his back, pushing forward his jaw. '*Grrr*eat Patriotic War.' He lifted up his jacket and shirt to reveal his scrawny chest. Just below the ribcage, a couple of inches beneath his heart, was a small round purple wound, evidently made by a bullet.

'You were lucky,' I said, and pointed higher up. 'Had the bullet hit you here . . .'

The old soldier dropped his jacket and shook his head. A smile formed in his rheumy eyes. It was a look that said 'But it didn't.' His name was Mikhail, his wife, Katrin. That wasn't the only tale they had to tell. Through mime and the smattering of shared language we managed to ascertain that they weren't Kyrgyz but Russian and, like Nicolai's grandparents, had been deported to Central Asia during Stalin's purges. When I asked why, he simply shrugged. They were up in the mountains for the summer, grazing, milking their animals, making butter and cheese to sell in the bazaar and eat through the winter. As we were leaving I asked what the strange white balls were, lying in the sun.

'*Kroot*,' he said, and took one from his pocket. He gave it to me to taste. As bitter as a lemon, with the texture of chalk, it was some kind of dried cheese; revolting to my taste, it took a great deal of willpower to refrain from spitting it out. The old couple stood at the entrance of their temporary home and cheerily waved us goodbye. They didn't mind the fact that we did it three times. They took the concept of cut-aways and close-ups with the same easy balance I expect they now took most things in life. If you've survived being shot by a German sniper and being subjected to Stalin's purges, little else is going to faze you.

We rode on through the afternoon. Most of the time the going was good – easy tracks and grassy trails – but at times the terrain became less even and the trail harder to see. Crossing one low pass we struck upon a coarse area of boulders and rock – glacial moraine – and were forced to slow down while the horses picked their way gingerly round the obstacles. Akylbek was having particular problems leading my old mule. Still huffing and puffing under the luggage, he was almost pulling Akylbek's arm out of its socket as his horse pushed to go faster.

'Hey, Jonny,' called an excited Sarah, with Murat laughing by her side. 'We have a name for this horse.'

'Yeah?' I shouted back, turning in my saddle. 'What's that?'

'He's always slowing down, stopping Akylbek . . . we think you should call him Anchor.'

And so the horse was christened.

After a while Akylbek stopped and tied Anchor's rope to his

horse's tail. At least that way he saved his arm.

Later in the afternoon we found ourselves back on a high ridge above a tumbling river. The land was split by deep troughs, caused by side streams, which cut directly across our path. Scrambling down the small ravines wasn't such a problem, but the ascent back out the other side was hard for the animals. On one occasion neither Akylbek nor Murat could make their horses attempt the climb. Hitting with their whips, kicking with their heels made no difference at all, the horses simply shied away from the acutely rising bank. Akylbek called me to the front and directed me to go first.

With the others out of the way I pushed Express on. Bursting with energy, with me leaning forward, hanging on to his chestnut mane, he powered up the ridge as though it were a gentle slope, and the others duly followed. After that I was given the job of scout. When the horses were thirsty I was sent ahead to find a suitable place to water them. When we needed a camp I rode on to find it. It was a job I greatly enjoyed.

We made camp that evening on a bowl of grass by a muddy river. No sooner had we dealt with the horses and got the tents up than the heavens opened and it began to pour. I had hoped to film the scene, but with hard rain driving in rods against the land I had to abandon the idea and take shelter with the others. And after a quick supper, produced hastily at the entrance to the mess tent, and another few shots of pure Kyrgyz vodka, I went to bed exhausted, with the loyal Yalki Palki. We'd ridden for ten hours that day.

When I woke the next morning I was surprised to see Akylbek scramble alone from the other modern tent.

13 The Gods Must Be Laughing

We rode on across an open plain.

With the sun high we were joined by two young herdsmen. With the same broad jaws, hollow cheeks and distant, pale-blue eyes, they were obviously brothers. Neither wore a hat, and beneath their long, lank hair their skin was grey and sallow. Slavic immigrants, they held their narrow lips in strange, contemptuous grins. They rode shabby hill ponies and slouched crookedly in their saddles. With no tack to talk of, they used old rope for reins, wooden pegs for bits and had slung chains for stirrups across their felt saddles. They'd been up since dawn, they informed us, searching the hills for some sheep that had strayed from the herd during the night. Driving the stragglers before them, they were now returning home. They invited us to join them.

They lived in a dwelling on the edge of a wide flat maidan at a junction of two valleys. The house looked dark and dingy, but was unusually large for the location. Built on two floors with an outside staircase and raised front veranda, it was covered in creosoted weatherboard, had a corrugated asbestos roof and a stable-style front door. There was no glass in the windows, just cloudy plastic sheeting that billowed and flapped against the morning breeze. Beside the house was a broken-down stone corral, a low haystack and a pile of rusting food troughs. As we approached I had a feeling of flashing back a hundred years or more, to the Klondike gold rush.

'Jesus,' whispered Sarah nervously, 'it's like finding ourselves in a scene from *Deliverance*.'

As we rode up to the entrance all hell broke loose. To the left of the house, by the stone corral, there erupted a deafening maelstrom of snapping jaws, bared teeth, fearsome barks and anguished yelps. Behind the quickly rising wall of dust it was hard to decipher exactly what was going on. There were certainly a few dogs involved; one in particular was an evil-looking brute. Huge, with a dark and stripy, thick fur coat, it had had its ears removed. What they were attacking I really couldn't tell.

With a pang of horror, I suddenly realised.

Murat flew past me, galloping his horse towards the chaos.

'My God,' screamed Sarah, 'they're killing Yalki Palki.'

'Shit,' I gasped, lowering the camera, forgetting in my horror to film the scene before me.

One of the two herders had dismounted. Having picked up stones, he threw them at the animals, trying to break them up. He wasn't very accurate, nor did he seem too concerned; there was a freakish smile on his twisted face. Murat, without much care for his own tender flesh, leapt from his horse and waded into the melee. Lashing out at the animals wildly with his boots and whip, he shrieked and yelled at the madness around him. At first little happened, as the dogs' teeth still tried to find their mark. Undeterred, Murat battled on, appearing almost as terrifying as the animals, and soon began to break them up. One dog, smaller and less keen than the others, caught a crack across the head and retired from the fray yelping, then another and another, leaving only the striped aggressor. With a well-directed right boot, Murat caught him square on the chin and reluctantly the stripy dog withdrew. He stood back, barking incessantly at a dishevelled Yalki Palki.

I was surprised to see him still alive. He'd endured a ferocious attack by four large dogs. Though he could hardly move, he continued to growl courageously, displaying his white teeth and blood-soaked gums.

I jumped from my horse and rushed over to him.

'Is he all right?' asked Sarah anxiously, her face pale. The event had obviously unnerved her.

Feeling Yalki Palki's front right paw, Murat said, 'I think broken.' He looked down sadly at the stricken animal that now lay across his knee, shaking wildly. Apart from the wounded leg there were also a number of cuts on his face, mainly above his eyes, and two across his back. Thankfully, though, none looked very deep.

Alerted by the noise of the fight, others had appeared from the house and now stood round us in a close circle of intrigue and concern. Four women – wives of the herdsmen, their mother and an aunt – whispered among themselves. They wore red shawls and conical hats, had creased faces and callused hands. They were ethnic Kyrgyz and by their knees four or five grubby-faced, mixed-race children stood, watching Murat and the dog in quiet contemplation.

'Get back,' stormed Sarah, shooing them away irritably with her hand. 'Get back, give us some space. It's not a freak show.'

Murat took Yalki Palki's paw and gently moved it at the joint. Though in obvious discomfort, Yalki Palki didn't howl with pain, just whimpered quietly. As he tried again, the dog leaned forward and licked his hand. It appeared the leg was only bruised. Murat put Yalki Palki down and watched him climb gingerly to this feet. Much relieved, we led him limping to a hay rack and tied him up. He'd be lame for a while, but he would survive.

The excitement over, we were ushered up a rickety flight of steps, through the stable-style door and into a long and narrow room. It was drab in the extreme. The walls were grey, devoid of paint, and the bare wooden floor was rugless. There was nothing in the way of decoration and only a little furniture. A low table and a couple of stools were pushed into the corner. On an oily chest of drawers sat a curious red plastic alarm clock, shaped like a church; a brass samovar steamed beneath the window, beside which was propped a hammer-action shotgun. We were asked to sit down while some of the women prepared yoghurt, butter, bread, some goat's cheese and bowls of hot tea. Those not involved huddled in round us, smiling, staring and whispering to each other. Sarah seemed on edge.

'What's wrong?' I asked.

'I don't like these people, they make me nervous.' She sat back and clenched her jaw. 'I wish they'd just back off a bit, give us some room . . . and stop bloody staring. And those men, they've got such strange faces. I don't trust them. They could have done more to save Yalki Palki. Did you see the way they just stood and laughed? If it hadn't been for Murat he'd probably be dead.' She looked up at the wild, grinning brothers and then at the wives. 'Good job they got some outside blood, if you ask me.'

I thought she was probably right.

We didn't stay long. Having drunk our tea and picked at some bread and cheese, we thanked our hosts, wandered back outside and climbed onto our horses. Leading a limping Yalki Palki, we headed on up the valley.

We had another pass to cross that day. Both high and steep, by all accounts Kashka Su was going to prove a tiring obstacle on the remote mountain trail. We were now entering a region known locally as Jaman Tau – the bad mountains. Murat informed me that the name wasn't simply derived from the punishing landscape. '*Gooligani*' or hooligans – mainly very poor herdsmen, hunters and farmers who had turned to crime as much from necessity as avarice – were known to frequent these mountain parts.

His words soon appeared prophetic.

The goat track lead over a ridge and into a camp of armed men. With rough faces and tattered clothes – long woollen coats, thick felt trousers, leather boots patched with strips of rubber – they made an ominous sight. One had a rifle slung across his shoulder; there were two more guns propped against a rock. They stopped us and proposed sharing their midday food and alcohol with us.

The four men were hunters. Camped by a stream in a low hovel made of piled stones and clods of earth they'd been up there for a month snaring marmots, shooting ibex, Marco Polo's sheep and wild mountain goat. Pelts of the animals hung from homemade racks like macabre trophies. Others covered in curing salt lay on the flat stones. The curved horns of an ibex poked out from behind a pile of rocks. Four ponies were tethered to a fallen tree and a fierce dog was chained to an iron stake. Yalki Palki wisely gave it a wide berth.

In front of the dwelling a low fire smouldered. We sat in a circle round it and, in exchange for our coffee and biscuits, drank their vodka from old tin cups.

'Pooh,' said Sarah, contorting her face as she brought the clear liquid up to her nose. 'Smells like meths to me . . . just like the stuff I use to clean my oil paints.' This wasn't the vodka one buys in a bottle. This was raw spirit, ninety-six per cent proof, carried in a five-litre plastic container and diluted in the cup with a small amount of water. Still, like its up-market relation, it had a pleasant warming effect and, having finished filming, I lay stretched out, resting on a elbow, head on my hand, and listened to our hosts and guides chew the fat in their beautiful Russian tongue. They were all young – in their early twenties – and had characterful Turkic faces. When Sarah pulled out a packet of Marlboro Lights they went quite wild, jumping forward in great excitement. They had only a bag of rough tobacco leaves, which they smoked rolled in paper pages torn from an exercise book. She must have handed out a packet. Conscious that the Kashka Su still lurked above us, we downed their rank and fiery brew and prepared to leave. They insisted on showing us the way.

As we rode from camp the vulnerability of our situation struck me. Here we were high in the mountains, heading for an isolated pass, in a region known to be frequented by outlaws, with unknown gunmen as our guides. They seemed friendly enough, laughing and chatting merrily to us as we rode along, but they'd seen the camera and would surely assume that two foreigners travelling in these parts would be carrying a great deal of cash; more, in all probability, than they'd see in many years hunting. If they turned their guns on us, we'd have little option but to give them whatever they wanted.

Descending from a grassy plain, we entered a dried-out river bed. Lying at the base of a narrow gorge, the bolder-strewn terrain was a nightmare for the horses, who picked their way delicately across the sharp, uneven rocks. It was made even worse when the heavens opened and it began to pour. High above us, lost behind the swirling mist, was the pass of Kashka Su. Sarah and I pulled our waterproof ponchos from our saddle bags and pushed on into the mounting storm.

After an hour, with the hard rain turned to a dismal drizzle, we came to a second camp. Smaller than the first, it consisted of one low, old-fashioned tent made of dirty white canvas, which was home to two more friends of our new escorts. One of them was surprisingly wearing a pair of Converse trainers. This time they offered us *kumis*, which again we thankfully accepted.

Pretending to check the girth of one of the horses, Murat called me over.

'This no good situation,' he said, his dark eyes darting back and forth between me and the group of hunters. 'Maybe these men bad.'

'I was wondering the same, but I think they look OK.'

'I tell them Akylbek, me, we Kyrgyz military, keep you safe from Japanese kidnap-men.' His face split into his trademark grin.

'Excellent.' It was a good ruse. 'Do you think they believed you?'

'Maybe . . .' Standing there in Sarah's wide-brimmed hat and his East German military greatcoat, he certainly looked the part.

I decided it would be safer to share Murat's concerns with Sarah, just in case a nasty situation suddenly blew up. I picked up the camera and walked back to where she was sitting by herself on a low rock. Having trained the lens on both of us, I pressed record.

'These guys,' I said, pointing towards the hunters, 'they're armed, they've got guns, knives and they seem to be accompanying us whether we like it or not. Murat and Akylbek have told them that they're soldiers of some sort, looking after us . . .'

'Murat and Akylbek are?'

'Yep, because it's only a little way from here, over these hills, that the Japanese are being held hostage.'

Sarah appeared shocked. 'Oh, thanks!' she scoffed indignantly, throwing back her head. 'Why the hell did you tell me that?'

'I thought you should know,' I said, nervously readjusting my hat. 'We should all be aware of these things, be careful.'

'Oh yeah, great . . . that makes me feel just a whole lot better.'

'Don't worry, I'm sure it'll be fine.' I stopped filming, stood up and walked away. Her unfriendly, even petulant, reaction irritated me. OK, so it wasn't the most cheering news in the world, but surely it wasn't that bad. Besides, what would she rather? That I tried to spare her feelings and keep her in the dark about such things, just as one would a small child? Did she really need such mollycoddling?

Five minutes later we were back in the saddle and underway again. On the dried-out river bed the going was terrible, made no easier by the rain. It was frustrating, was it as not only excruciatingly slow work zigzagging over the loose boulders but it made it impossible to film anything other than tiny snippets of the action. The hunters, sticking close to us, chatted and laughed among themselves, but much to our relief, at a split in the valley, they pointed to the left and sent us on our way alone.

An hour later we had emerged from the confined canyon and

were climbing an awkward slope. The path was steep and rough, formed by loose grey shale and crumbling rocks, and was exposed to the wind and descending cloud. Halfway up, where the land flattened a mighty bowl, we stopped and looked behind us. There, to our immense surprise – and mild alarm – we saw one of the hunters, following in hot pursuit. As he got closer we could see the gun he carried. He was shouting at us to stop.

'What the hell do you think he wants?' I asked Murat. 'I thought we'd seen the last of them.'

'I no know, not us, not money,' he said, squinting his eyes to get a better look, 'all bandit come for that. Maybe he want Sarah.' He turned towards her and laughed.

'Very funny,' she said mockingly.

On a fit horse that was used to the terrain, the hunter was eating up the ground at an incredible rate. We sat and waited. When he arrived, he did indeed go straight up to Sarah. But it wasn't her he wanted, or her money. He held out his hand and asked simply in his guttural tongue, 'One pack Marlboro Lights?'

Before us now stretched a mile-long plain of black gravel. Wanting to rest the horses before the final push, Akylbek suggested we should walk. Within moments the curious mountain weather changed again. Once more the clouds parted to reveal a rich and warming sun. But with it came the wind. Gentle at first, but by the time we reached the middle of the plain it was howling down from the mouth of Kashka Su, picking up ice and snow and throwing it in our faces. Heads down and eyes covered, we marched in a bedraggled column across the hostile land.

When we hit the pass, things became worse. At 3,500 metres it wasn't particularly high but, as we'd discovered near Torugart, the steep sides of pale slate and black gravel made every stride a nightmare. For each two metres that the horses climbed, floundering clumsily, they slid back one. All the while an icy wind flicked like whips at our faces. Murat and Akylbek, with two horses each, had a particularly hard time, driving one in front, dragging one behind. This time it was Torugart's turn to fall. Slipping on a sheet of rock, he lost his balance completely and rolled over, then miraculously stopped. In the process he had lost his load. It took us twenty minutes to pack the flustered animal up again and return him to the path.

Still we kept moving, inch by inch, foot by foot. At times the angle of the mountain was so severe that I was forced to crawl, my back against the rocks, dragging Kyrgyz Express behind me. It seemed strange, almost unbelievable, that we were on one of the main threads of the old Silk Road. We were struggling to get four young people and six fit horses over this ancient pass; caravans of camels laden with bulky goods were beyond my imagination. I figured somewhere along the way we'd taken a wrong turn.

At last we reached the top. The pass itself was a high wall of serrated rock, with a ridge just wide enough for one horse, along which we had to advance. Awe-struck we stood, squashed side by side, staring west across the plummeting slope, to where endless valleys dropped away only to rise up again far away in another silver chain of snowy peaks. 'Ferghanskaya,' Murat said. 'The Ferghana Range.'

If all went well, in four more days I knew we'd be standing on top of that snowy land staring down on the Ferghana Valley. Two hundred miles long, fifty miles wide, the valley is Central Asia's agricultural heartland. For us it would mark the end of the mountains and the beginning of the plains, the end of wilderness and the rebirth of civilisation. What wonders and troubles would that bring?

Looking back was impressive too. We could see the giant form of Kalkada, the great White Rock under which we'd camped that first cold night, and beyond that the Torugart Pass and China. But, with the afternoon sliding towards dusk, we had no time to stand and ponder. It was vital we moved on quickly.

For the first 200 metres the descent was even steeper than the climb. But this time the horses proved a help and not a hindrance. Holding firmly to the rope attached to their head collars, we were able to use them as anchors to slow us down and provide support when sliding on the loose rock. Kyrgyz Express, as sure-footed as ever, proved a master, carefully picking his way down the mountain's broken side, three or four times holding me back from a certain fall.

At the bottom of the steep scree slope a grassy glade, broken by a shallow stream, formed an entrance to a narrow valley that led the trail round a dogleg to the north. Murat and Akylbek climbed down quickly, and set about watering their horses. I followed just behind. Sarah had more problems. Halfway down her horse decided to go no further. Evidently angry with the harsh stones snapping around his heels, he stood there as stiff and motionless as a granite statue. Pulling at the reins, Sarah was shouting in frustration at the unwilling animal. Showing more dedication to the cause than I'd often given her credit for, she took out her camera . . .

Come on, please. We've got to get down this mountain . . . It's so cold. Look, they're all the way down at the bottom, they'll start worrying, 'Where's Sarah?' Please, come on, Younger. Chew . . . chew! – she screams, getting more and more irate – *Come on you fucking animal. MOVE!*

'Whip his arse, Sarah,' I bellowed from below.

This she did. Again the horse moved, but only a couple of paces before grinding to a stubborn halt.

'Hit him, Sarah,' I shouted up again.

'What do you think I'm doing?' She yelled back, her face a mask of contempt. 'Patting the fucking thing?'

'Yes,' I screamed in retort. That was exactly what she was doing. 'Hit him properly. Hard.' This time she ignored me, put away the camera and stood staring at the horse, as though force of mind might make him move. It didn't. Great, I thought despondently. I looked at Murat. He was paying no notice, laughing at some shared joke with Akylbek. Knowing there was nothing else for it, I dropped my whip, my horse's reins and, with a sinking heart, started back up the mountainside. It took me twenty minutes to reach Sarah and her horse. Embarrassed, she avoided my eyes and pointed to Younger's hooves.

'Look,' she said, 'he's cut his feet. That must be why he won't move.'

Showing against his dusty white socks were two or three flecks of blood. They were little bigger than pinpricks.

'They're nothing, Sarah,' I panted, trying to keep the exasperation out of my voice. I rubbed one hoof with my hand, checking there were no deeper lacerations, and then stood up. 'Nothing at all, he's probably just scared, or tired. Here, give me your whip.' She did so. 'You pull and I'll drive him along from behind.' And with that I gave him one firm crack across the rear. Sure enough he began to move. After another two strokes I found I didn't need to connect with his flesh – the snap of Sarah's whip was enough – and after fifteen minutes we reached the others. After giving Younger a drink, we continued on our way.

On a ridge above the river, where the valley before us widened, we came to a halt. To the left the cliffs rose starkly towards tall forests of juniper pines but to the right, beyond the river, the land fell away in gentle rolling hills. Half a mile down the winding track, we could see that the river took a sudden detour in a large bow to the right, forming, on its inside, a flat stretch of land sandwiched between the high rock walls and tumbling water. The land nearest to us was covered in stunted thorn bushes. At some point, not long ago, a fire had evidently swept across the narrow plain, for they were stripped of leaves and coated in charcoal. Naked, twisted, scorched by the heat and turned to silver by the evening light, they appeared like hideous claws rising from the ground. But on the land beside the river meander was an unbroken patch of lush green grass and pretty wild flowers. It was an exquisite place to make camp.

In the fading light we continued down the trail, forded the shallow river and rode up onto the narrow plateau. I wondered how many other Silk Road travellers must have sought a night of sanctuary here. We were not surprised to find at the centre of the cleared area a ring of stones and the remains of a freshly burnt-out fire.

Murat let out a whoop and jumped from his horse in a state of some excitement. Bending over, he quickly picked a bunch of purple flowers that were growing by a flattened rock and rushed over to Sarah. Standing proudly before her, he held them out in his big right hand.

Sitting in her saddle, the normally resolute Sarah appeared flustered, unsure quite what to do with herself. She looked around embarrassed and began to blush.

'I . . . umm . . .' Sarah stammered, before gaining some composure. 'Murat, what are you doing?' she asked.

'Doing?' Seemingly unaware of the embarrassment he was causing, he pushed the flowers closer to her. 'Smell,' he instructed.

Sarah took the flowers and did as she was asked. Her nose contorted, her eyes narrowed. 'It's mint. Peppermint.' She looked at me, then down at Murat. 'What are you giving these to me for?'

'*Chai*.'

'*Chai*?'

'*Da, chai*,' Murat's smile deepened. 'You women, we men. We make horses, fire, you *chai* . . . good mountain *chai*.' Watching the transition in her face, he burst out laughing.

'Sod you, Murat . . .' exploded Sarah, and threw the flowers back in his face. But then she began to laugh, much relieved it appeared.

Night brought with it a beautiful, clear and starry sky. We built a fire, made silly toasts over cups of neat, raw vodka and were once again entertained by a laughing Murat trying to explain his Russian jokes and stories. Anaesthetised by the alcohol and Murat's sing-song voice, and with insufficient light to film or make notes, I relaxed and unwound. I still felt frustrated by my and Sarah's inability to form a close rapport, but, staring into the fire or up at the starry sky, I managed to let the problems drift away and my mind become a void.

Sarah sat close to Murat, enjoying the guide's every word. She seemed very content and was evidently enjoying the whole experience enormously. Though she still scorned Murat when he teased her, acting angry or annoyed, it was obvious by now that it was just a game. There was no ignoring that over the last couple of days they appeared to have forged a strong bond. With Murat Sarah seemed to have the kind of warm friendship that I had hoped to share with my travelling partner should romance not be on the agenda, and I have to admit I was slightly irked by this. But it wasn't long before I realised that I'd managed to read that wrong as well. When Akylbek said goodnight and headed to his tent alone, and Sarah moved to rest herself against Murat's legs, at last the penny dropped.

Not quite able to believe that I was a gooseberry on my own dream journey, I too, bade them goodnight and, followed by Yalki

Palki, headed off to bed. Once inside my tent, my head in my hands, tears of mirth filling my eyes, I began quietly to chuckle. So, romance it seemed had been a possibility after all . . . it just wasn't going to be with me. I imagined my friends back home, hysterical at the situation . . . 'Jonny, you arse. You're the only man we know who could possibly take a girl on a romantic journey into the mountains of a distant, beautiful land with only a gold-toothed horse guide for company, and who does she choose . . . ?' There was no denying the irony. It was the final unravelling of a disastrous and unattainable fantasy I'd been desperately clinging to since the day I'd met Rachel. I shook my head, wiped my eyes and pulled myself into the sleeping bag.

As I drifted off to sleep I couldn't help but overhear their conversation.

'These star here Orion's belt,' whispered Murat.

Teaching her the stars indeed!

The following day we rode on another thirty kilometres. Late in the morning we came upon a high plateau. Riding across the mountain steppe, it was easy to see from where the Tian Shan took its name. Squashed between the fertile earth and sheltering sky, it was as though we were riding on top of the world, close to the sky, almost touching heaven.

Not that it felt much like heaven to me. With Murat and Sarah happy in each other's company, I found it a solitary ride. Normally, while travelling alone I suffer little from loneliness. It seemed ironic that on the first full trip I'd attempted with someone from home, I felt more alone than ever.

In the afternoon we pushed on down the valley and soon emerged once again onto a verdant steppe. Long yellow grass was punctuated by tall wild flowers of white and blue. On the flat the horses were full of themselves, particularly Kyrgyz Express, who fought to break into a gallop at any opportunity, pulling at my arms and also my patience. Finding ourselves on a glorious open prairie, twice I gave him his head and let him run in the hope of quietening him down. Unfortunately, it had the opposite effect. Releasing the pressure on the stretching reins in order to take my sunglasses from my pocket, I once again lost control. Tired and frustrated, I slammed my hand down hard across his head and wrestled him to a stop. All I gained was a pair of broken glasses and a cut hand. Express was as strong as ever.

Akylbek came up alongside me. 'Mr Jonny,' said the quiet man, 'it no good hit horse across the head . . . they remember very long.' I felt terrible. The truth was I had allowed myself to take out my own unrelated frustration on my innocent and trusty horse, and that was unforgivable.

Later in the day we stopped for *kumis* at a neglected cattle station. It consisted of a large complex of concrete sheds and pens, a two-storey wooden house, hay lofts and barns. Murat explained that in Soviet times there had been many such places in Kyrgyzstan that reared and held thousands of animals to provide milk or beef for the Union. But with lack of funding, maintenance and skilled personnel, they had fallen into disrepair and disuse. There were no cattle here now, just a handful of mangy-looking horses and an unkempt dog. Without upkeep, the walls of the liveries were crumbling fast, the roofs collapsing, the fences falling down. Even the electricity pylons that walked a path towards some distant habitation carried no wire; it had been taken down – stolen – and sold. An old woman and her retarded daughter now lived in the house as caretakers. They spoke only Kyrgyz. They gave us mare's milk and sold me a black sheepskin for my saddle. I had wanted one since Kashgar. As we left, the shaggy bitch, looking something like a dark-haired collie, spotted Yalki Palki and trotted over. Evidently impressed by what she found, she elected to flee the abandoned cattle range and joined our curious band. I christened her Han Shah, the little queen.

Early in the evening, with dark storm clouds rolling up the valley, we made camp above a deep gorge. Once again it started to rain the minute we had the store tent up. We crammed inside, drank vodka to keep us warm and ate a simple supper. Sarah and Murat sat close together, surreptitiously holding hands, stealing glances at each other. As the rain eased, I poured a large splash of vodka into my cup and wandered outside. My mirth from the previous evening had long since drained away. I felt empty and alone.

To the west of our camp was a high cliff. Pulling my jacket over my shoulders, and collar up around my neck, I climbed a steep and narrow goat trail, round a ridge – out of sight of the camp – and sat on a boulder, staring west towards the setting sun. With the rain now gone it was a stupendous sight: hues of red and orange, purple and blue were reflected off the billowing clouds and high Ferghana peaks. But downcast as I was, I saw little beauty in it. The same fears and insecurities that had plagued me months before while sitting alone in that Brixton flat consumed me again. And a familiar question returned to haunt me: what am I doing here?

On one level the answer was pretty obvious: as a travel writer I was successfully plying my trade by travelling and writing and making a film to boot. But is that who I really was – a travel writer? At heart was I even a traveller? I took a long gulp of the vodka, wiped my mouth with a cold wet hand and lit a cigarette.

It was ten years, almost to the day, since I had flown out to Bangkok to meet Melanie and started travelling again. But that journey hadn't been driven on my part by an urge to travel or even a profound curiosity about the world: it was simply a desire to be with her. In truth, since I'd been lucky enough to explore a reasonable portion of the globe in my late teens and early twenties, I was feeling ready to settle down. Melanie hadn't travelled and wanted to do so. And we wanted to be together.

But watching her die changed everything. Throwing up a whole gamut of emotions – horror, disbelief, fear, despair, anger and frustration – the feeling that burrowed deepest into my soul was the sense of just how fragile life was. If Melanie – young, carefree, beautiful Melanie – could simply be here one minute and gone the next, then so could we all. And if we can die tomorrow, I reasoned, surely it makes sense to live as hard and fast as we can today. I also realised on returning home from India that there was nothing left for me in London anyway. The home I'd made for us to share was now no home at all. All that remained in that lonely city were reminders of what might have been, and I wasn't brave enough for that. My desire to escape the torments of a stolen life with Melanie, and an unquenchable thirst to live this new one to the full, had thrown me into travel.

And I'd taken to it like a man possessed. Travelling to more that sixty countries, I'd crossed deserts and plains, mountains and seas, struggled through rainforests and jungles. I'd ventured in and out of war zones – sometimes deliberately, sometimes by chance – and lost myself in foreign cities and towns. I'd dined with princes in their castles and forts, shared meals with peasants on banana-leaf plates. I camped out under the stars more times than I could remember and slept in brothels, prisons, shop doorways, on charpoys, reed mats and four-poster beds. I'd been held by rebels armed with guns and grenades; I'd made love on a tropical beach. I'd seen rockets rain death from murderous skies; I'd named a pagan child, in a mountain hut.

Travelling. Always travelling.

In the past ten years, the longest period I'd actually spent in one place was seven months, and that had been in a small iron-roofed beach hut on the west coast of India writing a book – a temporary abode, by design. I'd had no job, voted in no election, paid no income tax, owned no car, mortgage, television licence, mobile phone or insurance, and seldom been forced to pay rent. Scraping by on three modest book advances, a trickle of royalties, sporadic bouts of journalism, and living at least seventy per cent of the decade in the much less expensive developing world, I'd survived. Two months after Melanie's death I'd moved out of our London flat, packed two large trunks with pictures, books and broken dreams and stashed them away at my parents' home. They'd remained there gathering dust ever since.

But now I could see that this life I'd made had come at a considerable cost. Despite barely a day passing without dreaming of sharing my life with someone again, for the last ten years I hadn't managed to hold on to a single meaningful relationship. Financially, I had little more to show for my thirty-five years than the scruffy clothes that hung from my back. I'd missed a brother's wedding and a best friend's funeral, godchildren's christenings and my parents' anniversaries . . . hell, even with a ticket to the Nou Camp, I'd missed Manchester United lifting the European Cup!

None of that would have mattered if the path I was following were the one my heart truly desired. But as I perched on that cold, wet rock, watching the crimson sky fading fast to black, I suddenly understood it was not. Ten years earlier there had been a valid and tragic reason for travelling. All my adventures and misadventures had had an honest purpose: to help escape a crushing loneliness, answer impossible questions and ultimately fill the terrible emptiness caused by Melanie's death. And, up to a point, so they had. But I was over that now, had been for some time – if nothing else, falling in love with Rachel proved that – and therefore what reason was there to be fighting my way across these lonely mountain lands? For a book and television film? They were more of a career move than a passion. For Sarah? A hollow laugh rose in my throat and I shook my head. What a joke that was. The girl I'd chosen to share my happy ending was now sharing the tent of the horse guide! What on earth did that say about me?

I hurriedly threw back a long draft of vodka and frowned.

What was worse was that I knew very well that history was repeating itself. Wasn't it just the same story with Rachel, and even with Amel? Hadn't I been guilty on both those occasions of charging blindly into fanciful relationships without stopping really to think about what the other person wanted to get out of it? Hadn't I been guilty then of selfishly assuming that I deserved, that I would gain by rights, another Melanie in my life? Of course neither relationship had worked out. Why on earth should my relationship – if I could even call it such – with Sarah? She wasn't here to play a supporting role in my life story . . . she quite obviously had her own path to follow.

No, as I sat there staring west towards an inky sky and the first bright stars of the night, I knew things had to change. Travelling the Silk Road was a fantastic adventure I had truly wanted to make, and I would. But cradled high in the Mountains of Heaven, I felt that when the journey had run its course the time would finally have come to hang up my boots and put down some roots – somewhere, anywhere – for at least a little while. After almost ten years, I knew it was time to rejoin the world and face up to London, life and being alone again.

I drew deeply on the cheap, filterless cigarette, warmed my throat on the last of the vodka and stumbled back down the track. By the fire I found Murat and Sarah snuggling up together, looking happy and content. I said goodnight and made my way to my tent.

'Don't forget your water bottle,' said Sarah sweetly. 'I left it by the stove.'

That collected, I whistled for Yalki Palki but tonight he didn't come. After a minute's search I found him just behind the camp, happily entwined in a warm furry ball with his new friend, Han Shah. It somehow seemed apt. I returned to my tent alone, crawled inside my sleeping bag and lay down to sleep. But even here there was one last poke in the eye from the fickle finger of fate to remind me of the sorry corner I'd painted myself into. Sarah had failed to replace the lid on my water bottle correctly and during the night it leaked. So, while she kept warm through a tried and trusted method, I was left alone in the middle of a very cold night to skate round my tent on a puddle of ice.

14 On to the Plains and into Trouble

The horses' hooves dragged uncertainly on the brittle earth as we trudged across the stubble field, leaving the hills a misty blue behind us. Approaching the village of Karakul Jar, we stumbled along like stragglers from a battle. The long journey through the mountains had taken its toll. Two of the horses – Torugart and Younger – were badly lame; the others were weak and tired. We were almost out of food, hadn't washed properly for more than two weeks and our clothes were torn and tatty. With Osh still seventy miles away, I wondered how we'd make it.

Passing a wooden barn, a grain silo and water tower, we aimed the horses' heads towards a row of single-storey whitewashed homes a hundred yards further on. To the left fields of rusty corn swayed against the breeze; to the right lay an abandoned cemetery. Enclosed by a tall wrought-iron fence and padlocked gate stood two tarnished mausoleums and a dozen smaller graves. It wasn't a Kyrgyz Muslim graveyard. Rising from the wispy grass that overran the sacred sight were the three-slatted crosses of the Russian Orthodox church. Settlers, no doubt, who'd lived and died in these foreign lands.

The last seven days had gone well enough. Riding high into the Ferghana Range we'd found ourselves in a world above that of humans. The vaguely discernible tracks that we'd followed had been made by wild goats, ibex, wolves and mountain bears. Forests of giant thistles, three metres high, often plagued our route. Dry and brittle, they crunched and shattered as we pushed a path between them. For four whole days we saw not another soul.

And so the landscape changed. Gone were the accessible wide-open mountain plains with low snow-speckled hills many miles apart. Here the valleys closed in around us in sharp V-shaped ravines, with our path rising and falling along the edge of steep cliff walls. Often the going was treacherous. At one point a smaller valley met ours, spewing a shelf of dirty ice across our track. Hidden from the sun for much of the day it formed a lethal bridge, some forty feet wide. On the other side of the path yawned a deep chasm down which a swirling torrent flowed. Once again the sure-footed Kyrgyz Express was summoned to the front. Dismounting – had he slipped, my added weight might well have pushed us both to a watery grave – I lead the horse delicately across. Once there I turned and watched a determined Sarah lead Younger safely across, followed by Murat with his two horses. But when Akylbek was halfway over, Torugart slipped and fell. For a dreadful moment it looked as though our valiant pack animal was going to slide off the ledge and into oblivion. Torugart desperately struggled to regain control of his feet, which splayed in all directions on the lethal ice. Akylbek grabbed his rope just in time, stopping his slide and giving him just enough support to regain his footing and stumble across.

Then, late one glorious afternoon, with a yellowing sun full in our faces, we crossed the 4,000-metre Kandrajak Pass. It was a stunning ride following freshly made wolf tracks in the snow, and as I pushed Kyrgyz Express over the ridge to begin the long journey down towards the distant plains, I felt happier than I had done in a long while. My reflections on the mountainside had brought me a fresh outlook. The cosy idea of a new home and more-settled future was just the tonic I needed to help drive myself forward over the mountains and across the deserts and plains that would follow.

I have to admit that though internally I was recovering some peace of mind, externally my behaviour towards my partner wasn't very friendly; in fact, much of the time it was remote and even cold. I was annoyed with Sarah, still slightly shocked by how events had turned out. Ignoring my earlier lecture to her, I didn't share my feelings with her but kept them inside . . . not that I had much choice. With Sarah and Murat happy in each other's company, I was often left on a solitary ride. Which, under the circumstances, suited me fine. Recognising that my own crazy plans had got me into this mess, I now saw in Sarah not just an incompatible partner I'd fallen out with, but a stark reflection of my own stupidity. And the less I had to face that ugly image each day, the better!

But I was also smouldering about the television series we'd been commissioned to make. It was supposed to be a fly-on-the-wall documentary about the relationship between two strangers on the Silk Road. Yet how was I to explain the near-total breakdown of that relationship? To do so I would have to spell out what was going on between her and the guide. And how could I do that? Sneak into their tent, camera running? Try to catch them holding hands? Even saying it to camera seemed too great a humiliation – for both of us. I wondered what Sarah was saying on tape. Every time she pulled her camera from the bag to do a diary piece, I found myself gripped by paranoia. Guessing she wouldn't be making any in-depth revelations about what was really going on, I imagined she was grumbling about the nightmare of travelling with an unfriendly, moody bastard! As it turned out, I wasn't far wrong.

This is the first time I've come into a home, or stopped as we do three or four times a day for kumis *and cream and bread, without Jonny . . . I just find his presence so, umm . . . intense, stressed. I can't relax and it's really nice to just be with this family . . . and not be able to join in but also not have the compunction to talk to him either.*

Safe to say, when we did have to communicate with each other, conversation was brief and fairly spiky.

But at last we tumbled from the hills and rejoined the land of humans. At first we passed small bee farms where the owners were kind and gave us honey, curds and cheese from their goats. But as the land flattened out and agriculture increased, so did an overwhelming sense of unease. Around the tobacco and maize farms that followed, hard-faced men began to hassle us. Walking beside us they'd grab our bridles and demand to know exactly who we were, where we'd come from, why we were there and what we were filming. Outside one farmstead a staggering drunk groped Sarah's leg and became aggressive when she kicked him violently away. By another, grubby kids threw stones at the horses and chained dogs snapped around their tired hooves. As the sky turned from soft azure to a harsh pale-blue and the snow-capped peaks melted away, I realised that for all the problems we'd encountered on our journey through the Mountains of Heaven, the Ferghana Valley would prove far worse. Civilisation, I could see, was not going to be easy.

Emerging from a column of silver birch, we joined Karakul Jar's only street. It wasn't asphalt but made of pale local hardcore, and dust climbed around the horses' hooves. On our left rose two more barns, overgrown with grass and creepers. By one, a middle-aged woman was hunched above a sieve. Dressed from head to toe in mourning black, she vigorously shook the wooden-framed implement to separate the wheat from the chaff. From a side street a fat man in a *kulpak* hat appeared on a donkey. He asked if we'd like to stay the night. It had just gone four, so, thanking him, we agreed and followed him back along the road from where he'd come.

Outside a tatty bungalow we dismounted. By the side door was a large blue truck with high wooden sides, and a wheelless pickup, perched on bricks. Washing hung like flags from a nylon line secured to a laden apple tree. Some of its weighty fruit had already fallen and lay rotting on the ground. Having filmed our arrival, I placed the camera on my saddle, knowing I'd soon need it again. Unfortunately, I forgot to disengage the tie mike I had attached to my collar and, when I stepped forward to bind Kyrgyz Express to a concrete post, I dragged the camera sharply forward, sending it crashing to the ground. Luckily my sheepskin fell as well, cushioning the camera's fall, but I was greatly concerned when I reached to pick it up. Much to my relief I found the camera itself was fine, if dented slightly and covered in dirt, but the sound box beneath – through which additional mikes could be attached – had not fared so well. The force of the impact had torn the tie-mike socket from the box and cracked the rim. Though I realised it would probably still work, without the socket, tie mikes would now have to be held physically or taped at a particular angle. It was very frustrating and I cursed myself for being so slapdash.

Having taken our boots off at the bungalow's entrance, we were led down a narrow corridor and into a plain room, about twelve feet square. At its centre was a long low table, covered by a plastic sheet, groaning with food – cheese, fruit, bread and cream – and around its edge sat a group of people: two middle-aged men, their wives, a granny and two kids. Making room for us, they invited us to sit on stools and help ourselves to the fare that lay before us.

The man at the head of the table was dressed in a shabby suit and large fur hat, and was called Gorban Tursumov. Small and wiry with a weathered face and watery eyes, he was the village schoolmaster and in decent English asked us about our journey.

'That is funny,' he said on hearing of our adventures and future plans. 'Two French people – man, wife – come through here three weeks before. They also ride horses to Uzbekistan.'

'Really?' I hadn't given the French couple another thought since Dom had told us about them two weeks earlier on the Torugart Pass. But now, as then, I found myself feeling slightly irritated that they were doing what seemed to be a very similar journey to our own. On the other hand, I quickly reasoned they might also help to smooth our passage. Though we hadn't had any awkward run-ins with the police so far – hardly surprising considering the remoteness of the region through which we'd just passed – in the Ferghana Valley, where widespread religious fanaticism is strictly monitored, it couldn't be long before we did. Trailblazing the roadblocks before us would surely help our own plight. Yes . . . and besides, I told myself, they were kindred spirits; it would be nice if we could meet them.

'Do you know where they are heading?' I asked.

'Khiva, I think,' he replied with a frown. 'There or the Caspian Sea.'

'How were they getting on?'

'They had problems with one horse,' he recalled. 'Stop here for two days. It lose shoe. Blacksmith here fixed new one.'

Little by little I could tell word was spreading that strangers were in town. The small room was filling fast. First to arrive was a young lad I took to be another son, and he was quickly followed by three more male youths. They all squashed into the room, squatted on their knees or rumps and stared at me and Sarah. We drank milky tea, seasoned with salt, and ate some bread and cheese. To toast a successful conclusion to our journey our hosts opened a half-litre bottle of vodka, which once again we drank at speed. In this wild part of the world it seemed the pleasure in alcohol was not gained from drinking, but from getting drunk.

Looking out of the window, I noticed the truck again and

suddenly, feeling rather tired, had an idea.

'Sarah,' I said, turning to my partner, 'what do you think about doing the last few miles to Osh by truck?'

'What . . . why?' She could just be bothered to turn my way.

'Well, two of the horses are lame, which is bound to slow us down. It's still another fifty-odd miles, most of which will be on the road, not much fun, and our visas run out in four days. I think it might be better to hire that truck out there, which could get us to Osh tomorrow morning. Akylbek can then use it to take Dom's horses back via Bishkek to his place for the winter, while we sell ours at the market on Sunday. It will also give us two free days in Osh.'

Time was now becoming a major issue, and not just because of visa restrictions. It was already well into the second half of September, yet we still had over two-thirds of the journey – almost 2,000 kilometres – left to travel. With the meagre state of our equipment, the Karakum Desert would become impassable by December when snow falls and temperatures plummet to thirty degrees below. As we'd left England so late, and been held up in Kashgar so long, I'd now resigned myself to the fact that we were never going to ride all the way to the Caspian Sea. Added to that, Murat didn't think the Uzbek authorities would take kindly to us trying to cross the border with horses. Despite a common trade arrangement with Kyrgyzstan, the Uzbek customs were apparently notoriously tricky, as were the Uzbek police. Because of all these problems, we'd agreed that the only course of action left open to us was to sell Torugart and Anchor at Osh's weekly animal bazaar, cross the border as simple backpackers and continue a little way on public transport.

'What about the film?' asked Sarah. 'It's supposed to be a riding trip. We're already going to travel by bus through part of the Ferghana Valley.'

'We'll just fake it . . . have a couple of shots of us riding into Osh, pick it up again when we next get horses or something . . . No one will know.'

'If we hadn't wasted so much time travelling to Kashgar by road . . .'

'But we did.' I was all too aware of that fact. I didn't need it spelt out.

She turned and looked vacantly out through the window. 'All right,' she said, testily. 'But once we get to Osh we'll have to find somewhere for the horses to stay.'

'Murat said there's some kind of horse hotel at the market. We can leave them there for a couple of days, until Sunday. We can then cross the border on Monday, the day before our visas expire.'

'Really?' she scoffed. 'A horse hotel?'

'Apparently so. It's no bad thing; a couple of days rest will give Torugart a chance to recover. We'll get a better price if the horses aren't lame.'

'You don't say,' she remarked and returned to drinking her tea.

The following morning we loaded all six horses onto the truck. With the high sides and wooden floor it was a good deal easier than our previous experience in China, and within half an hour they were all on board, their heads secured to a rail up front, peering serenely across the pale-blue cab and down the gravel road. We climbed into a hastily commandeered Lada, owned by Gorban Tursumov's brother, and followed. Not that the journey went altogether smoothly. Now travelling through the heavily populated Ferghana Valley, police roadblocks appeared every ten kilometres. Apparently, while we'd been travelling though the mountains, the situation in Batkent, where the armed band of Tajik Islamic rebels were holed up, had deteriorated badly. According to Gorban, it wasn't just four Japanese geologists the rebels were now holding hostage but two entire villages. Fearful of Islamic extremism spreading into their countries from neighbouring Afghanistan, the Uzbek and Kyrgyz governments had now launched a combined assault on the arid mountain region with large-scale troop deployments, helicopter gunships and even strafing jets. It was little wonder we were thrice stopped, questioned and made to show our papers.

On the outskirts of Osh, beside a large and dusty bowl that formed the animal bazaar, we found the horse hotel: a low-rise, pink-painted crew yard with a rusting iron roof, fifty metres long, capable of stabling a hundred or so animals. As it was Friday the place was still only half full, mainly with cattle and sheep that would be sold the following Sunday. The manager gave us an empty corner at one end of the building and, having been slipped $20, promised to look after our horses well for the next two days. With them safe and secure, we bade farewell to Akylbek, Dom's horses and the dogs. It was sad to see them go. The quiet horseman had been wonderfully reliable, never complaining and always with a shy smile close to his lips. I doubted I'd ever find a more reliable horse than Kyrgyz Express, and Yalki Palki had, for a while at least, seemed like my only friend. Once the truck had disappeared from view, Sarah, Murat and I climbed back into the Lada and headed into town.

Osh carried an overwhelming sense of the Soviet Union. The roads were wide, often four-laned, bordered by ugly concrete government offices, dreary shops and tenement flats that climbed grey and charmless against the hazy sky. Outside one large administrative centre stood an imposing black granite statue of Lenin; above the rooftops of the western town rose a huge metal-cut of the same bearded icon. I'd been lead to believe that the independent states of Central Asia had jettisoned their Soviet past as soon as the central hold on them was relaxed. But not Kyrgyzstan, if their statuary was anything to go by.

Dirty Ladas, old trucks and diesel buses bought cheaply from East Germany – often with German companies still advertised on their sides – spewed black smoke onto the busy streets. Suspended from the street lights, banners celebrated the town's 3000th year. This seemed rather a spurious anniversary, marked, I suspected, more for current commercial reasons than any serious relevance to history, as no one knows how old the town really is. Some say Osh was founded by King Solomon, others Alexander the Great, and it was certainly from here that Emperor Babur came to found his Afghan Mogul dynasty. Most of the residents claim it's been around longer than Rome. Sited as it is on the northern end of the rich and fertile Ferghana Valley, it was certainly an important crossroads on the old Silk Road and today still boasts one of the largest bazaars in Central Asia. The town obviously harbours some wealth. As we stopped at a set of traffic lights, a large black Mercedes swept arrogantly by.

To my surprise few of the men I saw plying the streets wore the traditional Kyrgyz *kalpacs*. Instead their shaved heads were covered in embroidered blue skullcaps, and over their shoulders hung the three-quarter-length Uzbek velvet cloaks, known as *chapins*. Though we were still in Kyrgyzstan, Murat explained that eighty per cent of the town's population was in fact Uzbek.

Before the 1917 revolution and the Bolshevik's bloody subjugation of Central Asia, when the area was governed by local leaders in much smaller Khanates, most Central Asians simply described themselves as Muslim, Turk, or Tajik, meaning of Persian origin. The Soviets believed that this left the region highly vulnerable as a breeding ground for Islamic fundamentalism and Pan-Turkic nationalism. In the 1920s and '30s Stalin therefore created – some say personally – Central Asia's national boundaries and imposed on each nation its own specific ethnic profile, history, language and territory. Where these didn't exist – or were not considered suitably distinct from others – they were invented and supplied by Moscow. Islam, perceived by the politburo as a threat to Soviet domination, was excised from each national make-up and suppressed. The legacy of this is that today each of the newly independent republics has inherited ethnic 'grow-bags'. Thus there are Kyrgyz villages in Tajikistan, Tajik communities living in the cities of Uzbekistan, Kazaks grazing cattle on the Kyrgyz steppes and Uzbek towns, such as Osh, in Kyrgyzstan.

We found a guesthouse owned and run by colleagues of Alex. It was a lovely place, away from the busy town centre, quiet and welcoming with a pretty courtyard and comfortable rooms. Once settled in, I found a phone and called Alex. Delighted to hear that we'd arrived safely, he decided to fly down early the following morning from Bishkek.

This was great news. It would be lovely to see him, for with nothing much to say to Sarah, I craved a decent conversation. But also I hoped he might be able to help with the film, which I feared was beginning to go seriously wrong. Without an explanation as to why we weren't getting on, in the lead story there was now a gaping hole. While up in the mountains I'd tried to fill this gap by focusing on the history of the Silk Road, the quirky characters that live and have lived upon it, as well as the various practical elements of our travels. In Osh I hoped to continue this endeavour by seeking out the Heavenly Horses whose giant hoof prints Murat had become so excited about in Tash Rabat. Perhaps in the barren hills that rose up to the south of town Alex would be able to show us the ancient rock paintings and even the hoof prints and in English explain their significance on film.

In a strange way I also felt a keen personal need to explore as fully as possible the myth of the Heavenly Horses. As almost every aspect of the journey seemed to be sliding inexorably into farce, so the relevance of the mythical steeds had increased in my mind. Though we had failed so far to find a nag that even remotely appeared to be celestially bred, the quest to substantiate the legend represented the one element of the adventure that remained pure and undimmed: the one thread of the story that Sarah couldn't undermine, that the French couldn't steal, the authorities hide or the seasons change. The Heavenly Horses were the one part of my ridiculous odyssey that still stood a chance of turning out well. I don't know, perhaps it was a pride thing, but if there was such an animal, even painted on a bloody rock, I was damn well going to find it.

The following morning Alex arrived bearing gifts: a much-needed Central Asian guidebook and two English language novels from Dom. They were a great present for I'd only bought *Dr Zhivago* and, wonderful novel though it is, on the third read through I was getting a little bored.

In the afternoon we hired a taxi and drove a few miles out of town to where a huge orange rock – not wholly dissimilar to Ayers Rock in Australia – skirted the border with Uzbekistan. Finding the famous paintings, it turned out, was easy, for Alex had taken a couple of French tourists to see them the previous summer. We pulled off the road, passing beneath a small timber arch, drove up a narrow track bordered with silver poplars and high stone walls, and parked beside a heavy wooden door. Almost at once it opened and an old man appeared behind it, beckoning us through into a lush green orchard of pregnant apple and pomegranate trees. We followed him along a well-worn path that led us by a small log cabin and up towards a towering cliff. At its base was a clear stream, where he stopped. While Sarah filmed Alex's and my expression, we followed the old man's wavering hand high up the side of the rust-coloured rock until our vision fell on the ancient depictions of two wild horses.

A mare and foal, the larger to the left protecting her small baby in front, facing east and the rising sun, their pale images seemed to be covered in leopard's spots. They were faded and mottled, with modern graffiti above and tufts of grass sprouting to the side, but, even so, it was immediately obvious that these were no ordinary horses. With long necks and refined heads, they were a far cry from the stocky battlers of the mountain steppes to which we'd become accustomed. Even in this state they were really very pretty.

'Who painted them . . . and right up there?' I asked. They were a hundred feet above the ground and twenty from the top of the cliff.

'Different ideas,' replied Alex, staring towards the portraits. 'Some say they were painted by Chinese travellers that had been sent by their emperor in search of the famous horses of the region –'

'Like Zhang Qian,' I said excitedly.

'Exactly . . . but others say they're local Turkic inscriptions, perhaps painted here as a place of prayer.'

'Heavenly Horses.' I nodded sagely. 'It would make sense to worship them.'

'Sure.'

'But are these Akhal Teke horses?' I asked. I'd read something about this famous breed that was said to be closely related to the Arab and English Thoroughbred, but remained somewhat confused as to whether or not they were considered the same animal as the Heavenly Horses of Ferghana.

'I'm not sure,' said Alex thoughtfully. 'Some say that the Akhal Tekes were really the Heavenly Horses of the Ferghana Valley, and that it was these horses that the Chinese emperor got so excited about. But others question this. The Akhal Tekes originate much further west, in the desert regions of Turkmenistan and, though I have never seen one, they are also apparently much lighter-boned than the horses of Ferghana. So for me they are two different breeds.' Looking at us once again, he smiled. 'But it's all so long ago, no one really knows.'

'Might we be able to find a couple of these Akhal Tekes in Turkmenistan?' asked Sarah, looking up hopefully from the monitor.

'Possibly,' said Alex, 'but I doubt you'll be able to ride them, and certainly not buy them. From what I understand, a pure-bred Akhal Teke can be worth as much as a hundred thousand dollars. There are very few left, even in Turkmenistan.' Seeing our disappointment, he added with a grin, 'But you might still find a Ferghana Heavenly Horse in Andijan or Kokand, or even north of Tajikistan as you continue your journey through the Ferghana Valley. Long ago they were renowned throughout the region.'

'Great,' I said, wrapping up the shot, 'then that's what we'll do. Wander on until we find some.'

The scene finished, Sarah handed me the camera. As she did so I noticed that the microphone was switched off. Checking the tape we discovered that she'd filmed the sequence without sound. It wasn't the first time. We spent half an hour re-shooting the conversation, then set about trying to find the giant horses' hoof prints. Sadly, no one we asked had even heard of them and, after a profitless hour searching among the hills, we gave up and headed back to town.

As fate would have it I didn't have to wait until Kokand, or even Andijan, to catch sight of my first Heavenly Horse. At 7.30 the next morning, at the Osh animal bazaar I ran right into one. With Sarah, Murat and Alex enjoying a cup of tea, and while I waited for the right moment to lead Torugart and Anchor into the fray, I decided to wander around and get some cut-aways of the people, the animals, the general hubbub. I was busy filming, pushing through the crowd, when the monitor was suddenly filled from side to side by an enormous beast. Looking up, I stood back, awestruck. There before me, right in the middle of the arena, rising from the filth and mayhem that simmered all around it, casting brilliant white against a pure blue sky, stood one of the most impressive animals I've ever seen. My jaw dropped.

He was magnificent. A dappled grey stallion, he stood well over sixteen hands tall, was broadly built, and had a fine arched chest and neck that just went on and on. His hindquarters tapered slightly and his legs were thick and strong. Seen from the front, his cannon bones were long and heavy, and unusually wide when seen sideways. His head was broad and regal, with proud ears picked rigidly forward, and bright, sparkling eyes. This wasn't an English

Thoroughbred and certainly no relation to any Arab horse I'd seen; he was far too heavy-boned for that. But he was still beautiful. He was the kind of animal a Disney cartoonist would use as a template for a fantasy animation: Pegasus without wings. Was this the horse from the ancient legend? Was it heavenly bred? For a Chinese emperor used to squat, shaggy ponies from the mountain steppes, I could imagine such a magnificent beast would indeed seem divine. Terribly excited – it was after all in the Ferghana Valley, perhaps even Osh, that Zhang Qian had first coined the phrase Heavenly Horses – I filmed some shots and did a quick piece to camera.

Sitting bareback across him, watching keenly, was a young boy, no more than eight, with his bandy legs barely reaching halfway down the horse's flanks. Having finished filming, I stepped forward, patted the horse's muscular neck, adjusted a lock of his long grey mane and scratched him softly behind his ears. He didn't mind; he was well-natured and nuzzled my chest. I smiled up at the boy.

'*Letch pour?*' I asked, assuming the animal was for sale.

The boy just shook his head, whether not interested or not comprehending, I wasn't sure. '*Asp, letch pour?*' I asked again. This time the boy pulled at the animal's head with the rope he had attached to the head collar, kicked his sides and, with an impudent grin, began to move away. The horse had a lovely stride.

Hurrying off I found Murat and Sarah at the far side of the bazaar. I tried to explain the importance of what I'd just seen, but they seemed rather uninterested. They were annoyed that I had been gone so long, reminding me we had our own horses to sell and that if we didn't get a move on we might not even manage that. So we hustled to the stable, collected Torugart and Anchor, did a couple of sneaky shots of us riding off the main road and into the mayhem, and dismounted among a busy throng. At once we were surrounded by scores of men and boys, potential buyers and curiosity seekers alike. As usual, making the deal was not easy. With Western faces at his side, and the absolute necessity to sell, even Murat could do little about being beaten down to a miserly price by the Uzbek traders. Including the swapping of Kara for a further $100, we'd paid in total nearly $700 for our three horses and all the equipment. After an hour's frustrating haggle with an old Uzbek and his oily son, I considered ourselves fortunate to get

$250 for the lot. The deal filmed, shaken upon, and the money paid, we watched them being led away. I wasn't too bothered about Anchor, I'd barely ridden him, but Torugart's departure left me a little downhearted. He'd quietly gone about his job, both as a pack animal and ridden horse, with strength, grace and abject good manners. Added to that we'd brought him 700 kilometres from his home in Kashgar and, like Kara, had now sold him in a foreign land. I hoped he'd be OK.

As they disappeared into the throng, I turned my attention to finding the mighty grey stallion. I desperately wanted Sarah, Murat and Alex to see it for themselves, to show them that the Heavenly Horses of Ferghana did still exist and just what magnificent beasts they were. But after a fruitless half hour, touring every corner of the market, I had to give up. My Heavenly Horse had flown away.

15 Final Fallout

Back at the guesthouse Sarah and I had something of a set-to. It wasn't very serious, but the altercation did little to help our already damaged relationship. For the previous two days both Murat and Alex had been putting the fear of God into Sarah about travelling across the border into Uzbekistan and onward through the Ferghana Valley and Tajikistan. According to them, Uzbekistan was a loathsome place, peopled by duplicitous bullies, capable of anything, and by plotting a course through Tajikistan we were striding gamely, yet very unwisely, into a deeply hostile and dangerous territory. The fighting in Batkent, which by travelling south-west towards Khodjent we would be circling, was, according to them, only the first of the problems we would be likely to encounter. The civil war that had raged since independence continued to be an issue in the south, with rebels from various factions still fighting each other and anyone else who happened to get in their way. Added to that, the army, unpaid for months by a bankrupt exchequer, could not be relied upon to smooth our passage and protect us; on the contrary, they would almost certainly prove an unwelcome and constant annoyance. And just to round things off, the Tajiks, they told us smugly – and totally unreasonably – were renowned for their thieving, hostage taking and murdering; according to them there was little doubt that bandits and renegades would stalk our every stride. In the end I'd told them both to shut up. This they did, but not before suggesting we should let them put us in touch with an affiliated Uzbek tour operator who could arrange everything – new horses, guides, food – and see us safely through the Ferghana Valley, a hundred-mile corridor of Tajikistan, and on to Samarkand. Sarah thought it a fine idea.

Tempting as it was, I did not. For one thing, such a commitment would cost thousands of dollars, far more than we could afford –

Alex, Murat and Akylbek on special friendly rates had cost us nearly $2,000 as it was, leaving us little more than $3,000 for the rest of the journey – and just as importantly it was not at all in the spirit of the adventure on which we'd embarked. I was already concerned we'd had it rather easy using Dom's contacts through Kyrgyzstan. To hire tour operators and therefore travel on little more than a glorified package holiday was definitely out of the question. And I told Sarah as much.

'Listen,' I said as we sat in the courtyard face to face, 'you can forget hiring some travel company to work it all out for us. To Lion TV this film is supposed to be about us travelling the old Silk Road as it used to be travelled, chancing our arm and going for it; not on a horse safari organised by Abercrombie and Kent.'

'Well, I don't care what bloody Lion TV think,' retorted Sarah angrily. 'You can tell them they either get us a guide and translator or they don't get me at all!'

I was tempted, believe me.

'Look, these guys haven't crossed the border into Uzbekistan for years, they've never been to Tajikistan' – I glanced at Alex and Murat, who smiled and shrugged – 'they haven't a clue what they're talking about. If you asked Uzbeks what they thought about the Kyrgyz, they'd probably tell you exactly the same.'

'I don't care, Jonny.' She pouted stubbornly, crossing her arms and stamping a foot. 'I'm not budging from here without a translator and a guide and an organised itinerary.'

I shook my head and sighed. 'OK . . .' I took off my cap and ran a hand through my hair. 'I'll find us a translator to help us across the border tomorrow and to stay with us through the Ferghana Valley. But as we're probably going to do most of that stage by bus, we don't need a guide holding our hands as well.'

'And what about the Tajik corridor?'

'I don't know, we're not there yet. But I'm sure something'll turn up.'

'Something will turn up!' She threw back her chin contemptuously. 'According to you, Jonny, never mind these two' – she jerked a thumb in our guides' direction – 'Tajikistan is the most dangerous country in Central Asia, a place swarming with bandits and rebels and God only knows what else. The civil war hasn't been finished long, and this is precisely where the Japanese are being held hostage. And you think something will just show up? Great!'

'The Japanese were up in the hills, not on the main road. And all the civil war stuff, that's in the mountains of the south, not in the Ferghana Valley.'

'Oh, and you know?'

I looked at her and sighed. It was no good. She wasn't going to take my word for it. And the worst of it was I knew she was right. Why should she trust my judgement? The truth was, I didn't know if we'd cross bandits or rebels or kidnappers or cutthroats. How could I? For me it was all part of the adventure and I was prepared to take the risk. But it was her life as well. I stood back and collapsed into a chair.

'I know someone in Tajikistan.' It was Alex who spoke. We both turned and looked at him.

'A tour operator . . . right?' I asked glumly.

'Well, not exactly . . . more a businessman. I mean he will cost you money, but not so much and he is reliable. He'll be able to find you a guide, horses, homes to stay in. As much or as little as you want. I can call him up, get him to meet you at the border.'

'What's his name?' asked Sarah.

'Saidullah,' he replied.

'And you're sure he's reliable?'

'He's a good man,' said Alex. 'He speaks English, will sort out your visas, anything really. I've put clients with him before.'

'And how many days will it take us to get through the Ferghana Valley?' This question she directed at me.

'We could do it by bus in a day, but if we want to get some decent footage, say three . . . maybe four.'

'I thought we were in a hurry.'

'Alright, three . . . Jesus.'

'Great. Thank you, Alex.' She turned her attention back to our mutual friend. 'You ring this associate of yours, Saidullah, and ask him to meet us at the border four days from today at, say, twelve o'clock, with two horses and a guide, and visas if we need them. We'll then –'

'Wait a minute,' I interrupted, 'what about if we want to buy horses in Andijan or Kokand?'

'Then when we meet him we'll tell him to send his away.' A caustic smile snaked across her lips.

'OK, Sarah,' I said, holding up my hands, knowing I was beaten. 'We'll do it your way. But when we do get this Saidullah bloke, we're only going to take the horses and a guide, not him or anyone else. I looked at her with the most determined look I could muster. 'I'm not prepared to have a bloody entourage following our every move, and lavish banquets laid on for us every night.'

'Fine.' She rested her hands on her hips. 'And where are you going to find a translator?'

'I'll find one,' I said stubbornly. 'Believe it or not I have a contact here in Osh. He used to be the translator for a friend of mine who worked for the BBC.'

'Then call him,' she replied.

'I will.'

And I did. Unfortunately he was busy and unable join us, but he knew a young man who could. After a couple of brief telephone conversations, he told me he'd send him along to meet us the following morning. That sorted, and a successful telephone call put through to Saidullah in Tajikistan, we settled down for supper. As it was the last one we'd share with Murat and Alex, we piled in the goodies, including wine and beer as well as vodka, stuffed ourselves and became very drunk. Not that the merriment helped Sarah and me put aside our differences. We sat at either end of the table, growling at each other.

We picked up our new translator in the main town square just before lunch. A quiet but pleasant lad called Nadir Bek, he was an English student from Osh University. As an ethnic Uzbek, and son of a local policeman, he didn't mind in the least the idea of travelling with us through the Ferghana Valley. We had a quick meal at a restaurant nearby and, unsure how long the formalities would take at the border, paid up and prepared to leave. As we hailed a taxi, Murat disappeared, begging us to wait. A moment later he returned with that huge golden smile covering his face and two *kalpacs*. Although with all our luggage the thoroughly impractical traditional Kyrgyz hats were as welcome as a stack of concrete breeze-blocks, it was a very sweet gesture. Taking his giant hand in my own meagre paw, I thanked him and pulled him into a friendly embrace. Inevitably, our relationship had suffered over the past two weeks under the strange circumstances of our shared adventure, which I considered a real shame. I knew he was a kind-hearted and interesting man. While Sarah and Murat made their farewells, I loaded Alex down with used video tapes and careful instructions to courier them to London, gave him an affectionate hug, and climbed into the taxi.

As we drove out of town and on towards the frontier, it seemed strange not to have our Kyrgyz horse guide with us. With the exception of Nadir Bek, who sat up front in silence, we were now as we'd been at the beginning of the trip, except that, with tension hanging almost visibly in the air between us, Sarah and I uttered hardly a word to one another. It was obvious that things couldn't go on like this for much longer and the storm would have to break.

Even without the horses, crossing the border into Uzbekistan took three hours. Searched enthusiastically by two stone-faced guards, we were then made to fill out currency declaration forms, stating exactly how much money we were carrying, what possessions we had – including all our camera gear – and the relative value of them. Getting a stamp in our passports again set the clock ticking, and my nerves jangling. Having been told categorically that we would not be allowed an extension to our one-month Uzbek visa, from that moment on we had just thirty-one days to get through the Ferghana Valley and the 100-mile corridor of Tajikistan, back across the border into Uzbekistan, on to Samarkand and Bukhara, before finally fleeing into Turkmenistan. Watching the officious customs men meticulously picking their way through our bags, I was pleased we'd decided to travel some of the way by bus.

We took another taxi the sixty kilometres to Andijan, where we arrived just after dark, and checked into a ugly, state-run hotel in the centre of town. Rooms organised and bags unloaded, we headed to an open-air café in the pleasure gardens just behind the hotel. It didn't take long for the fireworks to start.

With tension between us we started to drink; a small bottle of vodka at first, followed by beer, and soon we were quite drunk. I can't remember exactly what triggered it – I think something Sarah said to Nadir Bek about having a boyfriend back home, to whom she'd proposed just before she came away. Anyway, whatever it was, six weeks of pent-up frustration had finally come to the boil and when Nadir Bek, probably sensing war was about to break out, explained that he had to go back to the hotel to telephone his father, I exploded.

'What the fuck do you think of me, Sarah?'

'What?' She lifted her glass of beer and brought it casually to her lips.

'Because it can't be very much. You sit here, quite happily telling Nadir Bek, in a voice you must know I'll overhear, that you have a boyfriend back home who you've lived with for the past *six* years, who you're going to marry, who you fucking *proposed to* the night before you left England.' I shook my head. 'Are you deliberately *trying* to antagonise me?'

'What are you talking about, Jonny?' There was an apathetic, almost bored, tone to her words, as though the conversation that was sure to unfold was a familiar routine she had no wish to revisit.

'What am I talking about?' I lit the cigarette and blew out a great jet of smoke. 'I'll tell you what I'm talking about, Sarah; I'm talking about sending you home.' The words surprised me – and clearly shocked Sarah.

'What?' The nonchalant look was wiped from her face in an instant. 'But you can't do that.'

'Can't I?' I brought the cigarette to my mouth again and dragged deeply. 'If you think I'm going to sit through another two months of this shit, you're insane.'

'And you're angry because I proposed to my boyfriend the night before we left?' She asked, eyes wide with amazement. 'That means nothing, we're always talking about getting married. Besides, he turned me down.'

'I don't blame him.'

'Hah-hah.' She twisted her mouth sourly.

'Have you forgotten what we talked about in the pub in London, before I chose you to come with me? Have you forgotten what you told me about the state of your relationship, Sarah? Because I haven't: "My boyfriend is a workaholic, Jonny"' – in a childish, squeaky way I imitated her voice – '"I hardly ever see him; he's off to work before I get up and doesn't return home until past ten. At weekends he wants to see his friends while I want to see mine; he's a banker, I want to be a traveller." Do you remember that, Sarah? 'Cause I do.'

'Yes, I remember' – she studied her fingers nervously – 'and now you feel . . . shortchanged?'

'You could say that,' I hissed. 'And what were you doing with Murat?'

'What the hell's that got to do with you.' She jerked back, looking flabbergasted, and hurriedly lit her own cigarette.

'What's it got to do with me? Have you totally forgotten what we're here for? We're supposed to be making a documentary about how two strangers get on, on a journey across Central Asia. Fly-on-the-wall . . . warts and all. Remember?'

'So . . .'

'So! Do you really imagine, even in your wildest dreams, that I was going to be overjoyed, have a cheerful and jolly time, choosing a woman who first of all refuses to talk to me, preferring instead to read her book at dinner and sit on the e-mail for three hours a –'

'I explained that: I was homesick.'

'Who then can't be arsed to use the camera she's told me she so proficient at using. Someone who refuses point blank to share a tent with me. I mean did you think I was going to jump on you?' I gave her no time to answer. 'And then, as if to throw contempt in my face, once we've had a chat to clear the air and made a pact to be more "together", spends the next two weeks shacked up with the horse guide!'

'I wasn't "shacked up" with the horse guide; your tent was too small.'

'Yeah, right,' I sneered contemptuously. 'Don't treat me like a total fucking moron.'

'Well, you were so bloody moody and heavy and uncommunicative, drifting around like a big black shadow.' Now she was getting angry. Muscles flinched on her jawbone. Her voice began to tremble. 'Murat was the only one to make it any fun. He was warm and funny and made me laugh.'

'Ha!'

'Yes. All you think about is this film, this bloody film, which you don't let me get involved in. You've never really let me get involved in it. You're always the one who decides what we shoot and how we shoot it, where we put the camera and how we position the mikes. If I do try to do something myself, all you do is criticise.'

'Bollocks . . . you've shown virtually no interest in helping to make this film . . . which I thought was the whole reason you wanted to come on this trip. Bar a few video diaries, you only do it when I hand you the camera and make you do it.'

'That's because that's the only time you *let* me do it.'

'Listen,' I growled, 'I can't help it if I know more about photography than you, Sarah. How many times have I told you that you can't point the camera straight into the sun? How many times have I had to remind you to turn the microphone on before filming and to check the sound levels? How many times have I had to ask you to squat or stand on something to film from a more interesting angle? What am I supposed to do, stand back and watch you film shit . . . mute shit at that?'

'Oh, and like you're so fucking perfect at it! Great shot of us crossing that river, Jonny,' she whined sarcastically. 'How many times did you make us do it? Three? Four? And you hadn't even turned the bloody camera on!' She sat back and dragged proudly on her cigarette.

I stared at her. Despite knowing that some of what she said was true – I had made mistakes, and not just with the filming – at that moment I felt nothing but contempt for her, for myself, for the whole damn mess. Things looked so bleak, so broken, I wondered if it would be possible to rectify the situation. Perhaps, I pondered, it really would be better if we went our separate ways.

'Jesus, Sarah,' I said more calmly, taking my last drag and stubbing out my cigarette, 'what are we going to do now?'

She said nothing and for a while there was silence. A waiter walked past carrying a tray of kebabs. They smelt burnt.

I poured some beer into our glasses and drank a long draught. And, after a few minutes, strangely I began to feel better. Having at last spoken my mind, fully and freely, holding nothing back, a calm relief washed over me. Having felt utterly frustrated, one way or another, for most of the past month, it felt good to have finally thrown it from my chest. However things continued there was no denying that this was a major watershed; everything would be different from now on.

Sarah removed her glasses. Just for a moment I thought she was crying, but she'd simply got smoke in her eyes. Having rubbed them better and replaced her dark-rimmed specs, she moved forward and leant on the table. Finding herself in a tight spot, her aggression suddenly seemed to seep away. She spoke quietly. 'So what *are* you going to do now?' she asked.

'I don't know.' I watched as the waiter scurried by again. 'I really don't know. But the way I see it, there are only two things we can do.' Sarah nodded. 'One, we can split up, you go home, whatever . . .'

'Oh, no, we can't do that . . .' She looked at me beseechingly. 'Please . . .'

'I would then either carry on alone or try to get someone else to join me in Samarkand, from England.'

'Someone else?'

'Sure, why not?' I still had the note from Lucy tucked safely into a pocket of my waistcoat.

Her head dropped.

'Or we go on and try once more to build something that will see us through the next two months.' I stared off into the night. 'If the second option is possible, and I really don't know if it is, we'd have to make something up for the camera, something that will explain to the viewer our lack of friendship over the last few weeks.'

'Why . . . what does it matter? We just didn't get on.'

'But we haven't explained why. Now there's a huge hole in the main story of the film. The whole thing was set up as a wild blind date, and yet neither of us has said anything about why we are hating each other's guts. We can turn it into a travel documentary to a certain degree, but without some explanation the film won't follow through on what it promised to deliver.'

'Yes.' she said softly.

'Maybe you could explain at this juncture that you have a boyfriend back home, that you've just told me about him, and that, I don't know, you'd promised him you wouldn't share a tent with me . . . stuff like that. It's a bit of a lie, but I don't suppose that'll matter.'

'Yes, OK . . . that would work.' She tapped on the table with anxious fingers and joined my gaze towards the trees. 'I could say that I wanted to come on the trip so badly I lied about that in the interview, having a boyfriend I mean, and that was why I couldn't get close to you, allow you to get close to me, and that made you feel shortchanged and pissed off.'

'Yeah, well, don't go overboard . . . besides, I don't know if even that'll work. Regardless of the film, we still have to get through the next two months.'

'Yes . . .'

And I knew that would not be easy. When a relationship sinks so low that all respect, trust and understanding has gone – as I feared was the case with ours – it's usually impossible to salvage anything other than a superficial farce. But I knew inside I simply didn't have the stomach to end it all there and send her home. Dealing with a broken Sarah, then an angry Lion TV, explaining everything to camera, and confronting my own sense of guilt and frustration, was all just too much to contemplate. Not only that but continuing alone would be boring, for me and the viewer, and even if Lucy were prepared to fly out to Samarkand to meet me, what guarantee was there that the same problems wouldn't arise with her? No. However things were destined to pan out, sitting in Andijan with a head full of booze, it seemed a whole lot easier simply to let things ride.

'You'll have to make the piece to camera convincing, Sarah, as will I . . .'

'Oh I will, I will.' Her face broke into a beaming smile. In my jaundiced mood, it seemed to say, 'Huh, so, I've won again . . . sucker.'

PART FOUR
A Game of Snakes and Ladders

'Experience is the name everyone gives to their mistakes'
Oscar Wilde

16 Audience with the KGB

By two the following afternoon we were on board a rickety bus cutting a course through the heart of the Ferghana Valley. Beyond the grimy windows endless cotton fields stretched towards the pale horizon. Among the mottled, dusty plants, rows of labourers toiled under the autumn sun. Though it looked hard graft I imagined the workers were grateful for the employment. Over the course of the next two months the more proficient among them would pick some three tons of cotton, at a rate of 8 Uzbek *sums* per kilogram, earning a total somewhere in the region of 300 US dollars, a small fortune in post-Soviet Central Asia. Every few minutes we passed collection depots where great white pyramids rose against the shimmering sky, like cumulus clouds fallen to earth.

Sarah and I sat apart. We both knew it was going to take a long time to heal the scars we'd inflicted on each other and form any sort of friendship. And though there was a realisation, and acceptance, that like it or not we were now stuck with each other for the remainder of the trip, after the angry tongue-lashing we'd given each other the previous evening we both needed our space. Earlier that morning we'd done our video diaries – Sarah explaining that she had a boyfriend, while I bemoaned the fact that my recent bad luck with women was continuing, and I'd got it wrong again. Whether they'd work or not in the context of the television series I really wasn't sure, but at least there was now something on tape explaining why we weren't getting on. That done, we'd gone to the bazaar in search of Heavenly Horses to buy or rent, only to be informed that because of the cotton harvest the animal markets of the region were closed for the next two months. It was in reality something of a relief for it gave us the perfect excuse to continue through the Ferghana Valley by bus, knowing that in three days' time we'd pick up Saidullah's horses on the Tajik border.

Even utilising public transport, the next three days were, however, among the trickiest we had to negotiate, as we spent much of our time trying to avoid police or being interrogated by them. For the most part the Ferghana Valley felt like an occupied territory. Every ten kilometres steel gates, nail boards and concrete slabs blocked the road. By the checkpoints heavily armed soldiers searched all traffic, paying particular attention to our bags and documents. Though they were generally friendly and polite, accepting us for what we were, we began to feel harried. At each hotel we were questioned thoroughly by security staff; whenever sightseeing in towns, waiting in bus terminals or eating in restaurants we were hassled by plain-clothes cops, and in the border town of Besharik, on 24 September – my birthday – we were finally arrested. Our crime was nothing more sinister than food shopping, but with the heightened tensions in the mountains around Batkent, the Uzbek authorities were more tetchy than ever and clearly two Westerners buying bread and vodka in the town's deserted mall was too damn fishy by half. After an unsuccessful ten minutes trying to plead our innocence, we were bundled into a car and driven off to police headquarters.

Lacking any beauty or elegance, the large grey building, set behind an imposing fence of iron railings, was a purely functional establishment; just right for a good interrogation. Police officers, some in uniform, others not, sauntered in and out. Our arresting officer – a young tyke with weeping acne – jumped from the car and, like a prospector who'd just found gold, led us smiling through the gate, up the steps and into the reception.

Here we were greeted by an enormous man, fat and bald, with a strawberry nose and soulless eyes. His paunch stretched the buttonholes on his uniform shirt, his gun hung threateningly at his side. He stood, sour-faced, and listened to the guard before pointing to two plastic chairs and telling us to sit. He then picked up the phone. I stood, allowing Nadir Bek to rest his legs. I never could take an order.

A moment later another man entered. He could hardly have been more different. Short, sharp-featured, with pale, narrow lips and silvering hair, he was dressed in an elegant charcoal suit and smart black shoes. He had a tiny hammer-and-sickle badge pinned to his lapel, which surprised me, and he could have had KGB stamped across his forehead. He smiled patronisingly and, in a quiet voice, smooth yet sinister, introduced himself as Colonel Lobkov. Having studied us intently for a moment through his inquisitive, clear grey eyes, he turned and told us to follow him down a darkened corridor.

We all stood up. He told Nadir Bek to wait.

As our feet beat out a rhythm on the linoleum floor, echoing hollowly through the autocratic halls, I still felt reasonably calm. We were near the border now, planning to cross it the very next day. In my experience, once the police have established that you're nothing more sinister than a tourist, they're happy to have you off their turf as quickly as possible and into another's jurisdiction. Then again, I'd never been the guest of the KGB before.

Pushing open the door to a small office, Colonel Lobkov stood to one side and ushered us in. No larger than three metres square, the grey walls were lined with old grey filing cabinets, their tops cluttered with piles of papers, faded folders, passports – some still carrying the CCCP inscription of the Soviet Union, others Uzbek – and identification cards. What wasn't hidden by the clutter was covered in sheets of Xerox paper depicting the images of haunted men, staring blankly towards the camera. Though the words above and below were printed in Cyrillic script and therefore illegible to me, it was obvious what they were: wanted posters for others who had transgressed the state's intractable laws. At the far end, beneath a grimy window, stood a dented metal desk. Lying by the plastic phone and pen holder was a revolver. Colonel Lobkov glided smoothly past us and, as though embarrassed, removed it with his thin right hand and slipped it into the bottom draw. Having offered us two wooden seats opposite, he sat down and lit a cigarette.

'So,' he said, eyeing us keenly. He gave the impression of being no stranger to interrogation cells. He exhaled a jet of bluish smoke. Even in this gloomy light I could make out nicotine stains on the first two fingers of his right hand and a yellowing patch in his falling fringe. On the knuckles of the same hand '1961' had been tattooed. I smiled at him, saying nothing, with the most innocent look that I could muster.

'What are you doing here?' His English was excellent, with barely an accent.

'We are riding horses along the Silk Road,' I answered. Though my eyes were wide and expressionless, I could feel my heart begin to pound more heavily behind my ribcage. I told myself to relax, calm down . . . I had nothing much to hide. He pulled a pad from the top drawer and began to write intricate notes. 'We started in Kashgar,' I continued, 'two months ago and are hoping to make it all the way to the Caspian Sea. Tomorrow we will cross into Tajikistan.'

'Why?'

'Why . . . because we are heading to Samarkand. It's the shortest way.'

'No.' He looked up from the page. 'Why are you making this journey?'

I thought for a moment before answering. 'Because we are tourists, travellers, we enjoy seeing other parts of the world. The Silk Road is one of the most famous trade routes in the history of the world and we wanted to experience it as it used to be . . . as much as we could.' I smiled simply, shrugged my shoulders and raised my hands. It was an expression that was supposed to say, 'Hey, you know us in the West . . . all a bit bourgeois and crazy!' The smile was not returned.

'You are aware of the situation in Batkent?'

'Yes, of course . . . kind of.'

'What do you know?'

'Well,' I paused again. It was a delicate situation. To say too much might make him suspicious; not enough and he might think I was holding back. The last thing we needed was to be arrested as spies. He was staring at me, waiting. 'As I understand it a group of Islamic rebels, possibly backed by Wahabis, have crossed the border from Afghanistan, taken control of the area around Batkent and are hoping to set up some sort of purified Muslim homeland.'

He looked up and for the first time a thin smile spread across his face. 'You are well informed.' I could sense Sarah twitching nervously beside me.

'I read the English-language papers,' I answered carefully.

'And what do you know of these people . . . these Wahabis?' He looked me straight in the eye.

'Nothing much. Except, I'm told, that they can marry their

seventh daughter . . . if they have one, which seems . . . rather odd.' I tailed off and laughed nervously; he didn't. His face was cold, deliberate.

'So would you say they are good people?'

Coming from him it was such a ridiculous question that just for one crazy moment I thought it might be a trick. Could he be a supporter, a sympathiser, of the radical Islamists? There was absolutely no hint of an expression on his face. I said nothing and watched as he stubbed out one cigarette and lit another. Noticing that I was watching, he offered one to me. Rather too hastily, I accepted.

Biding time, I nervously pulled on the harsh tobacco. It was hot and stuffy in the tiny, airless room. My palms were damp. I could hear blood rushing in my ears. Suddenly I remembered his name: Lobkov. Russian, not Uzbek. He was unlikely to be Muslim, much less a fundamentalist sympathiser. He worked for the government. For the government! For Christ's sake, Jonny, pull yourself together!

'No,' I said at last. 'Though I try not to concern myself with politics while travelling, I don't think they are good people. I can see that they are causing your country, as well as Tajikistan and Kyrgyzstan, a great deal of trouble. They are doing the same in Afghanistan and many other Islamic countries. Mostly these people are terrorists. And many good Muslims would agree with me.'

Lobkov stood up. 'Exactly,' he hissed, animated for the first time. I breathed a sigh of relief. 'These people are animals. They come into our homeland, kill, take innocent people – Western people, like yourselves – hostage. And bring disgrace to us all. Did you know they have captured two whole villages, demanding a ransom for all the people who live there?' He shook his head. 'They try to force their religion, their medieval ways on others. Our reports tell us there are Arabians, Afghans, Pakistanis, Uyghurs, Tajiks, Uzbeks, even Chechens, even Algerians. What right do these people have to invade our countries and cause this . . . distress?' He sat down again and angrily flicked the ash from his cigarette. A trail of wispy smoke climbed towards the ceiling. 'But our army will beat them,' he said in a calmer tone. 'Today we were using jets, you know.' He smiled with a sense of triumph. 'They will not win.'

'I'm sure they won't.'

If I had hoped that that was to be the end of our experience with the KGB, I was to be disappointed. For the next two hours he asked us a barrage of inane – and insane – questions. He started with me: my name, date and place of birth (smiling and offering congratulations on seeing it was my birthday), home address, father's name and address, brothers' and sister's names, their professions, home addresses and how many children they had. Each answer he wrote down scrupulously in his pad, weighing their relevance and plausibility. When he finally got round to asking my profession I told the truth. A man as well-trained as Lobkov would have eaten me for breakfast had I tried to lie. Though I neglected to tell him about the TV series, I did tell him I was hoping to write a book about our experiences. He didn't seem particularly perturbed by this, and merely asked what I thought of his adopted country, Uzbekistan. It was as well he wasn't asking a month later or the answer might have been very different, but for then I managed, with almost total sincerity, to tell him that I thought it a fine place.

During the entire interview thus far Sarah had been sitting nervously in silence, waiting for her turn. The first few questions she handled fine, but as he became more ambiguous and intrusive, I could sense her tighten up. It made me nervous as well. Sarah's forthright and dismissive approach to anyone who annoyed her would not, I feared, be tolerated here.

'And what do you think of the position of women in this country?' asked Lobkov, suddenly holding her gaze. I held my breath.

'I . . . er . . . well . . .' stuttered Sarah, stealing a glance in my direction. 'Women, fine . . .' she shrugged. 'I mean they work all day in the fields, which must be hard, breaking their backs picking the cotton and things, having to deal with the scorpions and heat and stuff, and then they have to do all the housework when they get home . . .' – oh shit, I thought, here she goes – 'they also have to look after the children while the men just sit around on their backsides all day and drink vodka and chat and do noth –'

'Just as it is in so much of the world,' I interrupted, chuckling loudly towards Lobkov. Much to my relief, he laughed too.

Finally he asked whether any of our museums in London had any artefacts, traditional costumes or displays from Uzbekistan; how well-known was his country in the West and how much Russian news was covered by the BBC. He seemed intrigued by how Central Asia was perceived by the West, how well the political situation was understood and how great were the chances of an increase in trade and hence for local economic growth. It was hard work answering positively.

In the end he put his pen down and sat back in his chair. I let out a long sigh. It seemed as though we had passed the test. 'So,' he said, tapping his pen against the pad. 'I have asked you so many questions, perhaps you would like to ask some of me?'

That was a surprise, but why not. 'Sure,' I answered. 'What does the tattoo mean on your knuckles? I have seen it on many other people's hands as well.'

He stretched out his fingers and regarded his hand with a smile. 'This is the year I was born. 1961. We all do it in the army.'

'And are you KGB?' asked Sarah. I looked at her, almost unable to believe my ears.

But Lobkov only laughed. 'That is something you are not allowed to ask. Besides, we do not have KGB any more, only the NSS, National Security Service.' And with a wink towards Sarah, he stood, indicating that the interview was over and that we were free to leave.

The next morning we were both relieved to cross the border into Tajikistan.

Saidullah looked nothing like what I'd imagined. To my mind the name had conjured an image of an ethnic Tajik, a tall and swarthy man with olive skin and angled features dressed in traditional flowing robes. The reality could hardly have been more different. Short and squat, with a thatch of thick white hair and pallid skin – like Boris Yeltsin or Slobodan Milošević – wearing poorly cut jeans, badly made trainers and a beige Harrington jacket, he was evidently Slavic. Luckily he spotted us and rushed from his car to greet us. Having introduced himself, he informed us, in tortured English, that the horses and guide were waiting for us at a small *chaikhana*, just beyond the village of Kanibadam, a mile or so down the road. A businessman, as Alex had warned, the moment we were seated in the car he explained that for the four-day journey down to Khodjent he would require $500. I agreed. Though in Tajikistan it was a great deal of money, I figured it could have been worse. Alex, it seemed, had done us proud.

When we arrived in Kanibadam a few minutes later, I was once again surprised. Not by the outdoor restaurant, that was normal enough, or by the horses, they looked convincing – strong and stocky, just right for the journey – but by the horse guide. If I harboured any concern about my partner's penchant for men with such employment, I dismissed them immediately: he was old enough to be her grandfather. He had a proud mahogany face, with bright, clear eyes and a great hooked nose above a wispy moustache. His head was shrouded in a filthy green turban, his sinewy body in an old and tatty robe. As was the style of the region, his baggy black pants were tucked into knee-length leather boots. In his gnarled left hand he carried a whip. I couldn't wait to film him.

'Is he going to be up to it?' Sarah asked Saidullah dubiously, as we climbed from the car. 'Three horses to look after; it's quite a lot of work, you know.'

'There no man is better, for than Ismael Bek in aaaall Tojikiston,' came the somewhat confusing, yet confident reply.

I walked over and, remembering some Farsi I'd picked up in Afghanistan, offered the plethora of greetings: '*Khair Khairyat*, Ismael Bek,' I said, bowing politely with my right hand held across my heart. '*Khobaste, Jon Joorast, Mondana Bashi, Chitouri . . . Al 'hamdul 'illah.*' As I spoke his wizened old face split into an enormous, toothless grin. His eyes disappeared behind folds of weathered skin and his shoulders shook like a little boy's. He had evidently not been expecting to hear his favoured tongue and seemed to appreciate the effort. Unfortunately, though he took it as a sign that I could actually speak Farsi and having offered the pleasantries back – 'Is all well with you, Sahib? Is your body good? May you never be tired. May you live forever. Praise be to God' – he continued to rabbit away with great animation, for at least a minute, before grinding to a baffled halt. This left me feeling rather foolish, and Ismael Bek looking rather confused. Not that it mattered. My heart had melted. At last, on the Tajik–Uzbek border, I'd found an authentic Central Asian cowboy. Smiling broadly, I clasped his arm and shook his hand. It was as firm and strong as iron.

Saidullah then introduced us to a man of about forty, called Serge. Tall, broad and blond, he appeared the archetypal Soviet hero; the type who appeared in posters in the thirties and forties wielding a pickaxe or hammer. He had a pleasant, open face and, like his boss, was dressed in cheap European clothes. In the restaurant, beside the road, beneath the arms of a mulberry tree, we all sat down for lunch.

Having been served sweet green tea, Saidullah explained – again in lumbering and confused English – that the following day he had to travel back to his home in Panjikent to take care of some other business, and that from then on Serge would look after our safety and deliver us to Khodjent, where Saidullah would meet us in four days' time. He pointed to a small orange motorcycle on which he said Serge would track our progress. I told him that was fine by us – even though Serge spoke not a word of English – but as far as possible we wanted to be left alone to let the fates take their course. Saidullah then informed us that, following Alex's instructions, he'd organised our accommodation for that night at the small town of Lakhuti, two hours' ride down the road, but after that we could do as we pleased. If we wanted to veer off the main road with Ismael Bek, we were free to do so. In his company we would be safe. He knew many different routes and had friends and family along the way with whom we could stay. Sarah was happy with this arrangement. She hated riding on metalled roads and now with a guide felt safe. He gave us each a letter in Cyrillic script, which he informed us were our visas, and after a quick bowl of *laghmann* we climbed astride our new mounts and set off down the road at a leisurely walk.

It was beautiful afternoon with thin high clouds riding lazily on a gentle breeze. All three horses seemed fit and healthy and were comfortable rides and, although the road was somewhat busier than either of us would have liked, I found myself in an easy frame of mind. After two hours we arrived in the small frontier town of Lakhuti and on the main street found Saidullah standing by his car between a row of black weatherboarded bungalows. Waving his arms flamboyantly, he directed us under an arch and into someone's home opposite.

It was a grand place. Around a central forecourt single-storey buildings formed a large L. The space in between, stretching before us, had been cultivated with fruit trees, maize and vegetables. We dismounted and, having been introduced to the owner and his wife, led our horses to a patch of grass in the far corner, beside a well and haystack, and tied them to a railing. After we had taken the obligatory close-ups and cut-aways, we were ushered towards the house. We took off our boots at the entrance and were lead down a narrow corridor and into a room twenty-foot square. Three of the four walls were covered from floor to ceiling in gaudy velvet drapes of deep reds, blues and greens. Across the fourth was a mural depicting a forest scene with deer and bears, a badger and a fox. The room felt stuffy and, with net curtains hanging before the small closed windows, dark. It put me in mind of a gypsy caravan. Sarah's thoughts led her elsewhere: 'Like re-entering the womb,' she grumbled, dropping some bags in a heap at her feet.

At the centre of the room a plastic sheet had been laid out and covered with overflowing bowls of pomegranates, apricots, melons and grapes. There were others groaning under piles of almonds and walnuts, bread and cheese, biscuits and chocolates, even cream, brown sugar and boiled sweets. Inside, I sighed. We sat leaning against the walls on silky cushions. Almost at once the town's bigwigs appeared and introduced themselves with great formality. Sarah and I, understanding barely a word, turned to Saidullah for help, but sensing himself well out of his depth, he just smiled idiotically and looked at the floor. They then seated themselves cross-legged in a circle around us and immediately picked up the bowls and pushed them into our faces, with the single order we now knew well, '*Yeshte, yeshte* . . . Eat, eat!'

We did as we were told.

Then, much to our relief, the town's secondary-school English teacher, Khalil Khamarov, arrived and the introductions began all over again. First there was the leader of the local council, then the president of the town's co-operative farm, then three other grey beards – all council members – whose occupations I didn't catch, and lastly the butcher. Khalil Khamarov's presence was a very welcome addition as I was beginning to realise that Saidullah's English was limited. He was one of those people who figure that as long as you use enough words in any one sentence you can

sound, at least to yourself, almost fluent, no matter in which particular order they come or that eighty-five per cent of the sentence
consisted of the same five words. Any explanation from Saidullah
took a great deal of time to leave his lips and even longer for us
to comprehend. The English teacher was a lot more illuminating.

'I think in your England country,' he said, with serious eyes, 'you
have an expression, "When it rains . . . it only pours".' He pointed
to the window.

'Yes,' answered Sarah sweetly. 'It *never* rains, it pours. Why?'

'Ah,' said Khalil, nodding wisely, 'this is good. You know until
two weeks ago Lakhuti had never seen a tourist. Or if it had, it
had not known.'

'Really?' said Sarah.

'The few that come this way pass straight through to the border.
Why stop here? There is no hotel, no guesthouse . . . nothing to
see. But then two weeks ago a French couple, husband and wife,
passed through on horseback, much like yourselves. They, too,
stayed here, at Ikram Khoja's house, and now it has happened
again. It is strange, no?'

'Like the number 19,' I muttered despondently.

Sarah snorted a laugh.

'Indeed,' I agreed. 'We have heard about them before. Do you
remember where they were heading?'

'Khodjent,' he answered with a shrug. 'There is nowhere else to
go. And from there Samarkand and Bukhara. But I don't know
where they are going after that.' I looked at Sarah with a resigned
grin; her expression told me she felt the same. There was no getting
away from it; it looked as if we might well be following the French
all the way to the Caspian Sea.

A moment later there was a knock at the door and our host's
wife stuck her head round the corner. In her hands were two bowls
of steaming food. Serge jumped to his feet, took them from her
and placed them before Sarah and myself. Swimming in a dark
and oily liquid was a great lump of fatty meat.

'Jesus,' Sarah whispered under her breath. 'What the hell is that?'

'Looks like broth and . . . goat or mutton,' I answered uneasily.
'Best not ask. Try and eat what you can, it's rude not to.'

Once everyone had been served, Ismael Bek, as the eldest and hence most respected man present, embarked on a rather lengthy grace. Eventually, he said, '*Al hamdul 'illah* – Praise be to God,' and opened his eyes. In Tajikistan Islam is, however, considerably more relaxed than in other parts of the Muslim realm. No sooner had Ismael Bek finished the expansive benediction than he was cracking the seal on a bottle of vodka and breaking one of Islam's most forthright rules. With a childish chuckle he poured the drink into all our cups and, noticing my questioning eyes, shrugged. 'I am Muslim,' he said evenly. 'I am Tajik. I love Allah, I like vodka . . . I pray, I drink . . . is 50/50, good and bad; this is life, what can we do?' He then began to toast all and sundry.

Everyone ate, everyone drank, and as the spirit flowed so did the conversation. We discussed the situation in Batkent and whether the Japanese geologists had any chance of getting out alive. They all thought not. We talked about the civil war, the state of Tajikistan's battered economy, of the former Soviet Union and the politics of the region. They were agreed that in almost every walk of life things were now far worse than they had been. The situation was best summarised by the story of Ismael Bek. He told us that for forty-three years he had been a cowboy, working on a co-operative ranch in the foothills of the Pamir mountains, herding cattle that produced fine quality beef for places as far off as Kiev and Vladivostok. But when the Union fell, the Russian administrators packed their bags and headed home. With no management the contracts dried up, the cattle were sold and within two years the place was closed. Two hundred and thirty people had worked with Ismael Bek; all bar three had lost their jobs.

To our utter amazement, and considerable horror, halfway through a rather tedious lament by another old man, our host's wife returned, again proffering great bowls of food, this time chicken on a bed of rice and sultanas. We were both overfull from dutifully eating the goat. We'd had no inkling that it was a starter. I glanced at Sarah and began to laugh. She looked as if she could have cried.

'It's not surprising they're all so bloody fat,' she hissed quietly. 'Look at that guy next to you . . . looks as though he's swallowed a medicine ball.'

Having eaten all I could, I filmed the scene for fifteen minutes

– more from a feeling of guilt than thinking I'd actually get anything usable – and then put the camera away. Sarah, making the excuse that she wanted to film the women in the kitchen, slipped out for a cigarette. An hour later, the guests gone and the refuse from dinner cleared away, we made beds from quilts that were stacked in the corner and lay down, potbellied, to sleep.

'Fuck,' groaned Sarah, turning awkwardly on to her side, 'if we go on eating like this, I'll need two horses to carry me.'

Most of the next day we were alone. Departing Lakhuti shortly after nine – following a breakfast that consisted of boiled eggs, wedges of bread and cheese (most of which we shoved into our pockets) and another bowl of steaming *laghmann* – the three of us offered our thanks to our host, bade farewell to Saidullah and Serge, and headed out of town. This time, however, rather than continuing along the busy main road, we took a turning to the left just beyond a huge derelict factory and headed down a dusty side track. At its end was a narrow concrete canal running parallel and at half a mile's distance to the main road, cutting a line across the land for miles in both directions. Along its right bank was a tow path. It was exceptionally quiet and tranquil. Turning right, Sarah and I smiled towards Ismael Bek.

'*Horosho?*' he asked. 'Good?'

'*Bolshoi horosho,*' we answered in unison. 'Big good.' We hadn't even worked out the word for 'very'.

Beyond the canal a flat and arid plain stretched towards the mountains of Batkent. At eleven we caught a glimpse of just how seriously the government was taking the situation in and around the troubled town. At an altitude of no more that 500 metres, scaring the horses and ourselves, three Uzbek MiG fighters tore violently above our heads. Having brought the horses under control, we turned in our saddles and watched as the killing machines banked to the south to begin their strafing missions.

It was dusk by the time we arrived at Ismael Bek's cousin's house. The scene that greeted us, however, was not a very pretty one and it caused me to despair. Though there was no sign of Saidullah – he'd taken himself off to Panjikent as he'd told us he would – there were plenty of other worried faces. Serge was the first to rush from the house bellowing something about kidnaps and injured horses, followed by a suited driver. Hard on their heels came two more men and a spotty youth, all dressed in traditional Uzbek clothes, and in the background stood two anxious women.

'Serge, what are you doing here?' I groaned. 'We're supposed to be on our own.'

He smiled disconcertingly and told us that they had been gravely worried about our safety, that they had been expecting us hours ago, that they thought we had been kidnapped or involved in an accident or that the army had arrested us . . . and that we didn't have any mineral water.

With such genuine concern and so little mutual language it was impossible to be angry. I just smiled resignedly and climbed down from the saddle.

But when the horses had been dealt with, and introductions to the family had been completed, once again we were encouraged to eat from bowls of fruit and nuts. I picked up the map, went to sit with Sarah on the canal bank and smoked a cigarette.

'You know this can't go on, Sarah,' I said, staring across the flat plain, watching the last of the day merge into night. 'A guide's great, but we don't need three or four men chaperoning us. Mineral water, indeed!'

Sarah chuckled.

'Whenever we arrive at a home, because of all the people and all the food, it's so bloody obvious it's been prearranged that I can't be bothered to use the camera.' I gestured to where Serge and the others were sitting, knowing the wild, spontaneous film I'd been so determined to make, littered with glorious images of yesteryear, was falling to pieces before my eyes. 'I understand you're worried about us travelling on our own,' I said, 'but this is becoming ridiculous. With them involved we're never going to do anything interesting or adventurous. Honestly, we're not making a series about an epic journey on the Silk Road any more but an episode of *The Holiday Show*.'

She laughed again, taking my cigarette and having a drag. 'What do you suggest?'

'Well, a different route might help.' I spread the map out before us. 'What I think we should do is abandon the idea of heading immediately back into Uzbekistan when we reach the end of the Ferghana Valley, here at Khodjent, but instead turn due south, taking this road' – I pointed with my finger – 'through this place called Aratabey and over the mountains to Panjikent. It's a journey of about 250 kilometres, through the Fan Range, part of the Pamir Alays. From there we can reach Samarkand easily, it's just across the border, and from there ride on to Bukhara.'

'I like the idea of heading back into the mountains,' said Sarah. 'The main road and the bloody Ferghana Valley are a real pain up the arse. We'll get away from people as well. Yes, I agree, even here along these tracks it's pretty boring.' She frowned. 'But what about the horses . . . and Ismael Bek? Do you mean to keep them?'

'No. I'm sure he won't want to come with us all that way. He's already grumbling about a sore back.'

'I'm not surprised, poor old bugger.'

'I think we should buy some more horses instead.'

'That may not be easy, given that the animal bazaars are all closed.'

'No, but it should be possible. There'll be private sellers.' I studied the map again. 'Maybe here in Nau, or even Khodjent. I'm sure Saidullah can help us sort it out.'

'Okay, but this country could still be dangerous, Jonny. I don't mind going without a tour operator as backup – without Serge and what have you – but I'm not going without a guide. Someone who knows the way and can speak the language.'

'I wouldn't expect you to. We'll ask Saidullah to find us someone else.' I stubbed out my cigarette on the dusty ground beside me. 'What I also like about this route is that it's not the most obvious. Hopefully, therefore, we might be able to avoid following the French. That's beginning to piss me off.'

'Sure . . .' she said. 'All I want are the mountains.'

17 The Den of Thieves

Cold and damp, our collars turned against the falling rain, we rode in single file through the dismal streets of Aratabey.

Climbing once again into the wild Central Asian highlands, now well beyond the relative prosperity of the Ferghana Valley, the town appeared desperately sad and washed up in the early morning drizzle. No black Mercedes cruised these ruined streets, no trams, few trucks or buses, and the only cars to bump and crash through the endless potholes were worn-out, rusting taxis. You could tell at once that there was little employment. Beside the muddy road large groups of men huddled beneath canvas awnings, plastic sheeting, holey shawls or boards of sodden cardboard. Their hair was lank, clothes were threadbare and plastic shoes often laceless and ill-fitting. None of them waved to us or shouted or rushed over to exchange friendly banter. Appearing beaten and dejected, while some eyed us vacantly, others just stared at the ground. I'd been told Tajikistan was the poorest country in the Commonwealth of Independent States; I could believe it.

Since Khodjent, all had gone to plan. With Ismael Bek we'd ridden on to Nau, where Saidullah had introduced us to an Uzbek butcher-cum-horse dealer by the name of Kasop, who'd put us up for the night and in the morning sold us two horses. Neither beast was particularly sublime and, given our host's bizarre dual employment, I wondered whether we had in fact saved them from the sausage factory. Not that he'd have gained much *kolbasa* from Sarah's new mount. Thin and rather dainty, similar in shape to Younger, her black gelding was only four or five years old and barely thirteen hands. For reasons known only to herself, she christened him Titanic. On the other hand, my bay stallion was tall, thickset and strong-looking – called Sputnik, thanks to a large white star on his forehead – but at fifteen years was a good deal longer in the tooth than I would have wished. Not that we'd been given much choice. With the animal bazaars closed, the wily butcher knew he had us by the proverbials and only offered the two horses for sale – no doubt the lamest ducks in the yard – and, after a lengthy haggle, charged us $600 for the pair. It was ridiculous. Even including the well-worn tack he had thrown in, I doubt a Tajik would have paid more than $200. It was also rather annoying as Kasop actually owned a Heavenly Horse. Called Larchin, the fine black stallion was almost identical in stature to the mighty grey in the Osh bazaar. In ancient times, Kasop poetically informed me, it was believed that when such a horse died their spirit didn't rush off to some horse paradise or heavenly stable, but waited above the house of its master until the day he died. Then, spreading its ethereal wings, it carried its master off to the Elysian Fields, where it remained with him for all time.

'And is he for sale?' I'd asked pointlessly.

'Never,' Kasop had replied with a smile. 'How else will I reach paradise?'

Still, he did at least fix us up with Abror, an ethnic Tajik horseman, who, for a further $50, agreed to lead us over the 3,500-metre Sakhristan Pass in the heart of the Fan mountains, and on as far as Khoshikat. Here, Abror told us he would find us another guide to take us to Panjikent, from where it was short hop to Samarkand. Everything sorted, we'd said farewell to Ismael Bek, Saidullah and Serge – agreeing to meet the latter two in Panjikent – and ridden to Aratabey.

Soon we were out of town, riding south towards the mountains. It wasn't a busy route. The odd truck carrying cotton, vegetables or tobacco from the Ferghana Valley down to Dushanbe, and a few buses full of workers heading in the opposite direction, trundled slowly past, but for long stretches we walked along in peace and quiet, watching eagles and buzzards rise above the rolling hills. In the afternoon the road began to climb more steeply. Pines began to appear, crystal brooks cut through the land and the snow-capped peaks of the Fan Mountains rose serenely all around us. By a copse of willows we stopped at a wooden shack and again were offered *kumis*. There was little arable agriculture here, just long grass plains bordering the road, on which sheep and cattle grazed. At times we were able to leave the road and ride across the softer ground. But it was a risky business. Twice we found our route blocked by natural irrigation channels and had to backtrack miles to rejoin the road before we could continue.

We arrived in the village of Boragen with the long day drawing to a close. Abror told us he had friends here with whom we could stay the night. With a golden sun burnishing our faces, we crossed a field of stubbled maize and entered an avenue of tall white poplars. Autumn was well advanced and the leaves had turned a vibrant ochre gold. Some had fallen and lay in drifts against the low stone wall. We followed the narrow track between rows of neat stone dwellings and animal pens, corrals and fields. Children ran amuck, hitting goats with sticks and stones. They stopped and fell silent as we passed. At the end of the track we came to a large homestead. A low building, half hidden by fruit trees and a haystack, rose from a wet and muddy yard. To the left was a grass paddock, to the right, stables. Some brown sheep foraged in the dirt.

A young man emerged from the bungalow and walked across the yard towards us. Short, with slanted eyes, and wearing a *kalpac*, he was unmistakably Kyrgyz. Behind him scampered two small children and a woman in a shawl.

'*Asalam u aleykum*,' said Abror with a smile as he climbed down from his horse. He greeted his friend with a hug.

Half an hour later, the horses fed and taken care of, we were invited into their small, wooden-walled guest room. Rough goat's wool carpets covered the floor. Cushions and quilts were stacked in the corner, and we lay them out to sit on. Very quickly the room filled with brothers and wives, children and grannies. Our host, Abdul Azar, explained they were smallholders, growing barley and maize but mainly dealing in livestock. His grandfather had moved to Boragen from Özgön, near Osh, in Soviet times. The family had been here ever since. When dinner arrived, it filled me with joy. Just a bowl of broth, some boiled potatoes and chunks of tired bread. Arriving unannounced, without the fanfare of a semi-organised tour, we were witnessing a local family as they really lived, just as it had been on the few occasions we'd stumbled upon such lonely dwellings up in the Mountains of Heaven. It was exactly how I liked it: staying with an ordinary family, a local guide, our own horses tethered outside with the golden road to Samarkand stretching over the hills before us. Having filmed for an hour, I sat back and let an optimism I hadn't felt for a long time wash over me. It felt like a new beginning.

As usual our high spirits were lamentably short-lived. At eleven the following morning the proprietor of a small roadside *chaikhana* merrily informed us that a French couple had stopped at his modest establishment just two weeks earlier. This meant we were now fated to be travelling in their hoof prints at least as far as Bukhara. But, as annoying as this news was, it was nothing compared to what followed. While sharing a pot of sugary tea, Abror casually announced he'd had enough and was heading home to Nau. With our lack of shared language, it was impossible to ascertain what had made him renege on his deal, much less persuade him not to. The best we could do was insist he find us someone else.

'This man will take you,' he said grumpily, pointing to a man sitting next to him. The stranger was about the same age as Abror, lighter skinned, with greying hair and soft clear eyes. He was dressed in a tatty suit, with a dirty bobble hat on his head and plastic plimsolls on his sockless feet. He smiled amicably, displaying a mottled set of golden plastic dentures.

'Who is this man?' I asked incredulously.

'He's a farmer. He lives in Khoshikat. His name is Tolly Boy.'

'Tolly Boy?' It was an odd name.

'*Da* . . . He here on business, now he go home. Is good for you . . . he says you stay with his family in Khoshikat.'

I was so dumbfounded I hardly knew what to say.

'Where's his horse?' I asked.

'No horse . . .' Abror said. 'He walk.'

With clouds moving in up the valley, I threw him my waterproof poncho. A few minutes later we were underway again.

The higher we climbed, the worse the weather turned, and before long it began to rain. By midday thunder boomed and crashed overhead, black clouds rolled across the sky and wild forks of lightning slammed against the earth. For much of the way I led Sputnik by the reins. Walking at his side not only rested his legs but sheltered me and helped to keep me warm. In single file we wandered on, climbing through the deep canyons of reddish rock, around hairpin bends, over the ever-rising knolls and hills. It wasn't much fun and most of the while we walked along in silence.

When we reached a grey breeze-block truckstop that sat at the foot of the pass, Tolly Boy lead us off the main road and on to a grassy track.

'Where are we going?' I asked our new guide.

'This way good,' he said. 'Main road three hour. This road only one.'

'Really?' I was sceptical. How could there be such a difference? After all, the height of the pass would be roughly the same whichever way we went. On the other hand, I figured, as a native to the region and someone who'd crossed the Sakhristan Pass many times, Tolly Boy should know. I looked up into the drizzle and saw the road lead right into the sky. The distant pass was veiled in mist. It did not appear inviting.

I checked my watch, and saw it had already gone two. 'Perhaps we should stay here tonight' – I pointed towards the grey *chaikhana* – 'and leave again early in the morning.'

'No. This no good place to stay,' he said, shaking his head knowingly. 'No beds. No covers. No place to stay. We go on.' He pointed away down the dirt track that led straight into the sodden hills. 'This way good. Top of pass by four o'clock. *Chaikhana* ten kilometres other side. Good place. We make it there by six.'

I looked at Sarah. 'Do you want to go on?' I asked openly.

'Sure,' she said with a shrug. 'It's a little early to stop now and he seems to know what he's doing.' She looked towards the sky. 'The rain's almost stopped. Besides, you've been saying we need some more adventure. It could go well with the footage you've taken this morning.'

That was certainly true. By wrapping the camera in a plastic bag, I had finally managed to take some dramatic shots in the rain. And after the dull and monotonous Ferghana Valley, the film would benefit from some adventure. 'Okay,' I said, 'let's do it.'

Ten minutes later, after a quick cup of *chai*, we remounted and followed Tolly Boy down the muddy track beside a raging river. The rain had relented, but the light was wan and dismal.

To begin with, the trail was good, wide and firm, used by tractors and trailers, judging from the tracks, to carry yurts high into the mountains. It led out across a flat grass field towards a forest of vaulting pines. Steam rose from Sputnik's sides, filling my nostrils with a gorgeous musty scent.

Before long the path, wet and slippery from the rain which had again begun to fall, started to climb, gently at first then steeper the further we walked. Soon it was not much wider than a horse. We left the sheltering trees and passed through a narrow defile. Immediately to our right rose a steep cliff, covered in velvet moss, dripping brownish water; to our left the land fell away in a sheer twenty-foot drop to the swirling river torrent. I tried to film the tense scene as Tolly Boy and Sarah struggled along in front. With the wet reins in my teeth, I used both hands to hold the camera steady and managed to gain some dramatic shots. But as we moved further into the dark gorge, where the rock wall soared a hundred feet above us, I was forced to pack the camera away and concentrate on riding. It was just as well that I did.

Sarah and Tolly Boy were out of sight around a shallow bend when Sputnik suddenly slipped and fell. As he collapsed onto his front knees, his long nose grinding hard into the soggy path, I was sent flying forward over his neck. Purely by the grace of God I was thrown to the right, up against the rock face, and received only grazed hands and a bruised right shoulder. Had I fallen the other way, a deathly plunge to the river would have greeted me. I hung on to the reins and helped a frightened Sputnik back to his feet. Cursing beneath my breath, I elected to walk and lead him.

As we emerged from the gorge, on to steep and slippery rising ground, I stopped and looked up towards the distant pass. All was lost behind the swirling clouds and thick translucent mist. I wiped my face with my damp bandanna and wondered miserably why we'd left the security of the dry *chaikhana* in the afternoon to cross a 3,500-metre pass, with a guide we didn't know, on an indecipherable track of mud.

Once Sarah had dismounted, I handed her the camera and told her to film.

She looked at me nervously, no doubt reading familiar fury in my eyes. But this time I had no axe to grind with her. On the contrary, she was taking the uncomfortable situation with perfect good grace.

'The pass, Tolly Boy,' I said curtly. 'Where is the pass?' At first he failed to understand my pathetic Russian, shook his head and stared at his feet. Cursing again, I grabbed one of the few words of Persian that had found a home in my head. '*Kotal* . . .' I said, unable to stop myself raising my voice. 'Sakhristan *Kotal*?' This time he understood and pointed to the left where a grassy ridge rose almost vertically into the stormy heavens. I could hardly believe what I was looking at. There was not a chance in the world of getting the horses over it. 'Fuck,' I spat venomously.

'*Horosho, horosho kotal,*' said Tolly Boy persistently beside me.

'No, it's not bloody *horosho*, Tolly Boy,' I boomed. 'This is a nightmare, Sarah.'

'Why?' she asked, trying to concentrate on filming. 'He seems to know the way.'

'For people on foot, maybe . . . not for us. This pass that he told us about, the one up there that supposedly only takes an hour to cross, is for humans not horses. There's no way horses will get over that, in one hour or four. Especially in this weather. Look at the ground, it's as lethal as ice.'

Removing my hat, I pushed a hand through my hair and swore again. Sputnik snorted derisively at my side and impatiently pulled at the reins. A crash of thunder rolled down the valley. I turned and half contemplated returning to the *chaikhana*, but the dark gorge, its lethal sides tempting disaster, quickly turned me back. The decision had been made. Like it or not we had to go on. 'Well, there's nothing for it now,' I said, pulling my hat back on. 'We'll have to find a route from here up to the road . . . this way, I presume.' I gestured to the right. 'Tolly Boy,' I said. 'Road?'

He smiled simply and nodded, seemingly agreeing with my directions. We couldn't see anything, for a sheer rock face blocked our view.

'How far?' I asked pointlessly.

'Not far,' he replied.

'Then that's what we'll do.' I turned back to Sarah. 'Is that all right with you? I reckon it beats going back, and if the worst happens and we have to sleep outside, we've got our sleeping bags and things; we'll just have to find a cave or something.'

'Sure,' she answered, still watching the scene as a film on the monitor. If she was worried, she certainly didn't show it and I was thankful for that.

'And I apologise now for getting us into this mess . . . we should never have left the *chaikhana*. It was madness.'

'Don't worry, it was my fault too.'

I nodded appreciatively. 'Right then, let's go.' I threw the reins back over Sputnik's head and climbed into the soggy saddle. Sarah stopped filming and handed back the camera. I kept it out, eager to record everything that happened. If nothing else, I was determined to catch this story.

When we rounded the spur of rock ten minutes later, we stopped and stared miserably before us. The clouds had lifted, the rain had eased and, thanks to two tiny trucks crawling like toys up towards the head of the pass, we could make out the road a thousand feet above us. But the terrain that reached it looked ominous. A mile in front, beyond a gently rising flat green plain covered in heather and twisted thorn, the earth climbed in a steep gravel escarpment on to a ledge of dirty snow. A hundred feet above that, carved out of the sheer cliff sides, and hanging like a snake, wove the mountain road. To cap it all, the road appeared to be guarded by concrete barriers. Whether the horses would be able to scale the ridge and struggle across the ice shelf was doubtful. But even if we did reach the road, would we find a gap in the crash defences? What was clear was that we had no choice but to try. And quickly too. The evening gloom was closing in fast.

Twenty minutes later we'd crossed the grassy plain and had started to climb. Much to our surprise we found a solid track presumably made by goats, yaks and other horsemen, which made the going easier than expected. Following its course we zigzagged right and left across the face of the mountain, climbing constantly towards the metalled road. It was still painfully slow work on the steep cliff and the horses' breathing became laboured. Explosions of frozen breath shot from their nostrils with every stride they struggled to make. Twice Sputnik tripped and almost fell, and the sharp stones cut his fetlocks. I encouraged him on, driving hard with my hands and heels, eager to reach the road. I knew he was strong; I felt sure he'd make it.

Turning to film the others, I saw Tolly Boy finding his own route up the gravel, marching easily across the land, but Sarah was struggling. Trying desperately to push Titanic forward, I could see her kicking his sides and thrashing his rear. With my own hands full there was little I could do to help her. She had to deal with whatever problems she was having on her own. I was pleased to see her take out her camera and record a short video diary.

> *Suddenly it's all turned rather arctic-looking. And I'm not very happy about it because it's really very cold. Maybe thirty or forty minutes till we reach the lip of snow. It looks deep, slippery –* she bites her bottom lip *– a struggle to get through.*

And even more impressed to see her point the lens in front of her when she'd finished, to catch the scene ahead.

After an hour we hit the snow line. Although I'd been expecting a treacherous walk, this time across an icy ridge, I was pleasantly surprised. Softened by the rain, the dirty snow yielded under the animals' weight, forming a easy cushion on which to plant their exhausted hooves. Again we followed a path, invisible from below, that directed us steadily upwards. And to my immense relief, halfway across the icy scree I saw that where the path joined the road the concrete crash barriers had been knocked away, leaving a tiny gap through which we could pass.

On the main road I hugged Sputnik's steaming sides, thanked him and dismounted. Looping the reins through my right arm, I stood and filmed the others as they trudged up the last hundred metres. It made an impressive shot: a dishevelled guide and lonesome horsewoman, black against the dull white snow, the mountains and the evening sky. When they reached the top they both beamed with relief.

'Well done, Sarah.' I grinned. 'That was fantastic.'

'I'm not sure Titanic would agree,' she huffed, quite out of breath, leaning forward in her saddle.

'No, I doubt it.'

'*Horasho*,' said Tolly Boy, happily. 'It is good route, yes?'

'That was the wrong thing to ask, Tolly Boy,' I answered in English, shaking my head. 'If I had a gun, I'd shoot you.'

Sarah laughed and so did Tolly Boy.

It was half past six by the time we reached the top of the Sakhristan Pass. On the ridge looking south we stood, cold and damp, shivering against the chilling breeze, and, full of wonder, watched the Fan Mountains cascade into a watery distance. The thick grey blanket of cloud that had hung so obstinately above our heads for the last twenty-four hours had mysteriously risen, dissipated and moved on. All that remained was a thin veil of wispy vapour, turned rosy pink by the setting sun. It had been a hard ride, but perhaps it had been worth it as for the first time in a long while we'd caught a dramatic story on tape. The last shot I took was of a truck driver rounding the corner and handing us some boiled potatoes. It was extraordinary how good they tasted.

With the sun gone, the temperature dropped alarmingly. Until then I hadn't really noticed my damp trousers and wet boots; now I did. Having put the camera away, I blew warm air into my cupped fist, red and raw from lack of gloves. I pulled a pair of thick socks from one of my bags and slipped them over my hands. They worked very well as mittens. Though cold to the bone, I didn't much care as I carried the warm sensation of a good day's work done.

As we rode on down the other side of the mountain, I soon became aware that the adventure was far from over. For all we had achieved that day, we were still 3,000 metres up, and now night was snapping at our heels. Tolly Boy had told us that the next *chaikhana* where we could seek refuge for the night lay only ten kilometres away. But was Tolly Boy to be relied upon? One hour to him could mean four or five for us . . . perhaps it was an hour's journey travelling straight down the mountain as he might go, but along the road with horses? With a sense of dread I realised it could be midnight before we found a place to stay.

It wasn't long before the stars were out and the night was velvet black. Trying to warm my cold and tired limbs, I dismounted and walked at Sputnik's side, using my torch for guidance. It was easy going downhill on the tarmac road against the cliff, but still we had to watch our step. If we lost concentration, potholes and fallen rocks made us trip and fall. Every so often a noisy truck would swing round a corner into our path, its two glaring headlamps flashing, horn blasting, scaring the horses and leaving us tense.

A new concern began to seed itself in my chest: fear of robbery, kidnap and murder. If there's one rule I've learned on my travels, it's never go wandering after dark, particularly in a potentially hostile country. Tajikistan was just such a lawless land, awash with bandits and brigands. Hadn't we been warned? In the dead of night armed gangs could be waiting around any of these corners; any one of these truck drivers could stop, hold us up and take anything he wanted. Once again I became angry with myself for not foreseeing the situation. The place felt isolated, wild and extremely dangerous.

On and on we wandered, in single file down the winding road. Like children on a long car journey, every so often one of us would senselessly ask Tolly Boy how much further he thought it might be, but he just smiled nervously and told us, very soon. In the end I lost my temper. 'What do you mean, very soon?' I yelled pointlessly in English. 'You've been telling us that for three hours. Do you have any clue where we are?' I knew it was wrong to be angry with him, but fatigue had got the better of me. We'd been on the road since six that morning. In that time we'd covered nearly seventy tough kilometres, mostly in the pouring rain.

It was almost ten by the time we saw lights far off down the valley; faint pinpricks that glowed like stars in the inky distance. Though they were still some miles off, the sight put a spring in all our steps and we pushed on hard to reach them. When we did, an hour later, we discovered that the dwelling was not the *chaikhana* of which Tolly Boy had informed us but a cottage of some kind, and we approached with trepidation.

The light we had seen came from two pale bulbs that hung outside, above a raised veranda. Inside, the house was in darkness and Tolly Boy didn't like it.

'We no stay here,' he said, his pale face looking gaunt in the shadows. 'We go on. *Chaikhana* very close.' He pointed off into the darkness.

'How close?' I asked.

'Here . . .' he said. 'Just here.' This time he gestured animatedly towards the lonely valley.

But I'd had enough. I no longer trusted Tolly Boy's estimation of what was close and, as it neared midnight, had no intention of walking another yard. 'No, Tolly Boy,' I said determinedly, 'we sleep here. We must wake up whoever is inside.'

There was no need. A pale light flickered from inside the dark house and a dirty face appeared at the window. A moment later the door creaked open and a tall man, stooped and threatening, carrying a hurricane lamp in one hand and a rifle in the other, appeared on the balcony. Sarah gasped. Dressed in torn overalls with a fur-lined jacket pulled tight across his shoulders, thick twisted hair falling over his darkened eyes, and a face full of harsh suspicion, he made a sinister sight. The flickering flame threw his huge shadow dancing across the wall behind him.

'Hello,' I said in Russian, forcing a friendly smile on to my face.

He grunted a similar greeting, but his angled eyes darted dubiously between us. They came to rest on Tolly Boy, whom he addressed in sharp, quickfire Russian.

After a short conversation, the bulk of which came from Tolly Boy's lips, explaining, I imagined, who we were and what we wanted, much to our relief the stranger placed his gun against the wall and stepped down from the veranda onto the road. Orange light from the hurricane lamp flashed in the horses' eyes. Sputnik kicked the road. Having shaken our hands, he took hold of Titanic's reins, undid the rope round his neck and tied him to a balustrade that connected the veranda to a corrugated iron roof.

'Is it all right for us to stay?' I asked Tolly Boy.

'*Da*' he said, smiling sheepishly.

Much relieved, I secured Sputnik to a pole at the far end of the building and removed my saddlebags. From our host I asked for buckets and, while Sarah silently measured out some oats, I gave both horses some water from a spring that ran constantly into a trough beside the house and out onto the road. That done we clambered up onto the veranda, dragging our possessions with us, walked through an open door into the outer storage area and then pushed open the living room door. Sarah bade me go first.

The room was small, no more than five metres long and four wide. To the right, beyond a cot bed, was a table where our host was now laying out some bread. For some reason there was no electric light inside the house; the room was lit by the hurricane lamp that he'd hung on a peg above the window. Also hanging from the walls, out of reach of mice and rats, were bags of wheat and vegetables. In the corner behind the wooden door an iron stove crackled, warming the room most efficiently. As we entered, two sleepy men raised themselves from a low platform at the far end, and, looking at us casually, started to pull themselves from old and oily sleeping bags. One of the men was in his fifties with grey hair and bloodshot eyes that he rubbed hard to adjust to the light; the other was young, barely twenty, with thick bristles covering his face like a new doormat. Not that they were enough to hide the livid purple scar that ran from his left eye to his jawline. I nodded a timid hello and let my bags fall to the floor. The man who'd greeted us directed us to sit at the table while he placed a kettle on the stove, which he stoked with a metal rod.

I could tell Sarah was anxious. She'd said nothing since we'd arrived, had gone about her chores like an automaton, and her face looked drawn and tired. I took some honey, cheese and sausage from one of my saddlebags and put them on the table. We'd eaten nothing all day. I sat next to Sarah on the edge of the sleeping platform and the others joined us. Without ceremony, they leant forward and began to gorge noisily on the food.

'Are you OK?' I asked Sarah quietly.

'Sure,' she said sarcastically, staring at the table. 'I just love spending the night in a den of thieves like this.' She took a piece of bread and dunked it in the honey. I chuckled. If she was eating, she couldn't be feeling too bad. Looking round the table it was hard to disagree with her assessment of our hosts – a rougher crew would have been hard to imagine – but I doubted we were in danger.

'I think it's a workman's cottage,' I said by way of reassurance. 'I imagine they're employed to keep the pass open, clear landslides and the like. I saw a bulldozer opposite the house when I was tying up Sputnik.' I cut myself some sausage. 'If I'm right and they work for the government, I doubt they'll do anything to us. But I suppose we should keep the camera gear close by when we sleep.'

For a moment we all sat in silence. Scar-face took the boiling kettle from the stove and filled some mugs with steaming, sweet, milky tea.

'Is there enough light in here to film?' asked Sarah, glancing sheepishly across the table to where our hosts seemed to be enjoying their impromptu midnight feast. 'These faces are incredible.'

The orange light from the hurricane lamp barely covered the table. 'Only if I stick the torch beam into their faces, and I'm not quite brave enough for that.'

She laughed dryly.

'We'll have to wrap the story up tomorrow morning when there's some light.'

'Never mind,' she said. 'At least we're off the road and in the warmth and probably quite safe.'

After we'd finished eating, I followed Sarah and Tolly Boy outside to check on the horses. Tied for all to see at the side of the road, I knew it wasn't just our camera gear that was at the mercy of mountain robbers. The horses, too, would need watching. Figuring it was Tolly Boy who held most of the responsibility for getting us into the situation, I dragged another rope bed from the small store room and told him to sleep outside on the veranda from where he could keep an eye on them. He didn't seem to mind and immediately prepared himself for a sleepy vigil. Sarah and I had a cigarette.

'You know what,' she said, once we'd both lit up, 'for all my nerves and anxieties, I'm really quite enjoying this.'

'Yeah? You didn't seem to be in there.'

'I am. Now. I mean if this isn't what I left England for, I don't know what is . . . an adventure, a real adventure; it's like being in a film or book. I told you I wish I'd been an explorer in the olden days. It must have been something like this.' She thought for a moment. 'The Kyrgyz steppes were beautiful, but this is just so raw and well . . . exciting.'

Having finished the cigarettes, we wandered back inside. We unrolled our sleeping bags and lay down side by side on the platform to search for much-needed sleep.

We woke just after dawn to find ourselves in an empty room. Relieved to find our throats unslit and all our possessions present and correct, we crawled out of our sleeping bags and wandered outside. Tolly Boy was looking smug. He'd already fed the horses and was sitting proudly on the edge of his rope bed, staring wistfully off down the valley. It was a stunning sight. Unknown to us, at some point the previous evening we had dropped below the tree line and all around stood majestic pines. The road, little more than a dirt track here, led away from the house, past the bulldozer and down into the valley. With clear skies we could see for miles to where it swung sharply to the right and thundered into a wall of distant rock. The morning star still shone bright and clear above the mighty peaks. We did some filming, explaining the events we had been unable to shoot the previous evening, and I washed and shaved in a narrow stream.

After breakfast we thanked our unusual hosts and followed Tolly Boy down the valley towards his home in Khoshikat. Judging by the map, it was roughly forty kilometres away. If all went well we'd be there by mid-afternoon, leaving us a leisurely two day ride to Panjikent where Saidullah and Serge would be waiting. We'd stay with them for a night or two before crossing the border back into Uzbekistan, and then ride on to Samarkand. Spending two full days in that mythical city would still leave us with a tight, but manageable, week left on our Uzbek visas to ride the 250 kilometres down to Bukhara, sell the horses and be away into Turkmenistan. We still had almost $1,500 in our pockets, our horses were sound, and over the past twenty-four hours we'd filmed some cracking footage. Added to that, and perhaps most amazing of all, Sarah and I were actually starting to get on. Though I found it hard to believe, things appeared to be going rather well. I patted Sputnik's flank and smiled up at the morning sun.

Two hundred yards below the workmen's hut was the *chaikhana*, just as Tolly Boy had predicted. As we passed the front door he couldn't help but throw me a victorious smile.

18 A Few Dollars More

All travellers who set out for Central Asia hold in their hearts the dream of reaching Samarkand. And we were no exception.

Centre of the Universe, Mirror of the World, Garden of the Soul, Pearl of the East, Jewel of Islam, this fabled oasis on the eastern edge of the Kyzylkum Desert has had merchants and soldiers, poets and pilgrims waxing lyrical for almost three millennia. In the third century BC Alexander the Great took Samarkand without a fight and declared, 'Everything I have heard about the beauty of the city is true, except that it is much more beautiful than I'd even imagined.' In the thirteenth century the celebrated Moroccan traveller, Ibn Battutah, discovered, 'one of the largest and most perfectly beautiful cities in the world.' And in 1898 Lord Curzon was to write, 'I know of nothing in the East approaching its simplicity and grandeur; and nothing in Europe which can even aspire to enter the competition.' Even today, after seventy years of intrusive Soviet industrialisation, the Pearl of the East still holds an enigmatic wonder. Standing in Registan Square, surrounded by exquisite fluted domes, mosaiced *madrassahs*, the majestic arches and towering minarets, the romantic mind drifts easily back to a mystical time of fables, myths and legend: to the world of Omar Khayyám and his famous *Rubáiyát*; to the colourful Sogdian and Samanid courts; to the slaughter streets of Genghis Khan and Tamerlane's renaissance; to the lands through which Marco Polo, Xuan Zang and a thousand other great travellers passed. For me, nowhere symbolised the romance of our journey more than Samarkand. Little wonder then, given the sadly unfulfilling nature of our trip so far, that our stay in the city of famous shadows, as it has also been known, turned into a nightmare.

We arrived on the outskirts of Samarkand early in the evening. Escorted by Boris, an English-speaking friend of Saidullah's whom we'd picked up on the Tajik–Uzbek border, we were taken to the Rakimovs' home. The two brothers, Ashok and Juragul, were warm, jovial-faced, middle-aged gentlemen, with bald pates beneath embroidered skullcaps, and large corpulent bellies, cloaked in beautiful, deep-blue velvet *chapins*. At dusk, by a large set of iron gates that formed the entrance to their compound, we climbed tiredly from our mounts and shook their chubby hands.

Their home was impressive. Set on a couple of acres of land, there were living rooms, sleeping quarters and kitchens, with verandas in front forming two sides of a square, and opposite them a garden, open water tank and stable. What made this place different to all the others we'd encountered was an enormous garage, a hundred metres long, twenty wide and twenty high, running the entire length of the right side of the holding. Boris explained that our host ran a coach company in town and it was here that they kept their buses. Ashok, the older of the two brothers, placed a friendly arm across my shoulder.

'But not tomorrow,' he chuckled merrily; I felt his body shake. 'Tomorrow it will be the venue for the biggest party we Rakimovs have seen for a long time.'

'Oh, yes?' It was obvious something was afoot. Crates of vodka bottles were stacked against the wall like milk at a primary school.

'Juragul's youngest son is getting married,' said Ashok, punching me playfully in the stomach, and smiling towards his brother. 'You will stay for this, I hope.'

'Certainly,' I answered, addressing them both. 'Thank you. We were hoping to stay for the weekend and leave on Monday – for Bukhara – if that's OK with you?'

'Excellent.' Ashok chortled.

At that moment two young boys, aged about six and seven, came rushing from the house, fighting each other with plastic swords. As they tore past, the taller of the two whacked me cheekily on the rear. Everyone laughed, especially the young boys.

'My grandchildren,' explained Juragul, grinning proudly. He tried to persuade them to come over and be introduced properly, but they both declined the offer, preferring instead to stick out their tongues and run away in stitches.

Having stabled and fed the horses, we were shown to a pleasant room with sleeping mats and quilts already rolled out on the floor. Juragul told us to wash, change and return for supper whenever we were ready. Though we were naturally impatient to explore the legendary sights of the city, as it was late we decided there was nothing to be gained by rushing into town in the fading evening light. Samarkand had been around for some 3,000 years. It would last another night.

At seven we ate a huge meal, drank and chatted merrily with Boris, the brothers and a number of guests and, brimming with excitement at the thought of what the following day would bring, were fast asleep by ten.

On first impressions Samarkand was indistinguishable from the other former-Soviet Central Asian cities through which we'd passed. Driving through the sprawling eastern suburbs we followed wide, tree-lined streets, populated by the same battered cars, orange trams and propane-propelled buses. The same uniformed policemen stood at junctions directing the traffic, and on the sidewalks the same skullcapped men and brightly dressed women wandered past the same dour office blocks, technical institutes, kebab sellers and high-rise concrete apartment blocks. As we approached the centre we spotted occasional crumbling, sandstone domes, spangled with tiny turquoise tiles, bulging from the earth like giant poisonous toad-stools, but not much else to remind us of the city's glorious past. It was rather disappointing.

At almost every junction rose billboards depicting the imperious bearded image of Tamerlane. On the surface the sheep-rustler-turned-emperor from Kesh, a small town south of Samarkand, seemed an odd choice as a national hero. A self-proclaimed descendant of Genghis Khan, Tamerlane, or Timor the Lame – so called after an arrow wound left him with a profound limp – is known to Western historians as the despot's despot. During his thirty-year reign, which saw his extensive conquests cast a shadow of death over Persia, Syria, Asia Minor, Afghanistan and India, an estimated 17 million people were put to the sword. Stories of his brutality are legendary.

It was only after wandering mesmerised down the shallow steps and across the beautifully patterned tiled floor of the exquisite

Registan Square that the other side of this strange, schizophrenic man appeared. Here lay the centre of Tamerlane's empire, and the paradox of the Emperor's heart. Now restored to its former glory, the Registan is one of most majestic and grandiose works of architecture in all the Islamic world. The shape, style and symmetry of the three madrassahs' facades is extraordinary; the attention to detail absorbing. Tiles, often no larger than a fifty-pence piece, glazed turquoise, gold, navy, purple, deep red and creamy white, cover the imperial walls in stunning mosaics of richly coloured geometric, floral and epigraphic patterns. Sarah and I stood at the centre of the Square, under a clear blue sky, surrounded by the arches, domes and minarets, with mouths wide open, gurgling inadequate expletives.

But as we meandered through the mosques and *madrassahs*, the question I was grappling with was why should such a vicious butcher of men bother to create so much perfect splendour? Some say Tamerlane was obsessed by his own ugliness and contrived to create the most exquisite city in the world so he could feast his eyes on beauty. Others say that he was motivated by megalomanic pomp and vanity. And there are those that think that he simply wanted a showcase for all his captured treasures. Whatever the motives behind the building of Tamerlane's Samarkand from his Mogul ancestors' ashes, it remains one of the strange and enduring mysteries of Central Asia that a man who spent so much of his life engaged in slaughter and destruction should have expended so much energy creating such beauty.

Before continuing our sightseeing we had a few chores to complete. First we popped into a bank and changed $200 into 200,000 Uzbek *sums* – enough, we figured, to see us through the country – and then visited the telephone exchange. We had to put through a call to Bishkek to check that our Turkmen visas were going ahead – unlike our Kyrgyz and Uzbek ones, we'd had no time to get them in England – and much to our relief were assured by Samat, Alex's assistant, that they were. He told us a woman called Makri would be waiting with them at the border around noon on the 26th. And finally we found an Internet café. We had had no contact with Lion TV since we'd given the first batch of tapes to Alex to send from Osh, and we were eager to see what Lion had made of them. Both the BBC and Channel Four were holding back on a deal until they had seen how we were shaping up on tape. We both hoped that by now they would have signed a contract. But the news that was waiting for us could hardly have been more dispiriting. Bridget, a new series producer at Lion TV that neither of us had heard of, had sent us a long diatribe of criticism that left us both reeling. Though it started positively enough, saying, 'Well done, you're both doing a really good job in what are obviously very difficult circumstances . . .' it was soon lambasting almost every angle of our work. 'Where are the video-diary pieces,' she asked, '. . . the ten minutes each day when you are supposed to talk privately to camera? When you do talk to camera about personal things you're both guarded, hiding something it seems . . .' Shit, had it been that obvious, I wondered miserably. 'We need to know what's going on and why. And why nothing after dark? Don't you have a torch? And the sound: Sarah, too many times when you're filming there is no sound at all. Use your headphones and check the levels . . . this leaves really good bits unusable.' But the biggest criticism was thrown squarely in my direction. 'Jonny,' she wrote, 'a lot of the film work you're shooting is very good indeed, all the long shots, the studious attention to cut-aways and close-ups, but it's what you're missing that's the problem. It seems all the time you're trying to capture a preconceived script of your own, often hiding what's really happening. This is a video diary' – the phrase was underlined – 'a reflection of what really happens, not what you hoped might happen. You are not travelling in order to make a film. The reverse is true. The camera is there to record what happens on your travels. If you don't change this quickly, and really tell the camera what's going on, it will be very unlikely that we will be able to get a commission.'

Had she jumped from the computer screen and slapped us round the face, I doubt she could have hurt us more. It had barely entered my head that they wouldn't manage to secure a deal. Both the BBC and Channel Four had been so positive before we'd left I'd figured it was only a matter of 'when', not 'if'. It was a depressing thought indeed. For one thing, why else were we there now if not to make a broadcast-quality film? And second, whatever Sarah and I were doing wrong, none of it was for lack of effort. On average we were shooting more than two hours of tape every day, and if we weren't actually filming we were thinking about it. From the moment I woke up until the moment I closed my eyes to sleep at night, the camera was at my side, poised for action. The letter came like punch to the stomach. I felt hurt; Sarah went ballistic.

'Fuck her!' she spat, incandescent with rage. 'Really, fuck her. What the hell does she know anyway? She's wrong. What we've been getting is great. We had loads of excellent stories, all that fantastic scenery, the horses in the Kashgar bazaar, Tash Rabat, the Heavenly Horses in Osh . . .'

But I knew the producer was right. All that Sarah mentioned was peripheral. The emotional story, which, whatever we might have liked to imagine, still represented the crux of the programme, had not been recorded at all through the Mountains of Heaven. Added to that, I knew very well – now it had been spelled out in black and white – that all along I *had* been trying to tell the story the way I wanted it told; I *was* guilty of hiding aspects that didn't fit with my precise, rose-tinted image of a Central Asian horse trek: the truck, bus and taxi journeys, the lavish meals, intrusive tour operators, and many more things besides. Ever since Kashgar, when I'd tried to persuade Sarah out of her purple plastic crash helmet and beige jodhpurs and into something that sat more accurately with *my* image of an adventuring horsewoman, I'd been fighting a losing battle to capture the romantic odyssey on the old Silk Road for which my quixotic heart had yearned.

As we wandered back outside, I was struck by an even more curious thought. Was this blind and delusive ambition to make a perfect film actually only a symptom of a greater problem? On the surface I'd wanted to avoid filming these scenes because they didn't fit in with my image of what we were supposed to be doing. Yet now I wondered if there was another, more deep-rooted, reason for my editing. Was the manipulation of the film merely a reflection of the distorted way I'd begun to live my life? By undertaking a decade of romantic and adventurous travel writing, and now this film, had I become so driven by the concept of what makes a good story that I'd slipped into some illusory parallel universe where I believed I could control my destiny simply by attaching it to a perfect, sonorous tale? In short, was the film not just a piece of celluloid but a twisted hidden metaphor for a life that I was fighting desperately, and rather unsuccessfully, to control? If so, I knew it threw up a number of very awkward and intriguing questions. Would I have fallen for Rachel had I met her at a boring London dinner party, or was it because I knew intrinsically that a journey with her on the Silk Road could be turned into another literary adventure? Had I invited Amel back to England to live with me and be my wife entirely because of an honest and genuine desire to be with her, or had my decision been partly affected by the knowledge that doing so would help to give my first book the ideal ending? And if I went back all the way, had Melanie and I really shared such a truly blissful and unproblematic relationship, or had I been guilty of glorifying it, at least to some degree, for the sake of a perfect love story? I lit a cigarette and tried to push these unpalatable and confusing thoughts from my mind.

We both felt very flat and spent the rest of the afternoon touring the sights more out of duty than any real desire. We climbed the 240 steps to the top of a minaret at the Bibi Khanum's mosque to film Samarkand's rooftops, wandered a necropolis of mausoleums know as the Shah-i-Zinda and, with the producer's angry words ringing in my ears, even filmed ourselves with a group of French tourists at Tamerlane's tomb . . . reality, not fiction. Sarah appeared particularly mournful and having sat at a café in silence for some time, she disappeared with the camera.

I walked into a hotel earlier today, one of those swanky ones for rich foreign tourists, to find a loo and I saw a group of English tourists. It just made me feel so cut off and lonely. An overwhelming homesickness hit me and made me wonder if I had the strength to carry on. We're two-thirds of the way through the journey, but I just feel shattered, not physically but mentally . . . the problems day after day, the riding, the agro, the filming. I just feel so depressed. I don't know what's wrong with me. As a group of kids hustle around her, she drops her head dejectedly. *It really is very difficult.*

By the time we arrived at the Rakimovs', the wedding celebrations were already underway. The giant hangar, empty and bare when we'd left for town that morning, had been transformed into a party venue. Where before the exposed-brick, high-ceilinged, oil-stained construction had harboured as much atmosphere as – well, a bus depot – now, filled with noisy revellers, it was a glittering banqueting hall. Dozens of benches and trellis tables covered in cloth, and carrying fruits, sweets, bread and bottles of vodka, stretched from one end of the hall to the other. Covering the walls were colourful banners, drapes and twisted lengths of gold and silver tinsel. At the far end, raised on a stage, a cheesy electronic band squeezed out a dubious tune. No one sat as yet. Milling around in groups, segregated by their sex, the guests stood chatting. The bride and groom were not to be seen.

Avoiding the crowds, we slipped quietly through a side door of the house, passed the patio where eight huge cauldrons of food bubbled above gas fires, crossed the veranda and entered our room. Having pulled on our smartest clothes and grabbed a handful of fresh video tapes, we headed back towards the party. Before leaving, I hid the 200,000 sums I'd collected from the bank in the far corner of the room, beneath the cushion of a chair, and locked the door. The $1,200 we had left was safely zipped in the trouser pocket of the combat trousers I was wearing.

We arrived back at the hangar just in time to join the other guests as they moved outside. In front of the giant roller door, pulled high to let in the warm night air, a great bonfire had been lit. A buzz of expectation rose among the crowd. Mikhail, Ashok's English-speaking nephew whom we'd met the previous evening, spotted us and came over.

'What's going on here?' I asked the young translator.

'The couple are arriving.'

'And the fire?'

'It is tradition,' he answered. 'They must walk round the fire . . . it will bring them good luck.'

'And many children.'

'Very many.' He laughed.

A moment later the couple appeared out of the darkness, as if from nowhere, and a huge cheer went up. Ali, the groom, wore a flowing midnight-blue velvet *chapin*, a smart grey suit, and an embroidered skullcap on his head. His bride wore a sugary white bouffant dress. Behind a thin veil she had a round attractive face, but appeared terrified, pale, as though she'd seen a ghost. Four men held a ceremonial cloth above their heads. Theatrically clothed dancers and musicians stood before them, and, as the assembled crowd clapped out a rhythm, the happy couple began their ceremonial walk towards matrimonial bliss.

The bride and groom then moved inside, pushing their way through a throng of smiling faces. They climbed onto a raised platform at the side of the building to sit alone beneath a banner on which their names had been embroidered. Once they were seated the rest of us followed, again segregated by our sexes, and the feast began.

I was lucky. With Mikhail at my side I could talk to my neighbours and soon discovered that most had very interesting tales to tell. Gordie, a young Uzbek of Russian blood, explained that his grandfather had been deported to Samarkand under Stalin's purges in the fifties, and Victor's great-grandfather had been a German prisoner of the First World War. Two of Rahman's ancestors, his multiple-great-uncles had been executed by the Russians when they first annexed Samarkand in 1868 – they'd been hung, he merrily informed me, in the middle of Registan Square – and Ali was an Iranian, studying engineering.

As we talked, we ate and drank. I tried to pace myself, but with little success. Every time my glass was empty it would be filled again by my new friends with the order, 'Drink, drink!'. Bottle after bottle of vodka was thrown down our necks, and it wasn't long before we were all very drunk. I didn't mind. Far from it. After the frustrations of Lion's e-mail, I needed to escape. Looking around, I saw Sarah was also enjoying herself, drinking vodka and laughing merrily with a young girl who seemed to speak some English. Everyone was in fine sprits, except for the bride and groom. Sitting above us like china ornaments on the mantelpiece, they rarely spoke, never smiled and appeared rather sad. Especially the bride. Head cast permanently down, looking as fragile as a little doll, she appeared a figure of anxious dread.

It was fortunate I was drunk. After the main dish had been cleared away, the band struck up and I was dragged to my feet by Juragul and, in what was obviously an Uzbek wedding custom, made to dance with him and his wife the length of the building, taking money from those we passed. If I'd hoped my earnings might help our battered budget, I was to be disappointed. I was then instructed to stand before the platform and hand all my earnings over to the bride and groom. This finally made them smile. The band then stopped, and I was asked to make a speech and toast the happy couple. As seriously as I was able, I thanked Juragul and Ashok for all their hospitality, praised Uzbekistan, and then wished the bride and groom all the happiness for the future. Finally, quoting an Indian proverb, I asked Allah to be bountiful and make the bride mother of a hundred sons.

Whether this was what the guests heard is another matter entirely. Seventeen-year-old Mikhail was far more drunk than I and had immense difficulty standing, never mind translating. Whatever he said, however, went down well enough, for I received rousing applause. The groom then rose, quietly thanked me for my kind words and everyone for coming, before accepting an even more raucous cheer as he led his bride from the platform and away into the night. The band then struck up again and, alternating between Uzbek pop and bizarre renditions of Lionel Richie and Whitney Houston numbers, jacked up the volume and filled the hall with music. Tables were cleared from an area at the far end and the dancing began in earnest. There was no segregation now. The women and men swarmed together in a merry muddle. Sarah danced with Ashok and Juragul, while I was thrown around by their wives with gay abandon.

After that, everything became something of a blur. An hour or so later, Ali the groom came charging back into the room and onto the middle of the dance floor, with a triumphant smile spread across his face and a bloodied sheet in his raised right hand. A great cheer went up. Ali was then hoisted onto the shoulders of four men who danced through the crowd.

'Is that what I think it is?' asked Sarah, shocked.

'I can't imagine it's anything else.'

'Barbarians . . .' she whispered.

Ali then drank, danced, fell over and threw up Mikhail threw up. Two others had a fight. Ashok tried to buy our horses, for about fifty bucks as I recall. I tripped over a bench and hurt my knee, but at some point managed to stagger to bed. I would say I slept the sleep of the dead, and for the most part I did, but during the night I was woken by one of Juragul's sons creeping around our room. As he was backing out of the door, I shone my torch into his face. He apologised and held up a blanket. He needed it for sleeping. Thinking nothing more of it, I crashed my drunken head back on my pillow and returned to heavy sleep.

The moment I woke up I knew something wasn't quite right . . . and it had nothing to do with the hundred jackhammers pounding in my skull. My trousers, which should have been by my sleeping mat on the floor, where I always left them, were lying by the door.

What were they doing there, I wondered painfully. Sitting up, I rubbed my face and looked across the gloomy room. I tried to think. It wasn't easy. My brain felt as though it had been split in two by an axe. My mouth was dry and rancid, as fetid as a vulture's crotch, my tongue swollen and mouldy. Grappling in the dim light I found my water bottle, clumsily removed the lid and took a long slug. I tried to think again. Had I really been so drunk that I'd flung off my trousers any old how? No, I . . . yes . . . I'm sure I, no . . . It was useless. The pain of trying to picture the last few moments of the night before was simply too great. Leaning to my left I picked up my shirt, gingerly pulled it over my head and, checking I was still wearing underpants, climbed to my feet. I stumbled awkwardly across the floor. More bemused than anxious, I reached the door, picked up my trousers and prepared to put them on. And then, only then, did my heart stop. I knew in an instant that they were too light. Desperately groping at the flaccid right leg, I found the pocket and saw the zip was open. The pocket empty. My mouth seized like a vice. Blood rushed to my head; I heard it pounding like waves in my ears. I dropped my trousers and sank to the floor. The last twelve hundred dollars, the money that was to see us from Bukhara to the Caspian, our future and our security, was gone.

Sarah stirred. Propping herself on her elbows, she sat up and squinted. 'What's going on . . . you all right?'

'Yeah . . . yeah,' I lied hopelessly. I tried to swallow and failed. I coughed. 'I'm fine . . . sorry.' She lay back down and rolled over.

Well, what was I supposed to say? That I, the self-appointed responsible one, the one designated to look after the money, the person with the future of our trip in his hands, had got so plastered that he'd somehow managed to lose all our money . . . more than a THOUSAND FUCKING DOLLARS! I cupped my head in my hands. What did it mean? With no money how could we go on? Would Lion TV bail us out? If they really thought we were doing such a hapless job of filming, perhaps they'd consider it pointless throwing good money after bad and refuse. And even if they did, or if I found some extra myself, how could we get it to Samarkand? This wasn't the EU we were talking about. I couldn't just pop along to a cashpoint machine. Could I withdraw money, dollars, from a bank on my credit card? If not, it was the end of the journey.

I looked around desperately, and a flicker of hope suddenly danced in my heart. Did I empty the pocket myself? In some unlikely inebriated rush of sagacity did I take the money from my pocket, along with my notebook and pen, and place them somewhere safe? Did I put it with the used video tapes? Did I hide it somewhere? With hope rising, I jumped to my feet . . . had a terrible head-rush and sat back down. Trying again, more cautiously, I moved slowly across the room to the low table next to my bed. The notebook and pen were there, as was a pile of other documents from the pocket – my passport, vaccination certificate, Sputnik's ownership details – but no money. Desperately I sorted through the papers again . . . with the same depressing result. I checked my bum bag, my waistcoat pockets, my other trousers. I looked under my pillow, my sleeping bag, the cushion of the chair – where I found the 200,000 sums – but no dollars.

Sarah stirred again. 'Whatever is it?' she asked, blinking. 'You're like a rat on speed, rummaging through everything.' She took her glasses from beside her and placed them on her face.

'The money,' I said flatly, 'it's gone.' Embarrassed, I turned my head to the floor.

'The money's gone?' she repeated questioningly. 'What? The sums?'

'Oh, I wish . . . no, the dollars.'

'The dollars?' She weighed the words carefully and then whispered, 'Oh shit.'

For a moment we sat in silence, the gravity of the situation hanging like a guillotine blade between us. Once again I knew we should be filming. Reluctantly, I put the camera on the tripod, attached the microphone and set it to record.

'Are you sure it's gone?' Sarah asked hopefully.

'I'm sure.' I patted my combat trouser leg. 'It was in this pocket last night. It's not there now. I can only assume it's been nicked.'

'Are you sure it was in your pocket?'

The poisoned way I felt I wasn't very sure of anything. If all my other documents were scattered across the table, it was perfectly possible that I had removed the money from my pocket and placed it there with them. But if so, when? And how could I have been so stupid? 'I think so,' I answered lamely.

'Then who could have nicked it?'

'I don't know . . .'

'I mean the room was locked all evening and . . .'

'I suppose I could have been pickpocketed at the wedding, or somebody could have sneaked in here after we'd –' I stopped mid-sentence. A vague image of a nervous face, lit by torchlight, burst into my mind. Juragul's son. Had he really been looking for a blanket to sleep under? At the time it had made sense, it was his room we were using, but now . . .

'What?' said Sarah, studying me carefully. 'What is it?'

'Last night . . . late . . . one of Juragul's sons, you know, the one with fat lips, looks like Portillo . . .'

'I know, Mahmet. The bastard tried to catch me having a shower yesterday.'

'He sneaked in here last night while we were asleep.'

'What? How do you know?'

'I woke up just as he was leaving, shone my torch in his face. He explained he was looking for a blanket. He could have been; this is his room.'

'Bollocks,' she snapped. 'The bastard must have taken it.'

It did seem likely, but I knew, whatever the truth, that short of finding the money on his person we would have absolutely no way of proving it. Couldn't I have been pickpocketed? Couldn't someone else have come to our room last night? With my memory fragmented by alcohol, I had no answer to these questions.

Sarah stood up and pulled on her trousers. 'Well, the first thing we've got to do is see Juragul. Tell him what's happened.'

'What? And explain that on the day after his son's wedding his other son has abused his guests and stolen their money? Whatever we might think, we have no proof and no way of getting it. Added to that, we can't call the police because foreigners aren't allowed to stay in private homes like this, only licensed hotels, so at best they'd tell us it was as much as we deserved, at worst they could deport us. No. Forget it, the money's gone. What we have to think about now is whether or not it means the end of the trip.'

'End of the trip!' cried Sarah indignantly. 'Pull yourself together, Jonny, for Christ's sake. It's bad, but it's not that bad. We're insured, right? I mean Lion's policy is bound to be pretty watertight and cover cash as well.'

'Insurance?' I mumbled pathetically. It was the first time the thought had crossed my mind.

'They must have realised we might be robbed while travelling. Shit, on a trip like this sooner or later it was almost bound to happen. We can call them tomorrow morning, and if they say that it's OK we can try to take another $1,200 out of the bank in the afternoon. This is Samarkand, it's a huge place – used to tourists – there must be a bank or hotel. You do still have your credit cards, don't you?'

'Sure . . . he only took the cash.'

'Good, then that's what we'll do.'

'I just hope they'll let us take out dollars. Sums will be no use. We won't be able to change those again once we arrive in Turkmenistan.'

Evidently suffering as well, Sarah stopped listening and brought her hand to her forehead. 'One thing's for sure,' she said coldly, 'with that bastard Mahmet hanging around I don't feel like staying here all day. I'd rather take a wander round town.'

We switched the camera off and walked outside. Much to our surprise we found a grey, ill-looking groom and his newly deflowered bride sitting at the breakfast table. As before, her eyes were cast to the floor. For the next month she was not to raise her eyes and look at anyone in public. Sarah and I bade them as smiley a good morning as we were able, and tucked into bread and fig jam.

But Juragul's two grandchildren, dressed in smart new shirts and clip-on ties, ruined the meal by flying around on brand new bicycles, crashing into the table, shrieking and hollering as they went.

Any thought we might have had of escaping the party fallout was very soon dashed. During breakfast many of the male party revellers, including some new grey beards I hadn't noticed from the previous evening, started to gather in the hangar and round our breakfast table. Juragul and his wife came out, dressed again in all their finery, followed soon after by Ashok. I tried to ask the Rakimov elder brother what all the excitement was about and received a curious response. He wiggled his index finger between his legs, as though it were a penis, and with the other hand appeared to snip it off. He then pointed to the children. 'Quite right,' I said, nodding my head appreciatively. 'Just what they need. Noisy little buggers.'

Mikhail appeared, looking as dishevelled as everyone else, and explained. 'Child circumcision. On the day after wedding it is custom for the youngest males in family to be circumcised,' he said matter-of-factly.

'But where?' I asked. 'They're going to be taken to hospital somewhere?'

'No,' he said cheerfully, 'here.' He pointed to a room next to ours, beneath the long veranda.

Juragul's arm was suddenly over my shoulder. 'You official photographer,' he whispered quietly. 'You must film ceremony.' I looked beseechingly into his face. He had to be joking . . . He was not. I regarded the six- and seven-year-old boys again and was overcome with pity.

A few minutes later they were hoisted from their bikes and into the arms of their grandfather. Still smiling, shouting, waving their hands, seemingly totally unaware of the fate that awaited them, they were carried through a throng of cheering men, one on each shoulder, like lambs to the slaughter. I switched on the camera and began to film. From the hangar we marched past the table, under a canopy of rich, red roses and onto the veranda. Following the village mullah, dressed dramatically in a long white turban and flowing black robes, five grey-beards and a crowd of young and middle-aged men swept through a door and into the long thin room. It was already packed with men and boys, chanting, grinning and theatrically waving their fists in the air. To obscure the scene from the women the curtains had been drawn, leaving the room gloomy and dim, stuffy and claustrophobic.

The boys, apparently assuming they were so gorgeous that they deserved such attention, continued to laugh and clap and sing and shout while riding their grandfather's shoulders. At the far end of the room two cushions lay side by side on a wide sheet-covered quilt. Both boys looked at each other and their smiles began to drain away. Things did not look right.

Without ado, Juragul handed the boys to two elders who stood them side by side. The boys' eyes darted anxiously now around the room, seeking reassurance, but no one caught their glances. In a lightning move the men pulled the boys' trousers to their ankles and forced them to lie down. At their feet squatted the mullah. He placed a cloth over the knees of the lad closest to me, and knelt on either end, pinning down the child's trembling legs. The old man at his head pulled up the lad's shirt and held him tightly by his shoulders. The young boy's tiny shaft flapped like a little worm.

Now horror flashed across the child's face. The mullah pulled at the foreskin with one hand while picking up a cutthroat razor with the other. He then began to pray, 'Allah u Akbar . . .' The lad raised his head and screamed as he saw the silver blade flash in the gloomy light. A third man raised a round loaf of bread before the child's eyes as though to distract him. It made little difference. He shrieked with dread, writhed uncontrollably, pulled and kicked at those holding him down. Knowing he was next, his petrified brother also began to holler. Three more men held him secure. Now both boys were screaming at the top of their lungs, wriggling, trying desperately to be free, but there was no escape. I tried to concentrate on filming, but the shocking cries turned my stomach and I felt bile rising in my throat. The heat, the smell of sweat and fear, closed in round me. I turned away, disgusted, only to see a macabre, gold-toothed, wrinkled face grinning freakishly at me.

Turning back, I watched the little stalk through the garish colour monitor. I saw the mullah tug once again at the little chap's flaccid foreskin and stretch it as far beyond the head of the penis as it would go. He then folded it over the razor blade and, with an expert flick of the hand, and to the stomach-churning sound of soft meat tearing, sliced through the flesh. The animal wail could have shattered glass.

Fearing I was in danger of vomiting my breakfast over the mullah or the unfortunate boys, I scrambled to my feet and, without care for cut-aways and close-ups, pushed through the crowd. I reached the door and burst through, from darkness to light, like a man escaping a grave of freaks and goblins.

After a few moments to collect my wits, I turned and looked up towards our room. To my surprise I saw Boris standing on the veranda, in the shade, talking to Sarah. Of course, he'd come to pick up our excess baggage, to take it by taxi to Bukhara. Feeling more composed I walked steadily towards them.

'. . . but that's just it,' Sarah was saying, 'we think we know who took the money – Mahmet, one of Juragul's bastard sons – trouble is we can't prove it.'

'Hi, Boris,' I said.

'Hello.' He smiled and shook his head. 'This was bad situation, no?'

'It's nothing compared to what I've just witnessed.' He regarded me uncertainly. 'It doesn't matter. Listen, is there a bank in town that will allow us to withdraw dollars on my credit card?'

'In Tashkent, yes, here I'm not sure.' He shrugged. 'Even now, in the former Soviet Union it is hard to find dollars. Except with the gangsters. Most tourists bring what they need with them.'

'So did we,' scoffed Sarah.

'Indeed,' said Boris. 'I will help you look tomorrow. If not here, then you come with me to Tashkent.'

19 Even Cowgirls get the Blues

By dusk we'd ridden fifteen kilometres and cleared the city limits. It hadn't been a particularly pleasant ride through the southern suburbs and out of town along the hard shoulder of the busy dual carriageway, but neither of us was especially concerned about that. Having found a bank that had given us dollars, we were just relieved to be heading onwards to Bukhara and the setting sun, and not penniless towards Tashkent. Besides, having studied the map the previous evening, we both felt confident that we'd be able strike out across the smaller tracks and trails that wove their way across the flat, empty plains as soon as we found a guide. Following this less direct route we knew the journey would take a little longer, and with intermittent water supplies it represented more of a risk, but away from the main road we also imagined life in the saddle would be a good deal more filmic – six days on the motorway would surely have given Stanley Kubrick problems – not to mention less of a grind on our fractious nerves. Quite where this helpful guide was suddenly going to spring from, I hadn't a clue. But for the time being neither of us cared. Once again we were just thankful to continue on our way.

There were no hotels or *chaikhanas* beside the busy road, only low-rise bungalows, smallholdings and market gardens growing produce for the city. There were people though, many of them, milling about with little else to do, it seemed, but watch the passing traffic.

It was with locals like these that I had hoped we'd find lodgings for the next few nights of our travels. But now I wasn't so sure. With my twenty words of Russian and smattering of Uzbek I felt embarrassed to stride over and clumsily request a bed for the night. I had expected to find men on horseback and, with something in common, wait for an invitation; perhaps they'd also agree to guide us. But on the busy road there were no horsemen to be seen. We had our sleeping bags and roll mats in case we were forced to sleep rough, but to save the horses as much weight as possible we'd dispatched most of our camping gear – along with anything else we felt we didn't need – with Boris in a taxi to Bukhara. In our saddlebags was enough corn to last the horses for six days, a few sausages and loaves of bread for us, but not much else. If we did have to sleep out it wouldn't be very pleasant. Still, knowing it was my idea that we should do this stage of the journey without backup of any kind, I felt I couldn't allow my nerve to fail me. With night closing in, we needed to find some accommodation. Spotting a group of men sitting on the far side of the road, I handed Sarah the camera and asked her to film.

They watched me keenly as I approached.

'Hello,' I said tentatively in Russian. After three months I still hadn't really worked out how to say this improbably long word.

There were four men, three in their sixties to guess by their appearance, and the other in his early forties. Dressed in scruffy Western clothes they all appeared Russian and replied cheerfully in kind. The youngest stood, took hold of Sputnik's bridle with an amused smile, and began to stroke the horse's head.

'*Horosho*,' he said, turning my way. 'Your horse is beautiful.'

'Thank you,' I answered, and then looked at the sky. 'Night, now. You home, us stay?' It wasn't very polite, or even very comprehensible, and it took the man a few moments to work out what I was requesting. But when the light dawned he didn't seem surprised or angered by the request. He casually nodded, turned, uttered something to his mates, and started to wander off down the broken pavement. With no real knowledge of what was going on, I gestured to Sarah to cross the road and join us.

After a hundred yards a prefabricated, concrete wall rose up next to the pavement. From the saddle I could see over its uneven top into a large estate of tenement housing. Rising to six floors, eight identical dark-grey structures bordered a central park the size of a football pitch. On the grassless earth a group of poorly dressed children shrieked and cried as they spun a paint-chipped roundabout, scaled a rusty climbing frame and swung on a row of hazardous swings. My heart sank. He couldn't seriously expect us to stay here. What on earth would we do with the horses?

Where the pavement joined the gravel entrance we turned through a gap in the wall and passed a collection of overflowing rubbish bins, two old cars and a high-sided, flat-backed truck. We lumbered on between some golden-leafed sycamore trees and up towards a wooden bench. On it sat another group of middle-aged men. On seeing us approach, one of them jumped to his feet and with great excitement rushed over to greet us. He was a kind-looking man, about the same age as our guide, if a little more tatty round the edges. His chin was a field of thick stubble, his hair messy, and his white string vest fought a losing battle to contain his podgy belly. His trousers fell down low on his hips, and on his feet he wore slippers. Still highly dubious about our prospects of finding suitable accommodation, I remained in the saddle while the two men spoke in Russian. Some of the children had now stopped their playing and were watching us carefully, the more curious among them edging slowly across the park towards us.

'*Da . . . da*!' shouted the kind-looking man suddenly, and in simple Russian explained, 'My name is Ali Jan and I am president of the housing association.' Proudly puffing out his chest, he pointed to the apartment blocks that surrounded us. Then, in an attempt to make himself more respectable, he pulled up his trousers and pushed a hand through his thick black hair. 'Of course you stay the night.'

'Thank you,' I said, leaning over to shake his outstretched hand. 'It's very kind . . . but what about the horses?'

'No problem,' he replied, and pointed beyond the flats to some open ground. Unsure quite where he meant, I indicated that he should show us. He led the way along the gravel track, round to the right of the furthest set of apartments, past a dusty basketball court and up to a house much like the Rakimovs'.

At the entrance we dismounted and led the horses through the iron gates, beneath an arch and into the compound. Sensing something exciting, most of the children were now happily following us. In a mischievous rabble they scurried beside us, over a small bridge that crossed an irrigation channel and down to an orchard. It was a perfect place for the horses. Secure and safe and with grass at their feet.

'Oh *horosho, horosho* . . .' I said to Ali Jan, who was evidently delighted that we liked the place so much.

'*Da, da . . . horosho.*' He laughed. From a low branch he pulled a bright red pomegranate and handed it to me. '*Grrran-aad,*' he smiled, taking another from the tree. Then, pretending to pull the pin on a hand grenade with his teeth, he bit the stem and lobbed the ripe fruit, soldier-style, towards the far end of the field. As it landed he made an explosive bang and crouched towards the ground. The children shrieked with laughter.

We tied the horses loosely to a couple of trees, untacked them, gave them hay from a nearby stack and water from the channel. We then collected our belongings and followed Ali Jan back towards the flats. By now word had spread throughout the estate. Hundreds of kids ran around us, screaming and shouting, jumping up and pulling at our possessions. There was nothing threatening in their behaviour, or even particularly annoying, they all just wanted to be involved. Like kids the world over, before long their main preoccupation was fighting each other to push their grubby faces up against the camera lens. More than once Sarah, trying to film, swore at them in English. For me, enjoying the freedom of being filmed rather than doing the camera work, playing with the laughing kids made me feel like the Pied Piper.

At an entrance to one of the apartment blocks we escaped the mayhem by following Ali Jan into the dark stairwell. On the second landing we reached a white door. Figuring she'd done enough, I took the camera from Sarah and filmed our entrance into the tiny flat and our introductions to Ali Jan's son, daughter and his startled wife. We all shook hands and moved into the living room. In the corner by the window, a black and white television was playing an old cartoon. They showed us through to a small, light room beyond, with french windows that opened onto a narrow balcony that faced the playground. We thanked them again, dropped our luggage and collapsed onto two single beds that were pushed against the walls.

Dinner was a rowdy affair. Seemingly very proud of his new guests, Ali Jan invited extended members of his family as well as his neighbours to join us for a drunken meal. Twelve of us squashed around the tiny table at the end of the cramped living room. Luckily one of them – a young lad called Yuktam – spoke some English. Ali

Jan cracked open the first bottle of vodka and proposed a jolly toast. With a resigned glance towards each other, Sarah and I joined the rest downing the spirit in one. We had long since learnt that people here had little to celebrate, and when strangers showed up, it was all the excuse they needed. It would have been rude not to join in.

Realising that this was an interesting part of the story we'd been shooting earlier in the evening, I attached the camera to the tripod, placed it in the corner of the room and, checking everyone was in shot, set it to record. Much to my surprise nothing happened. I pressed the red button again. Still nothing. I looked at the camera a little bemusedly and tried again.

'What's up?' Sarah asked.

'I don't know . . . but it won't turn on.'

'Perhaps the battery's flat.'

I checked and it wasn't. I checked the tape, the lens, the monitor, but nothing made a difference. I shook it and slapped it, and for a second or two it flickered back to life. But a moment later it died again. I looked over at Sarah and shrugged.

'I don't know what's up with it,' I said anxiously. 'I'll look at it properly after supper. We'll use yours now.'

The four other men Ali Jan had invited were typical of the region. They were all well-educated professionals – a lawyer, a teacher, a bank clerk and a technical engineer – but none of them had any work, at least not in their chosen professions. Moreover, they had resigned themselves to the fact that for them, in their middle age, things would probably never get any better. Two of them now drove taxis in the city centre; two others traded what they could in the bazaar. Beyond the day-to-day running of the estate, Ali Jan had no work at all.

Though I commiserated with them and tried to listen sympathetically to their sorry tales, I was rather preoccupied with the broken camera. I stopped drinking, ate quickly and, as soon as I felt it was not rude, excused myself from the table and disappeared into our bedroom to give the camera a thorough check. Sitting on my bed, I tried to get it working again, but nothing I attempted made the slightest difference. After twenty minutes I knew I had to face reality: the camera was dead.

I slouched back against the wall, holding it in my hands. I wasn't surprised that it had broken. In fact, given the hammering it had received – multiple drops, constant dust, being soaked, heated and frozen – it was astonishing it had survived as long as it had. Not that that was any consolation. Without a main camera, things would be difficult. Sarah's camera was good enough for video diaries and incidental cut-aways, but that was about it. No additional microphones, lenses or filters could be attached to it, and the quality of the pictures it recorded was generally far worse. If we wanted to continue to record the story all the way to the end of the road, there was no doubt we'd need another. But how would we get one? While waiting for the bank to give me dollars on my credit cards earlier that day, we'd e-mailed Lion and discovered that our cash had been insured. The camera would be, too. But how would they get a new one out to us? I really hadn't a clue. I dropped the camera on the bed beside me and glanced out of the window. I felt defeated again.

Sarah entered the room. 'Is it OK?'

'No,' I sighed, 'it's fucked.'

'Shit.' She sat down opposite. 'What are we going to do about it?'

'Right now I really don't know.'

Armed with Sarah's camera to record the continuing story, by noon the next day I was back in Samarkand making a telephone call to London. Within seconds I was put through to Bridget, our new series producer, and I explained what had happened. Again I wondered if she'd tell us to call it a day and come home. I think a part of me hoped she might.

'You're not having much luck, are you?' she said with charming simplicity.

'You can say that twice.'

'Don't worry,' she continued, 'it'll be covered by insurance as well.'

I spelt out that the whole sorry mess was complicated further by the fact that we had only six days left on our Uzbek visas. We agreed they'd be hard pushed to buy and dispatch a new camera to us in that time and, even if they could, where to exactly? Again she was very sweet and told me not to worry, that under the circumstances all we could do was continue on to Bukhara using Sarah's camera as best we could and call again from there. Given time, they'd think of something.

Back at the housing estate I found Sarah sitting on a bench in the playground, drawing a pretty young girl. Turning the camera to record, I told her what Bridget and I had decided, but, noticing the battery light below the lens flashing, I cut the explanation short. Keen to record the sequence as one and wrap that part of the story, we returned to the flat so Sarah could collect one of her spare batteries. A few minutes later she slunk sheepishly from the bedroom.

'What is it?' I asked.

'The spare batteries . . . they're not here.'

'What do you mean they're not here . . . where are they?'

'I sent them in the luggage to Bukhara.'

'That wasn't very sensible. Never mind, we can charge this one up and do the shot later.'

'No,' she whispered. 'We can't.'

'Why, Sarah?' I had a nasty feeling I already knew the answer.

'Because that's in Bukhara, too.'

My mouth fell open. I looked at her dumbfounded. 'Oh great, just fucking great.' I slapped my palm against the side of my head. 'You sent your two spare batteries *and* the charger off to Bukhara, giving you what . . . two hours' worth of filming time for the entire six-day journey?' I could hardly believe it. I slumped back against the wall and slid down onto my arse.

'I'm sorry,' she bleated. 'It was a mistake.'

'A mistake?' I sighed deeply. 'So what do we do now? We have six days left in the country before our visas run out, five from tomorrow. We can't hang around here another day, yet to go on without the camera is pointless.' I turned my face towards the ceiling and closed my eyes. I tried to think, but my mind was more weary than it had ever been and I found the effort too great. Permanently surrounded by incomprehensible Uzbek and Russian, constantly worried about time, weather, the film, police, horses, camera and a faltering relationship, my brain felt like an overused punchbag and simply wouldn't register any more. I rubbed my eyes and forced myself to concentrate. 'There's only one thing for it. You'll have to go by taxi tomorrow to Bukhara, find the guesthouse where Boris has taken our things and bring the batteries and charger back here.' I stopped as another consideration seeped into my thoughts. 'But that still won't give us time to ride all the way – it's a four-day journey from here, minimum, five at our pace. Shit. I'll have to hire another truck, drive the horses to Navoyi or some-thing . . .' I stared at my partner. 'Jesus Christ, Sarah, isn't this trip hard enough without you carelessly fucking things up?'

Her chin began to wobble, her shoulders shook and behind her glasses her large eyes filled with tears. A moment later she began to sob. Sarah – tough, self-confident, determined Sarah – began to cry like a child. I was shocked. She was always so bloody sure of herself, so forthright and in control, if not lambasting me then usually pointing derision at someone else. I'd expected to be told to go to hell rather than having her break down on me. Watching her snivelling, biting her lower lip, it was impossible not to feel sympathy for her. Standing there, staring unfocused at the ground, she suddenly looked terribly young, no longer the cocksure 26-year-old but a frightened little girl. Putting a hand to her face she turned away and slouched miserably out into the balcony.

'Oh, bloody hell . . .' I whispered to myself, suddenly feeling guilty and wondering what to do. In any normal situation I imagine my natural response would have been to rush out and comfort her, put my arm around her, let her sob on my shoulder. But I didn't. The idea of Sarah and me sharing any physical contact, whatever the circumstances, was so bizarre as to be absurd. Though we had established more friendly relations over the last month, we'd both kept our distance and *good* friends we still were not. Besides, there was another issue. Sarah's breaking down was undeniably a poignant filmic moment. And though I did feel rather heartless, balancing it up, the film felt more important. So I grabbed the camera and, hoping there was enough juice left in the battery to record whatever might happen next, followed her outside. Leaning over the railing next to her, I held the camera out at arm's length, the lens pointing back at us, and pressed record. She didn't flinch or recoil, just stared vacantly into the distance.

'I'm sorry, Sarah,' I shrugged. 'I didn't mean to flip out and upset you like that.'

'It's not you,' she sobbed, tears streaming down her cheeks. 'It's not you, it's this, this place, this country . . . everything.'

'Yeah, well the last few days haven't exactly been easy.'

'I keep messing things up, getting things wrong, I . . .'

'Don't be ridiculous, of course you don't. At least no more than me. We've both made mistakes from time to time – who was responsible for the money? Besides, with all the pressure it's only to be expected.'

'It's not just that, I'm just fed up with the whole thing. Things being stolen, the camera breaking, Bridget and her bloody e-mail. I'm just tired, tired . . . really fucking tired. It's just not working out like I thought . . . I want to go home.' She lifted her glasses and wiped away the tears on the back of her sleeve.

In front of us stretched the playground. A handful of kids swung on the swings, slid down a slide. Beside the truck two men stood and talked. Sarah continued to sob quietly at my side.

'I'm not surprised you want to go home,' I said. 'So do I. To tell you the truth there's nothing in the world I'd rather do. I've been thinking of it for some time, wondering if all these hassles were really worth it.'

'Really?' she sniffled. 'I thought you just got on with it.'

'Well, I do. But that's not to say that a great deal of it doesn't really piss me off. But you know what keeps me going? Two things: the fear of failure and Registan Square – well, sights and situations like it. What an amazing place that was, Sarah.' She nodded. On the camera the power light started flashing double speed. 'We saw that, and not flying in like every other bloody tourist, or being carted around by aircon bus . . . we rode horses into Samarkand. Nobody you'll ever meet or ever know will be able to say they did that.'

'Except for the bloody French couple!'

'Ah, yes,' I chuckled, 'except for the French.' I put a tentative hand on her shoulder. It was the first time we'd touched deliberately since Hunza. 'In a few days' time we'll ride into Bukhara and that'll be just as great. This journey is proving infinitely harder than I'd ever imagined but, despite that, we are winning. We're doing pretty much what we set out to do, riding our horses along the Silk Road, most of it anyway, and having come this far I'm damned if I'm going to give up now. Not with the film and not with the journey. And now not even with you.'

'I know,' she said, wiping her nose on a tissue. 'It just seems like there's still so far to go. I wonder if I have the energy.'

'Not really,' I said. 'We'll soon be in our last country. And once we've sold Sputnik and Titanic in Bukhara we can be ordinary tourists for while. We can relax for a couple of days, even stay in a hotel.'

She managed to smile again.

'Really, once we reach Bukhara, it'll be downhill all the way.'

Little did I know.

For the next four days the motorway was our home. Eventually though, late on the fourth afternoon, with clear skies stretching far and wide across the land, we passed through another towering triumphal arch and entered Bukhara. Nearing a junction just beyond, I spotted two people on horseback, with a third pack horse in tow, riding north-west out of town towards Khiva. Obviously Westerners, I knew in an instant who they were.

'My God,' I exclaimed to Sarah, 'look, over there . . . it must be the French. Quick!' I dug my heels into Sputnik's side. Tired as he was, he barely responded at all, just coughed, shook his neck and farted. 'Come on, you old bastard, move your arse.' I kicked him again and slapped my reins across his withers. Reluctantly the old war-horse broke into a weary canter.

As I reached the road I shouted, 'Hey, Monsieur . . . Madame!' I had forgotten their names. Immediately they reined in, stopped and turned on their tracks. I slowed to trot, and then a walk. Though we had heard about them on an annoyingly regular basis, I couldn't think of any reason why they should have heard of us, except via Dom three months ago. But long before we reached them, I could see they were both smiling.

'So,' cried the man as we approached, 'Les Anglais, I presume.'

'Bien sûr,' I responded cheerily. 'Et les Français, je crois!' And a moment later we all crashed headlong into a merry muddle, shaking hands, clasping shoulders, laughing and smiling, every one of us talking at once. Even our horses started nuzzling each other. He was called Sylvian and was a lovely-looking man with a thick mop of curly fair hair, John Lennon specs and an unkempt beard. And Prescilla, his wife, as Dom had reported, was very easy to look at indeed. In a floppy green hat and tie-dyed T-shirt, she had watery blue eyes, long strawberry-blonde hair and, in a 1960s hippie kind of way, reminded me rather of a young Bardot. I struggled to take my eyes off her.

'Amazing,' I exclaimed excitedly. 'We really thought we'd never reach you. Did you know we've been travelling in your footsteps since before Osh?'

'We were told about you guys way back in Izzi-kul by your Italian friend.'

'Dom.'

'Yes, Dominico.'

'But at least you haven't had people telling you every night, "Oh, the French were here last week!"' I chided him.

'No,' he conceded, 'we have not, but we have had people telling us all along which route you had taken and that that you were catching us up.' Who these mystery informers were exactly, he didn't explain. 'We were starting to think it was becoming a race!'

'Are you going to the Caspian as well?' asked Sarah.

'No, we are leaving now for Khiva, and then the Aral Sea . . . that's where we finish.'

'What a shame,' I said sadly. 'You sure you can't hang out here with us for a day or two?'

'I wish we could, Bukhara is a beautiful city,' said Prescilla.

'Nicer than Samarkand?' asked Sarah.

'Oh, much.'

'Unfortunately we have to get on,' continued Sylvian. 'Khiva is still three weeks away, the Aral Sea a week beyond that and winter is approaching.'

'Tell me about it.'

And so we chatted on the side of the road. A married couple from Paris, taking six months out to do a journey they'd both longed to do, by their cheery account Sylvian and Prescilla had made a truly epic trip. The horses they were riding were the same ones they'd bought in Almaty, Kazakhstan, way back in July. Unlike us they'd ridden every inch of the way, crossed every border on horseback, camped almost every night. They hadn't employed the services of any tour operators or travelled a single mile on the side of a motorway; they'd found guides to direct them cross-country, via the all-important watering holes. Moreover, unlike us they'd even managed to persuade the obdurate Uzbek authorities to grant them two-month visas, leaving the onset of winter their only time concern. Buying one set of horses and not having lost any belongings, they had done the whole journey for a fraction of what it had cost us. With no film to make they had been able to enjoy the people they'd met, and each country through which they'd passed, without distractions. And as Prescilla spoke fluent Russian, they'd had few problems with any of the locals, the army or police. In short, they'd had a thoroughly successful and deeply fascinating trip.

Our story could hardly have been more different.

At first I was eager to hear all their tales, sitting forward smiling in my saddle, but, the more they both talked, the happier I was to know they were heading out of town that day. I felt embarrassed, sheepishly trying to explain why we'd had so many horses; why at times we'd had to carry them in trucks, ourselves in buses and taxis; how much money the whole trip had cost us; why for so much of the time the journey had been frustrating, irritating and even a crashing bore. We tried to justify our decision to buy and sell horses, to use trucks, our having things stolen, by explaining the hassles of making a film, the one-month visa restrictions, our leaving England so late and the problems of riding from Kashgar. But even though Sylvian and Prescilla were very sweet, nodding sympathetically, I knew deep down I was only making excuses . . . they were living proof of that. They had started planning the trip a year before they'd set out, they'd departed a month before us, and as a married couple had had none of the extended aggravation that Sarah and I had both endured. But beyond that there wasn't much of a difference. Our trip had been a shambles, theirs a rip-roaring success.

'So where are you going from here?' asked Prescilla.

'We're going to sell the horses tomorrow, hopefully in the bazaar, but from then on it all depends on getting the new camera. We'll certainly hang around here for a couple of days and then I guess head across the border, travel down to Merv and continue the trip from there.'

'All the way to the Caspian Sea?' asked Sylvian.

'We have to.'

He turned and looked towards Khiva, as though he could see all the way there. 'The weather is good for now, but we've already seen the cold and rain. If you want to ride all that way, you'll have to get a move on.'

After half an hour they apologised but said they had to leave. They wanted to be well clear of the city before nightfall. The orange sun was already low in the sky. Agreeing that we should all meet up in Paris or London for a proper debriefing in a few months' time, we scribbled down each other's addresses, shook hands, kissed and turned our separate ways.

As we rode off in the opposite direction, my sorry, defeated mood began to lift. So our trip had, for the most part, been a disaster. On the road we'd had a constant stream of problems, we had no idea if the film we'd gone to such pains to make would ever see the light of day and, for much of the journey, we'd have happily strangled each other. But, as I turned in my saddle and watched Sylvian and Prescilla riding off into the sunset, I realised that, for all the difficulties we'd endured, at least my instinct about the potential of the trip and romance of the travel had not been wrong: albeit in strangers' hands, my dream was still alive and kicking.

A successful traveller relies on luck and a following wind, previous trips had shown me that. But perhaps, I pondered, to earn that luck the motivation for the journey must also be true. The French couple were not writing books or making a film; ambition didn't drive them. They'd not picked each other out of a newspaper advert and gone off on some harebrained and desperate scheme to try to fall in love. They already were. They were doing it because it was simply something they'd longed to do. Watching them go, I could see now only too clearly that the inspiration for our trip had been artificial, rife with self-delusion and selfish fantasy, and born from dishonest intentions. With Rachel the plans had made at least some sense: I'd been in love with her and she was to some degree in love with me. But ever since she had dropped out and I'd picked Sarah – a girl who already had a boyfriend for goodness sake! – I'd been trying to trick the spirit of love and adventure into riding with me, on my terms, to my schedule and to fit neatly into my film. And things just don't work that way. The French had been granted the luck they richly deserved. So had we.

I smiled to myself. The Gods may be crazy, but they are seldom stupid.

20 City of Love

The morning after our arrival in Bukhara we sold Sputnik and Titanic, and for two days enjoyed Bukhara's fascinating sights. In the mornings, under lapis skies and a warm autumn sun, we wandered happily between the Kalyan Minaret – also known as the Tower of Death following its use in the nineteenth century, when the degenerate Emir Nasruddin Khan used it to execute his enemies by marching them up its 105 steps, stitching them into sacks so they wouldn't make a mess, and hurling them off the edge to their deaths – the mighty citadel or Ark, the bazaar, and the various mosques and *madrassahs*. In the afternoons we lounged around the ancient Labi-Hauz, a beautiful seventeenth-century plaza built around a tranquil pool, in the shade of the mulberry trees. And in the evenings at the traditional open-air restaurants we gorged ourselves on shashlik kebabs and the region's fruity wine. We felt wonderfully free not having any horses to look after. As Sarah remarked, being rid of Sputnik and Titanic was like off-loading the kids with the in-laws for a well-earned holiday. It was also liberating not to be staying as anyone's guest. For the first time since Kashgar we didn't have to worry about being polite, under-standing difficult foreign languages, or eating huge meals and drinking gallons of vodka we really didn't want. Beholden to no one, we could do exactly as we pleased.

The problems began when I scuttled off to make contact with the outside world. At Lion TV Bridget informed me that DHL took a minimum of two weeks to dispatch packages to Central Asia, making it impossible for her to get a new camera to us in Uzbekistan. Worse, the insurance company were reluctant to allow £2,000's worth of new equipment to be sent without a personal courier. Apparently, such things tend to 'go missing'. She was there-fore looking into the possibility of entrusting Launa, one of Lion's technical staff, with the mission of coming out to meet us in the

Turkmen capital, Ashkabat. She suggested we travel there directly and wait, with luck no more than a week, before backtracking to Merv to continue the last stage of the horse trek.

But the next phone call carried far more ominous news. Our Turkmen visas, which we'd arranged to pick up on the border, were not going to be there after all. On a crackling line, a desperately concerned Alex informed me that Makri, the Turkmen travel associate through whom he'd organised everything, had called him three days earlier to say that she'd failed to obtain our visas. Turkmenistan was about to commemorate its eighth year of independence and, apparently to celebrate the milestone, their autocratic leader, President Saparmurat Niyazov, had, for reasons known only to himself, suddenly decided to ban all foreigners from entering the country for two weeks. It was a disaster. Regardless of the fact that such news would obviously slow Launa down, and therefore seriously endanger our plans to ride all the way to the Caspian Sea, with little more than twenty-four hours left on our Uzbek visas we were in real danger of being stranded in Uzbekistan illegally.

I rushed a startled Sarah from the calm serenity of the Labi-Hauz back to our hotel, where we each seized a bag and fled to the bus station. There, with heavy hearts and tired heads, we bought two tickets for the night bus to Tashkent; we'd avoided the Uzbek capital once, but not a second time it seemed. While Sarah slept, I stared out at the darkness and tried to figure out where this extraordinary development left us. Our visas were valid until the 26th – it turned the 26th at midnight – but, though they were technically sound for the entire day, to be in this dogmatic part of the world without a valid air ticket to get us out of the country, I knew our visas were already as good as expired. If we were lucky enough to slip into the capital without being checked at one of the many roadblocks, we were unlikely to last long once there. Secret police, plain-clothes officers and regular uniformed cops patrolled all the key areas of the city: the streets, parks, trams, underground, bus stations, even markets, shops and arcades. Also we wouldn't be able to check into hotels as they always examined visas rigorously. We didn't dare ask the authorities for an Uzbek visa extension; knowing their reputation we'd simply be deported. The whole situation was a shambles.

As far as I could see, there was only one avenue left open to us.

If we could get a one-month Kyrgyz visa, which, under the CIS transit rules, allowed three days in any other Central Asian state, we'd have a little breathing space in which to sort things out. And if we really couldn't persuade the authorities at the Turkmen embassy to issue us visas in Tashkent, a Kyrgyz pass would also give us an escape hatch by allowing us to fly to Bishkek, Kyrgyzstan, and hole up there till the visas came through. Quite where it left the rest of the horse trip, I didn't care to dwell on.

It was then that I remembered another contact. While in Pakistan with Rachel, I'd met a very sweet guy called Richard Danziger, who worked for a UN migration agency. On my last trip to Islamabad, he'd given me his colleague's details in Ashkabat, a guy called Zlatko, who he said could help us if we found ourselves in trouble. Could Zlatko somehow get us permission to enter the country in which he worked? It had to be worth a try.

When the bus put us down, we jumped into a cab and without further ado made our way through the leafy streets to the Kyrgyz embassy. Here we explained our predicament to the jolly Kyrgyz missionary, who duly gave us a one-month visa while we waited. We could have kissed him.

Seventy-two hours. The clock was still ticking.

Next we found a telephone exchange from where I put through a call to Ashkabat. Unfortunately Zlatko was away in Tajikistan – working on the war in Batkent – but Valerie, his assistant, listened patiently to my troubled request and in perfect English explained that she would go and see the authorities and try to bring them round. She took our passport details and asked me to call back later in the afternoon.

We checked into the old Intourist Hotel, a grim leftover from the Soviet travel industry, and waited. The weather had turned once again, and for the next few hours we sat in our tiny room, looking out of the window at the dreary rain, watching the dirty trams clattering by, drinking coffee and smoking Russian cigarettes. We didn't talk much. With the grim spectre of a return to Kyrgyzstan hanging over our heads, there wasn't much to say. To be forced to travel back to the start of the journey when the end was in sight was dismaying. Moreover, as well as Alex, Murat lived in Bishkek. Sarah and I, if not exactly best mates, had at least managed to form an understanding that seemed to be getting us through the trip. Returning to Kyrgyzstan might jeopardise that. And how would Sarah feel about going back? Would she actually agree to such a loaded situation? Would she enjoy it? When we discussed the possibility, her dour expression told me she would not.

Luckily, the issue was never more than hypothetical. When we returned to the telephone exchange, a delighted Valerie informed me that by maintaining we were special guests of the UN – VIPs vital to the independence celebrations – she'd obtained exceptional leave for us to apply for visas. A fax from the Turkmen interior ministry would arrive at the embassy in Tashkent the following afternoon, allowing us to apply for a visa the day after that. So long as nothing went wrong this would give us some eighteen hours to travel the 600 kilometres to the Uzbek frontier and leave the country. Tight, but definitely possible.

Or so we thought.

Having applied at the Turkmen embassy on the morning in question, I was told by the consular official to pick up the passports at five that afternoon. But when we returned at four thirty the embassy doors were locked. After a frantic hour quizzing indifferent armed sentries, we discovered the entire embassy staff had gone to a party. Warming their hands over a charcoal stove, the guards happily informed us that the employees wouldn't be back until morning. Sarah, however, back to her best impression of a *memsahib*, was having none of it. In impressive Russian, far better that my own, she demanded that one of the guards should find out where this Turkmen soirée was going on, look up the number and call them. We simply had to speak to the head of the consular staff. It was a matter of life and death. And, much to my amazement, five minutes later I was standing in the sentry hut with a phone in my hand, connected to the right man.

'But I told you to be there at three,' the cold voice told me blankly down the other end of the line. 'I am now at an important party and cannot possibly leave.'

'But if you don't, by nine o'clock tomorrow morning it won't be Turkmenistan we'll be heading for but a filthy Uzbek jail. Please . . .' I begged.

He agreed to meet us there at ten. 'But don't be late,' he warned.

We were there at nine. Standing beside our taxi in the narrow, darkened street outside the quiet embassy, smoking cigarettes and stamping our feet against the cold, we waited. And waited. And waited. At a quarter to eleven a black Mercedes swung off the main road, glided towards us and pulled up next to the taxi. The rear window slid silently down and the official's gloved hand passed from the window a brown Manila envelope. Having checked the merchandise in the car headlights, I handed over $100, thanked him and stubbed out the remains of my cigarette. The experience had me feeling more like a character in a Le Carré novel than a latter-day Silk Road traveller. Much relieved, we climbed into the taxi and a moment later were racing south towards the border, Turkmenistan and freedom.

The inclement weather followed us to Ashkabat. As we emerged from the train a little after dawn, a thick layer of smoky cloud hung low in the sky and a light rain fell. It was cold, too, with a biting wind whipping off the Karakum desert. It was an unwelcome reminder that winter was marching inexorably towards us.

Valerie met us outside the station in a fat white Land Cruiser with IOM – International Organisation for Migration – painted in UN blue across the doors and bonnet, and a driver called Sasha sitting behind the wheel. She didn't take us to her office but instead drove directly through the centre of town to a narrow residential street and pulled up outside an apartment block. She told us her grandmother owned a vacant flat within the tall grey building, which we could rent for as long as we wanted. As we had no idea how long we were going to have to stay in the city, and there were apparently no budget hotels, it seemed a sensible option. With Sasha's help, we hauled our luggage through the entrance and up the dark staircase to the fourth floor lobby. Valerie unlocked and opened the door.

Though the hallway was gloomy, it was immediately obvious that this was a smarter home than others we'd seen. On either side off the central hall were spacious rooms, clean and light. To the left, as we entered, was a study filled with books, from whose windows we could look out across the city to the rugged, brown Kopet Dag escarpment, beyond whose crest Iran lay; and to the right was a formal living room furnished with piano, television and old gramophone player. There was also a beautifully bright dayroom, with tall windows running its entire length, from which we could see two more tenement blocks stretching away on either side towards the Trans-Caspian railway lines. As we stood there an endless freight train rumbled past. There were three bedrooms, a small bathroom and kitchen. It was all a little tired, with threadbare carpets and faded wallpaper, and the furniture was purely functional, but for us it was grand, a fine place to hole up for a while. There was even a telephone which Valerie said we could use for international calls. She gave us her home and office numbers and told us to call, once we'd rested. Had it not been for Valerie, we'd have been in Bishkek and 2,000 kilometres from the Caspian Sea. As it was we were in Ashkabat and less than 300 kilometres from our final destination. We couldn't thank her enough. Once she'd gone, we picked our rooms and crashed out on the big, soft beds.

As usual, our bubble of euphoria did not endure long. At midday I put through a call to Lion to find out what was happening with the new camera and listened with weary resignation as Bridget explained that Launa's trip had also fallen victim to President Niyazov's unfathomable foreign-visa ban, leaving her unable to apply for clearance to enter the country until after the festivities were completed. She was now pencilled in on a flight, via Istanbul, on 17 November, almost three weeks hence. Three weeks! I sat on a stool in the gloomy hall, head in my hands, wondering if I'd ever get to the Caspian Sea.

Much to my relief, Sarah took the bad news well, with nothing more than a resigned shrug. She told me she was so relieved not to be in Bishkek, or staying in some cruddy ex-Soviet hotel, or with some thieving family, or in a tent beside a motorway, that anything else was endurable. And to begin with everything went smoothly. We settled into an easy rhythm in our strange new home, shopping at the local supermarket and vegetable bazaar, cooking meals in our little kitchen, and drinking at a city centre bar with Valerie and her two female work colleagues, Ayna and Akja. We were to all extents and purposes a regular couple, living a normal life. Well, kind of. There was still a tangible distance between Sarah and myself, an emotional space that I doubted would ever be bridged. At no point over the last few weeks had either of us made any real effort to find out what was going on inside the other's head. With the exception of when Sarah had cried we'd discussed nothing very personal. In fact, not since the first few days of the adventure, back in Pakistan, had we tried to get to know each other better. Both aware of how terrible things had at one time been between us, I think we were just thankful to have made it this far, and that the end was now in sight.

As in Kashgar, we spent most of our time apart. I didn't mind this. Though I never discovered anything to justify Ashkabat's seductive and romantic name – city of love (from the Arabic *ashk*: to love) – it was none the less a fascinating place to wander. A few years earlier I imagine it would have looked very similar to all the uniform Central Asian towns through which we'd passed, with wide, tree-lined streets, Soviet proletariat buildings and spacious pleasure parks. But orchestrated by the flamboyant President Niyazov, and financed with millions of dollars of IMF from World Bank loans, and by oil and gas companies desperate to get their hands on Turkmenistan's sizeable natural energy reserves, in the last few years all manner of ostentatious buildings had sprung up, transforming the city into a strange hybrid of Eastern and Western pomposity.

The Niyazov personality cult was everywhere. From the Arch of Neutrality, whose apex is crowned with a twelve-metre high, revolving golden statue of the man, to the walls of all government buildings, shops and restaurants, centres of every park and square, President Niyazov looks down on his people. Streets, hospitals and universities are named after him. His face is on the money. He is the government. He is the country. In 1993, as if to underline this, he even took the modest name 'Turkmenbashi', meaning 'Father of all Turkmens', and coined the ubiquitous motto 'Halk, Watan, Turkmenbashi'. 'People, Nation, Me.'

There is another entity beside President Niyazov which the visitor to Ashkabat cannot fail to notice, one that had far greater significance to us. Its image is also seen on the money, it too has streets, hotels and buildings named after it, and, in an honour greater even than anything bestowed on the President, its likeness is carried at the centre of the nation's flag: it is the Akhal Teke horse, Turkmenistan's national symbol.

As one of the most ancient and distinctive breeds of horse in the world, forebear to the Arab and the English Thoroughbred, it is perhaps not surprising that the Akhal Teke is held in such high regard by the nomadic Turkmens. Originating around the Akhal oasis in southern Turkmenistan, reared and used by the Teke tribe, it is said to be descended not from heaven but from a wild steppe horse, known as Turanian – meaning 'horse of quality'. Renowned for their tremendous stamina and speed, Turkmen legend has it that they were used in the expansive military campaigns of King Darius of Persia and Alexander the Great. In the 1930s, to publicise their native breed, twenty Turkmen horsemen staged a 4,000-kilometre trek from Ashkabat to Moscow – including crossing 400 kilometres of baking Karakum desert – completing the journey in an incredible eighty-four days, which is just one of the long-distance records established by the horse.

Ayna told me that unfortunately there were only some 2,000 purebreds left in the world, half that number in the country and, in a bid to save those, all horse ownership was now tightly controlled. There were no bazaars where we could buy horses. If we wanted to ride from Merv, via Ashkabat, to the Caspian Sea, we'd have to rent some ordinary nags. And from where she hadn't a clue.

But finally it was time for luck to smile on us.

The last time I'd spoken with Alex he'd given me Makri's telephone number. Even though she'd been unable to secure us visas, he told me she was a good woman, very proficient in what she did and could be a useful contact. Wanting to sort out our transport for the last part of the journey as quickly as possible, three days after we arrived in town I put through a call to her office. Though much surprised to hear from us, she invited us to come round right away.

When we arrived we found a tall, attractive woman about forty-five years old, with dark wavy hair and smouldering green eyes. She proudly informed us that she ran her own tour company showing groups, mainly from Europe, around her country. She apologised for failing to get us into Turkmenistan and was furious that such a ludicrous decree had been passed.

'How will they court the tourist dollar,' she asked finally, shaking her head, 'if they treat tourists this way? I am pleased you had some other contacts.'

She then listened quietly as we explained our need for horses on which to complete our journey. Purely as a side issue, I explained that one of the threads of the television story referred to the Heavenly Horses, and that if it was at all possible we should love to see some of the famous Akhal Teke breed. We'd heard that there were some purebreds in or around the capital.

'Oh, I think we might be able to do better than that,' said Makri with a triumphant smile, picking up the phone. 'How do you say in England, kill two birds with a stone? Why not rent some Akhal Tekes for the last part of your journey? I know the very man. The government minister of equine affairs.' She winked seductively.

'You have to be joking,' I told her.

She said she was not.

The next morning, in yet another crumbling Lada, this time cherry red, we drove to the Hippodrome – a dirt racetrack on the edge of town – where we found some of the most exquisite horses I have ever seen, cantering around an oval bowl. Tall and lithe, with long backs and tapered necks, the willowy animals raced with grace and pride, lifting their fine hooves high as their supple legs criss-crossed like slender branches. There was an arrogance to them, a look of disdain in their large dark eyes, as if they knew their beauty and breeding and just how precious they were. Ridden by jockeys with reins pulled tight and stirrups short, they trained in groups of four and five. Alex had been right: the Akhal Tekes were nothing like as heavy-boned as Kasop's black stallion or the mighty grey in the Osh bazaar. They were much more elegant. They appeared like English Thoroughbreds, which was not wholly surprising, since it's through three stallions – the Godolphin Arabian, Darley Arabian and the Byerley Turk (the later, pure Akhal Teke) – brought to England at the beginning of the eighteenth century that the English Thoroughbred was born. Ancestors of the horses that now sped before us were directly responsible for such equine greats as Mill Reef, Lammtarra and Nijinsky. Little wonder they looked so impressive. Sarah clapped her hands in amazement.

'They're incredible, so beautiful . . . that colour!' Three of the animals' coats were the most startling shade of gold.

'This is unique to the Akhal Teke,' Makri explained proudly.

'God, I should love to ride one.'

'Dream on,' I chuckled, turning to Makri. 'They're never going to let us take any of these incredible animals away on a twenty-day trek,' I said dismissively. 'Not in a million years.'

'You never know,' she answered with a knowing smile. 'They might. The minister is a great friend of the President. If he likes the idea he can make it happen. Cross your fingers and hope for the best.' She smiled again, enjoying her knowledge of English idiom.

We arrived at the entrance to the grandstand and clubhouse where the minister's office was located. After ten minutes a large, government regulation black Mercedes appeared on the drive and swung round in front of the building. From the front jumped a shaven-headed chauffeur. He opened the rear door, allowing a pretty young woman to alight gracefully. 'His third wife,' Makri whispered gleefully in my ear. A moment later the minister let himself out.

He walked over to us, greeted Makri with a kiss on both cheeks and, with a broad smile, shook Sarah and me firmly by the hand. 'My friends call me Geldie,' he said in English with a heavy Slavic accent. It was an unfortunate name for the Minister of Equine Affairs.

Somewhere in his mid-forties, he was younger than I had expected, of medium height, with a thick sweep of jet-black hair and dark, audacious eyes. He was immaculately turned out in a tweed sports jacket with a government pin in his left lapel and a blue silk tie peppered with tiny golden horses' heads. Though there was something deeply intimidating about Geldie – he simply oozed ministerial power – I couldn't help but like him. You could see at once in his dangerous eyes that he was a man who liked to live.

His office was a long and narrow room. At one end a desk, cluttered with horse manuals, breeding books and sales brochures – from places as far afield as the USA and Ireland – abutted a conference table. Sliding into a large leather armchair behind his desk, Geldie gestured to us to sit round the table. He could have been a Mafia don at a meeting of hoodlums. He listened briefly as Makri divulged what we were requesting and then, holding up his hand, he cut her off.

'You explain.' He pointed at me.

'Well, sir, we are on an expedition,' I started cautiously, 'riding horses along the old Silk Road, from Kashgar to the Caspian Sea. We are making a film of our journey for the BBC, which we hope to show next year.' He nodded and smiled, as I'd hoped he might; there was vanity in his style. 'One of the main threads of this trip and the film has been trying to discover the origins of the famous Heavenly Horses of Central Asia. Some say these are the horses of the Ferghana Valley, others that they are your own national animal, the Akhal Teke. If we could hire two of your wonderful animals from the stables here, plus one of the grooms to guide us on the way, it would give our film, and therefore our entire journey, the most perfect ending.' The words seemed so audacious, I was surprised I'd even said them.

'The Heavenly Horse, these are definitely ours.' He chuckled towards Makri.

'So we've seen.' I nodded.

'And where you go from?' he asked. 'Here to Caspian?'

'No,' I answered ruefully. 'We must first travel back to Merv and begin our journey from there.'

'I see. And then ride to the Caspian?'

'Hopefully.'

'It is long way. When you want leave?'

'Unfortunately not for another two weeks, on the 18th of November.' I explained briefly about the camera.

'But this will be impossible.' He pointed to the window. 'It is already getting cold. By December snow will fall in Karakum.'

'Well,' I said, holding up my hands, 'as far as we can get.'

He sat back in his chair and thought for a moment. 'OK, this is what I do. I let you have two horses and guide – I know just the man for this: a local, Turkmen, very strong – you take them by truck to Merv and ride back to here, this will take ten days.' Once again I could barely believe my ears. I glanced across at Sarah, who was grinning broadly from ear to ear, like a young girl offered candy. 'If it is not too late, weather is good, you go further. If not,'

– as he smiled his dark eyes sparkled; it was no surprise he was a ladies man – 'I think you act like sensible peoples and take the train instead. *Da*?'

'*Da*,' I said, grinning. 'I mean, yes, sir.'

'But I ask you to do something for me.' He picked up a pen and waved it pointedly in my direction. 'I want get more tourist to come here, Turkmenistan, ride our horses –'

'Yes,' I rudely interrupted. 'Desert trekking – it would be fantastic.'

'Exactly. Through your film you must help me advertise this possibility.'

'Of course.' I looked excitedly at Sarah and then back at the minister. 'And I have a friend who runs horse trips in Kyrgyzstan, Morocco, other places . . . I'm sure his agency, Ride World Wide, would be very interested in offering holidays to ride Akhal Tekes. I'll tell them about your offer.'

'I'm sure you will.' He stood up indicating that the meeting was over and, walking round the desk, ominously placed a heavy hand on my shoulder. 'You will also pay me' – he thought for a moment – '$750.'

'Oh, umm, yes, of course,' I stuttered, trying to work out if we had enough money. 'That's a very reasonable price.'

'And I am reasonable man.' He laughed heartily and winked at his wife.

She turned away and giggled coquettishly.

Geldie told us to come back on the 17th, by which time all would be arranged.

So we waited. At first everything was fine in this strange 'city of love'. But, having organised the horses, there was no more planning to be done and, as the first week dragged slowly on into a second, so cracks in the calm began to appear. Ever since Kashgar, one way or another, we'd been constantly on the move. If we'd taken a day or two off, it had simply been to look round a famous town, co-ordinate plans and then move on. But now, with little more than 300 kilometres left to go, we had to face the fact that our troubled journey had spluttered and stalled.

For me this forced layoff wasn't too bad. I wanted to get the trip finished as quickly as possible, but when all was said and done it didn't really make much difference to me if we arrived back in the UK in late November or mid-December. I had no home to go to. There was no one missing me. But Sarah, she was frantic to be home.

Like myself, she'd called England soon after arriving in town. Bar brief e-mail correspondence in Samarkand, it had been the first communication either of us had had with our families in almost three months, and naturally they were delighted to hear from us. However, knowing how unsettling I find such long-distance conversations – they always make me homesick – my parents had been thoughtful enough to call only once. But for Sarah the phone barely stopped ringing. Mother, father, grandparents, sister and boyfriend called at all times of the night and day and, though I'm quite sure they thought they were helping strengthen her resolve by showing support, after a while the constant reminders of home began to take their toll, seriously undermining her determination to continue the trip. While I was out, she told the camera how she felt . . .

I just want to go home. I'm so sick of this place . . . this journey has just been too much. I want to go home to my family, get out of this. I never thought it would be this hard – she sniffs and wipes her nose – *I'm so sick of being so tired and now trying to fill the days in this god-forsaken Soviet town. Being bored is so trying, the only escape is sleep at night . . . There's just nothing to distract one and I've got another month. Even when we get out there there's only going to be desert. I feel like a robot. I can't remember what it's like to be excited by scenery, mountains. I feel like I'm programmed to get through every day in neutral. The actual riding feels like ages ago. Men with guns, the remoteness, the camping in the cold. Way back in Kyrgyzstan. That was tough . . . but easy. This isn't tough, apart from all the emotions . . . it's just nothing. I just don't know if I've got the strength to carry on for another month.* She pauses for a long time. *I feel so numb.*

When I returned to the apartment I found her huddled up on the sofa, her eyes puffy and red, streaming tears, chain-smoking cigarettes.

'Whatever is it?' I asked, sitting down beside her.

'I just want to go home,' she sobbed.

The trouble was there was very little to relieve the boredom. At the beginning of the second week we attended the independence-day celebrations at the football stadium, more in the hope of catching a glimpse of the reclusive President than any desire to witness kids in coloured tights running around waving pro-government propaganda banners. He never showed up; it was a tedious afternoon. We went to watch the horses training at the Hippodrome. We caught a bus to the weekly open-air bazaar out in the desert on the edge of town – the biggest in Central Asia – where in a moment of madness I tried to buy a motorcycle and sidecar. All we ended up with were two pairs of counterfeit jeans. We visited the museums and sights, again and again, and did a few personal pieces to camera. But with no new books, at least any that we could understand, a dwindling budget and tired minds, for a person aching to be home it must have been very frustrating. The Trans-Caspian Express that lumbered slowly past our flat window and out of town every second evening compounded the problem. She could have climbed aboard the train and been on the shores of the Caspian the following day. I think it nearly drove her mad.

'Why don't you go home?' I asked her. 'If things are really so bad.'

'Like you,' she answered, 'I just don't want to be beaten.'

Eventually Launa arrived and so Sarah's spirits rose. As well as the vital camera equipment and $800 cash from Lion TV – with Geldie's bill paid we were down to our last few hundred dollars – she'd also thoughtfully carried with her English newspapers and magazines, a pile of paperback novels, Belgium chocolate, a bottle of Scotch whisky and a carton of decent cigarettes. We felt like prisoners of war receiving a Red Cross package. But much more importantly Launa brought herself. So bored had we become of each other that we almost fell over at the chance to get at her, ravenous for different conversation. From the moment she landed neither of us left the poor girl alone. She must have wondered what mad environment she'd fallen into. Very sensibly, rather than staying in the flat, she checked into the Sheraton. My only regret was that her flying visit would be so short. However, with winter creeping ever nearer we couldn't enjoy her company for long; we would have to leave the next day.

That afternoon Sarah, Makri, Launa and myself headed back out to the Hippodrome, where Geldie showed us our horses. Both stallions, Sarah's was a stunning dappled grey with a dark mane and tail and shiny inquisitive eyes, while mine was shimmering black. Standing well over sixteen hands high, they were magnificent regal beasts and we could barely believe our good fortune. He also introduced us to Anah Konye, a hard-faced groom, who he said would guide us from Merv. Squat yet broad, with a jutting, stubble-covered jaw and twisted nose, he put me in mind of a troll. The previous evening he had apparently butchered a sheep, which was now cooked and preserved in sealed containers, ready for the road. I could hardly wait. We loaded the three Akhal Tekes and one pack horse onto a truck and watched them drive away.

Launa invited us out to dinner. We asked Valerie, Ayna, Akja and Zlatko, who had now returned from Tajikistan, to join us. Over a fabulous meal, Zlatko informed us he'd been working near Batkent helping refugees displaced by the fighting. That morning he'd heard that the four Japanese geologists had been released unharmed. We were amazed and drank to their health. After a spin round town we said our goodbyes, telling our IOM friends we'd be back in two weeks. We thanked Launa, hugged her as though she were a dear old mate and wished her *bon voyage*.

The next morning when I peered out of the window I saw that the rugged Kopet Dag escarpment was no longer its familiar oat-coloured hue. During the night the first snows of winter had fallen, leaving it covered in a blanket of sparkling light.

21 The Cold Desert

The sudden wind that heralds the rising sun whistled through the shack. Far away a lonely cry was carried across the sands as a muezzin called the faithful to prayer. Turning onto my back, I rubbed my eyes, stared into the darkness and listened. Deeply moving, evoking all the mysteries of the east, the haunting verse seeped like a spell through the cracks in the walls, the thorn-thatch roof, the ill-fitting window frames. It was the first time I'd heard the azan since Osh. '*Allah u Akbar . . .*' broke the distant voice again, '*La Illaha Illallah*' – 'There is no God but God . . . Stop your sleep and come to worship, prayer is better than sleep!' Unconvinced, I rolled over again. But in doing so I noticed Anah's bedroll was empty. Knowing our guide was not the pious type, I reluctantly eased myself from my sleeping bag, pulled on my clothes and boots and wandered outside.

The air was raw. I put on my fur hat and blew warmth into my hands. Before me stretched a flat courtyard, encircled by low mud walls, stables and a broken, roofless shed. By a haystack, two mangy camels chewed languorously. A goat drank from a twisted water trough. Somewhere nearby, a farm dog howled. Turning my face to the sky, I was relieved to see that the heavens were indigo-blue, still shimmering with crystal stars; the settled weather was holding. Looking east, however, where the compound wall was at its lowest, a jagged band of blood-red cloud seeped out above the village.

Moving silently like a ghost before me, Anah crossed the courtyard and entered one of the stables. In his arms he carried a saddle. I turned back towards the hut.

'Sarah.' My voice was magnified by the quiet of the desert dawn. 'You'd better get up. Looks like we're going to be away early this morning.'

From the darkness rose an anguished groan.

We worked quickly, aware that we had many miles to ride that day. Having led our mounts from the stables, we tied them to a hayrack, an old tractor and a balustrade by a crumbling wall, pulled off their felt rugs and began to tack them up. Throwing *numnahs* and saddles over shivering backs, checking hooves, fixing bridles, sliding down stirrups and packing saddlebags, we worked in silence. All well acquainted with the preparations for the road, we were soon ready to leave. We shook the hand of our old host and climbed easily into our saddles. Eager to be away, the fiery animals skipped and jumped nervously, their delicate hooves dancing on the frozen ground. In the dim dawn light, astride our elegant steeds, we made a timeless image: Cossack warriors on horses from heaven off to fight some distant battle; Silk Road travellers preparing to journey.

The old man pushed open the rusting metal gates. Before us, shimmering like a beacon, the morning star floated above the flat horizon. He bade us farewell, and against the wakening eastern skies we rode out into the desert.

I turned in my saddle and smiled at the rising sun. Today there would be silence.

The last four days hadn't been much fun. Once again stuck on the main road, the journey had been boring and monotonous in the extreme. Trudging along, hour after hour, the same screaming international trucks that had harried us on the road to Bukhara frayed our nerves once more. We tried to persuade Anah to branch off into the northern Karakum, or Black Sands, Desert, to follow the railway line on its quicker, more direct route towards Tojen and the capital, but he'd have none of it, simply shaking his head dismissively. 'Out there is only sand,' he warned darkly. 'No problem for a diesel train; big problem for a horse.'

It was a sad and lonely land. There were no trees, crops, few villages or towns, only tamarisk and stunted thorn managed to scavenge an existence from the miserly earth. Even the telegraph poles suffered, with the bases of the wooden structures devoured by termites. The ones not held vertical by sandwiching concrete pillars dangled uselessly from the cables overhead, like criminals swaying at the gallows. Occasionally a string of sand dunes, not black but muddy brown, bulged from the plain, bloated and fat, to shield us from the noisy traffic. But they never lasted long, always delivering us back to the edge of the tiresome road.

It was especially disappointing given our splendid mounts. Mine, called Moodri – meaning Wise – was a very spirited animal. A jet-black stallion with a light, graceful head, brawny neck and dark, expressive eyes, he was without doubt the most noble creature I had ever ridden. Carrying high withers, a long waist and elegant, well-developed legs, he walked with grace and stature. But, my god, he wasn't easy. Moodri was a purebred racehorse, a direct descendant of one of the most ancient and exceptional equine lineages on earth, with famous sporting ancestors dating back thousands of years. Needless to say, walking along a busy motorway didn't suit his style. He shied maniacally at the traffic, even when it was far away; unlike Kyrgyz Express, he wouldn't walk in a straight line when I dropped the reins to film from the saddle, but, more in the manner of Kara, veered drunkenly to the left and stopped; and if Sarah's horse came anywhere near, he'd swing round and angrily try to bite it – once succeeding in taking a mouthful of my startled partner's jacket. At times Moodri was so troublesome, I quite missed old Sputnik. Though there'd been little heavenly about my Tajik steed, he did at least have good manners.

To make matters worse, we were also desperately slow. On the famous trek to Moscow the Akhal Tekes were said to have travelled on average ninety kilometres a day. We barely managed fifty. Not that this was the fault of the horses Sarah and I rode. While Anah's mount was a half-breed Akhal Teke and quite capable of keeping up, the pack animal he led was a steppe pony from the Kopet Dag hills, and no faster than a mule.

Still, at least the weather held. Every morning, struggling from another strange abode – a closed motel, an asthmatics' sanatorium, a road workers' hut – I'd glance anxiously out across the arid land to see if winter had yet caught up with us. So far we'd been lucky with blue skies extending above us, and once the morning's chill had left the air, the days were warm and sunny.

The mild climate was not the only cheering situation. Much to my surprise and relief something fundamental seemed to have shifted in the relationship between Sarah and me. Where before we'd always been guarded with each other, now we were relaxed and enjoyed the other's company. We chatted properly, about life, the future, our fears and hopes. We shared jokes, laughed, even took the micky out of each other. Whether the change had occurred in me, in her, or in both of us, I wasn't sure, but it was a very pleasant transformation. For much of the journey our relationship had felt to me like that of an overbearing father chaperoning a wayward and unruly daughter, or, as I've remarked before, a boss and PA on a business trip. Now, all of a sudden, we were getting on like real friends. After so much aggravation, it seemed ironic that it was only as we neared the journey's end that we'd finally found the sense of camaraderie I'd been looking for from the start.

Nowhere was this better illustrated than on the fourth evening. Just before sundown we struck upon a small rural community just south of Tojen, and found lodgings with a farmer. Having stabled and fed the horses, I returned outside and, noticing a crescent moon above the western skies, was suddenly struck by a sad revelation. I slumped onto a bench, lit up a cigarette and wistfully prepared to watch the old day die.

Sarah came over, the map in her hand. Sensing something was up, she regarded me solemnly. 'What's wrong?' she asked.

'Nothing,' I said defensively, shaking my head and trying to smile. But something clearly was troubling me, it was obvious, and I wanted to share it. A month earlier I wouldn't have felt able. Now I did. 'Do you know, a few days ago was the tenth anniversary of Melanie's death.'

She sat down beside me. 'Your old girlfriend?'

'Yes.'

'Oh,' she sighed, 'I'm sorry.'

'No, no . . .' I continued hastily. 'I don't mean to tell you because it's sad, or I'm craving sympathy or anything. What's weird is that I forgot. I completely forgot the anniversary of her death. The tenth one, at that. I've never forgotten before. That's terrible, isn't it?'

'Well, I don't know. I'm not surprised. We have had our hands rather full of late.' She leant over and took my cigarette. 'Besides, I'm not sure that it is so bad. Actually, I imagine it's rather positive. What use is there really in anniversaries of this kind? They hold you back, stop you getting on. The fact that you didn't remember, perhaps says that it's over.' Tilting her head to one side, she raised her eyebrows and smiled. 'Yes, don't feel bad. I should say it's a good thing.' She took a drag and handed back my cigarette.

'Though I'm sure I can't even get close to understanding what something like that must feel like, everything has its time and passing: broken hearts, injury traumas, divorce, even death. I've never had a broken heart, not really, but I remember when my parents got divorced . . .' She paused, and a slight frown creased her forehead. 'Eventually you deal with things. You have to, that's all there is to it.'

'Sure, I know. It's just a silly thing.' For a moment we sat in quiet contemplation, watching the first stars of the night appear.

'Do you still miss her?' Sarah asked at last.

'Melanie?' I huffed. 'Evidently not that much.'

'No, really?'

'I don't know . . .' I looked towards the bright new moon. 'Yeah, I guess. I mean, I don't pine for her, think about her day and night, haven't done for years. Days, maybe even weeks, go by when I don't think of her at all; ten years is a long time and, like you say, things move on. But I miss being that close to someone, feeling comfortable with them, having someone to confide in, to share things with . . . being in love, I suppose.'

'Umm . . .' She borrowed the cigarette again.

'And what about you? Missed your boyfriend?'

'Of course.'

'And now are you itching to go home, get married, have kids?'

'Huh!' she cried. 'Six months ago I'd have snapped your head off for that. Now I'm not so sure,' she said in a calmer voice. '. . . maybe.'

'What about TV? I thought you wanted to be a travel TV presenter, the next Benedict Allen, Michael Palin.'

'I did, before this trip. You remember my Freya Stark documentary? I wanted to make that more than anything . . . now I'm not so sure. I don't know, the camera just seems to kill so many experiences, always getting in the way of us just being ourselves, living, travelling, experiencing things and people as they really are. I mean, how ridiculous having to get everyone we meet to shake hands five bloody times just to make sure we catch it right!'

Making the film, though an interesting experience, had indeed affected many aspects of the journey, including, I felt, our relationship. The pressure of shooting decent footage, the constant grind of filming every day, not to mention the inevitable artistic differences of opinion – and my controlling image of how the film should look – had undoubtedly placed a great strain upon us. Before leaving England, I'd imagined making the film would help bring us together by giving us a shared sense of purpose. In fact it had pushed us apart.

As we sat there quietly puffing on a single cigarette I couldn't help wondering how things might have worked out with Rachel. We'd known each other well, understood each other's make-up. The journey had not been mine but ours, with all aspects of it discussed, deliberated and agreed upon over a hundred conversations. With Rachel it would have undoubtedly been easier. But, that said, I couldn't help feeling that the pressure of filming, the constant intrusion of the camera lens, would have driven a wedge between us as well. However I looked at it, filming one's relationships could never be easy.

Ever since my scary insights in Samarkand I'd been pondering how much influence this film, the book I would soon be writing, and the others I'd written, had had on my life. Before this trip I'd seen them as a positive influence, but now I wasn't so sure. Over the last few weeks I'd often found myself grappling with this question: Which had come first, an adventurous life that made for good books, or ideas for good books that led me into adventures? After Melanie's death I'd headed off around Africa because I'd wanted to, needed to, for no other reason than the desire to throw myself into a challenging journey and learn from the experience; there'd been no thoughts of writing a book. But was the same true of my Afghan journey? I wasn't so sure. It certainly wasn't the case here. In this affair I had unquestionably allowed my actions to be governed by what would make an interesting tale. I'd known intrinsically there was no great story in travelling the Silk Road alone or with a platonic friend – I'd agreed with Lion TV that, for the sake of a good show, romance did have to be a possibility – so I'd placed an advert, taken Sarah, and my loneliest trip had ensued. The more I thought about it the more certain I felt. Writing books and making films about having adventures, confusing what was real life and what were simply good stories, had not led me to lasting happiness but further and further up a lonely dead-end street. Being a romantic travel writer had ultimately not alleviated the emptiness I'd felt after Melanie's death but, it seemed, had actually helped perpetuate it.

I sat back, rubbed my eyes and glanced sideways at my partner. 'You might find it hard going back to normal life, you know,' I said quietly. 'We haven't been away that long, but even so you're bound to have changed . . . and others at home won't have. It'll be hard for them to understand. Hard for you to adapt.'

'I know,' she said, stubbing out the cigarette beneath her boot. 'A part of me is dreading it.'

'Well, you'll cope, I'm sure of that. Hard to imagine you not coping with anything.'

'What do you mean?' She looked at me quickly.

'Well, you're not exactly what I'd call timid.'

She turned away again and was silent for a minute. 'I know what you think. That all my, what? – Forcefulness? Determination? Aggression? – is a show of confidence, but sometimes I honestly don't know where it comes from. I hear myself demanding things sometimes and hate myself for it. I'm not as assured as I sometimes make out.'

'Not many of us are.' I glanced at her hand. 'Anyway, what's with the map?'

'Well,' she said, smiling positively again, 'I think I've found a way for us to get off the damned road!'

'Good. Let's have a look.'

As the sun rose, we found ourselves riding through scrub. The sand beneath the horses' hooves was dark brown, crusted and cracked, and appeared like a dried-out river bed. Tufts of coarse, dry grass, brittle and dead, forced their way through the arid plain that stretched before us to where the Kopet Dag escarpment rose like a giant fortress wall on the far horizon. With the fair weather, the snow on its back had largely melted, leaving it mottled brown again. Beyond that lay Iran. Besides the creaking saddles and shuffling hooves, there was silence once again.

Just after eleven we reached the railway line. There was no need to ride directly along the track, in the lee of the escarpment; carried on an embankment the track was visible from half a mile away, and the ground before it was flat and wide, perfect for a ride.

Sarah and I became impatient to test out our racehorses.

'Look,' said Sarah, pointing towards the open land before us, 'it's just crying out to be charged across. We're on racehorses . . . why not?'

'I'm sure Anah could give you a thousand reasons,' I said, looking back at our silent guide, 'but I can't think of one.' I gathered up my reins, 'We'll canter, nothing more . . . OK?'

'OK.'

I stood in the saddle, pressed my heels to his sides, and a moment later Moodri was rushing forward. He was a highly excited, wound-up instrument of fine pulsating muscle and sinew; his pointed ears pricked forward, his nostrils quivered and his mane began to fly. This was what he was made for. This was what he wanted. Faster, with more purpose, his fleet feet began to skip across the sand. Faster, faster, with long, elastic, ravishing strides he ate up the ground, his vivid coat shining in the morning sun. Testing my strength, he pulled at the reins, but I held him firmly in a collected canter.

Suddenly, Sarah was alongside, whistling past, out of control. A racehorse to the last, Moodri was having none of it. With an irritated yank of the head, he tore free and a moment later his hooves spread wings and we were soaring above the desert floor. As the land danced past in a streaming blur, chill air thrashed my face, caught in my eyes and made them cry. At first I worried about having to explain a broken equine leg to Geldie, and fought with all my might to hold him in. Leaning back, pushing my feet deep into the stirrup irons, I heaved at the reins for all I was worth. It made no difference, so I accepted the inevitable, gave him his head and let my winged horse fly.

Unfortunately, full gallop was not a speed our saddlebags were made for. As we charged out of control across the desert, sleeping bags, coats, roll mats and water bottles were scattered liberally. When we finally came to a shuddering halt, laughing with exhilaration, we had to turn and wander back, shamefaced under Anah's withering looks, and pick up what we'd dropped.

In the afternoon our fleeting rations of luck ran out again. As we rode happily along, Anah called out from behind us. Sarah and I both turned in our saddle to see our guide pointing ahead. At first neither of us realised what he was trying to bring to our attention. To the untrained eye, the barren plain stretched innocently before us.

I asked him what was up.

'*Bolshaya problema*,' growled Anah, his face as grave as granite. '*Snyeg*.'

'What's "*snyeg*"?' I asked Sarah.

'Snow, I think,' she replied.

Again we studied the view ahead. Creeping menacingly over the dusty Kopet Dag escarpment and out across the plain – along the entire western horizon – rolled a dark and ominous sky. 'Bloody hell,' I whispered, 'a cold front! Looks like winter's finally arrived.'

Within an hour the blackened cloud had stretched across the land. With the sun gone, the temperature plummeted from twenty degrees to zero. Wind picked up the dust; it stung my eyes and I could taste it in my mouth. Brittle balls of thorn, torn from their roots, were thrown like tumbleweed across our path. We pulled on our coats, our fur hats, wrapped T-shirts round our necks and bandannas across our faces. But sitting high up, taking the full force of the mounting tempest, we were soon frozen through. I wondered where we'd find to sleep.

It began to snow, just occasional flurries, peppering us in giant flakes, but it was enough to remind us of the harsh extremes this desert environment could impart. We had no gloves, no proper scarves or waterproof leggings. Following Sarah's lead I rummaged through a saddlebag for my waterproof poncho, but it was nowhere to be found. Cursing under my breath, I realised I'd not seen it since I'd lent it to Tolly Boy, back in the mountains of Tajikistan. Trying to keep our provisions light, we hadn't even bothered to bring a tent. We had to find some shelter or freeze. For hours we wandered on into the blizzard. We didn't talk. We all knew the score. Then late in the afternoon, emerging like a mirage from the desolate wintry scene, we saw a water tower rising in the distance. As we drew nearer we could see a railway hut beneath it, with a trail of smoke seeping from a central chimney. We were all too cold to cheer, and just stumbled silently towards it.

Whitewashed, with a mud-thatch roof and a tiny covered porch, it wasn't much of an abode but it looked wonderful to us. Around it rose a mountain of clutter: piles of corrugated asbestos, plyboard sheeting, creosoted sleepers, railway tracks, and a defunct old car, which must at some time have been driven across the plain but now sprouted wild grass from its bonnet. Beside the entrance stooped a tall man, who was splitting logs. He turned and watched us as we climbed stiffly from our tired mounts.

Stepping awkwardly over logs and a pile of rusting metal stakes, he approached and shook our frozen hands. Close up, I could see he was badly burnt, his skin stretched taut across his face. It was impossible to tell how old he was, twenty-five or fifty-five. Hearing the commotion, another man emerged from the dwelling, pulling an ankle-length sheepskin coat over his shoulders. They were maintenance engineers, there to carry out some repair work on the track. They told us we were lucky. They'd only arrived that morning and there was no other refuge for many miles around. They showed us to the far side of the hut to a copse of lonely trees. The rough wind whistled among them, tearing the last dead leaves from the flailing branches. There was no other shelter for the horses. We tied them up as best we could and, having untacked and fed them, secured thick felt blankets to their shivering backs.

Inside, the only room was beautifully warm. On an iron stove our hosts fried chunks of pork belly and boiled up sweet, milky tea. They didn't talk to us but sat in the corner, chatting quietly to Anah. While I sat drinking tea, Sarah slipped outside with the camera and a torch.

Before this trip I'd have looked at somewhere like this and thought, God, I wouldn't stay there if you paid me. Home to strange-looking guys, it's rundown, it's ramshackle, practically derelict. But when you're on the trail, and you've nowhere to stay, and you're in the desert in the middle of nowhere, and there's a gale howling, and you're really on your last legs, and you don't think you can carry on for any longer, a place like this is heaven sent. It's not about choices any more . . . it's just about survival.

I woke to a curious rumbling. Growing steadily louder, denser, coming from the east, through my dispersing dreams the noise rose like distant thunder. Suddenly realising what it was, I jumped to my feet and grabbed the camera that was on the tripod by the door. There was no need to dress; I'd slept in my clothes. At the entrance I threw on my boots and bolted outside. I slipped and almost fell. An amazing scene awaited me. Snow had fallen through the night, and the world was now pure white. It took me a moment to get my bearings. The mounting reverberations drew me to the left of the hut, past the trees where the horses were tethered, and up to the railway track. Pointing the lens up at the shallow embankment, I positioned the camera and turned it to record just as the Trans-Caspian Express lumbered steadily past. The bright red engine and matching carriages trundling through the freshly fallen winter landscape made a staggering sight.

When I returned, Sarah was standing on the porch.

'Look at this snow,' she said, her voice a mixture of childlike fascination and adult despondency. Shivering slightly, she hugged herself against the cold.

'I know, and judging by these clouds, I should guess there'll be more.' The occasional giant flake, floating like a feather, continued to fall to earth from the heavy sky.

I positioned the camera so we were both in shot, then crouched to the ground and picked up a handful of snow.

'You know what it means, don't you?'

'What?'

'That the weather's finally beaten us. Even if we wanted to, and thought we could make it, there's no way Geldie will allow us to ride beyond Ashkabat now . . . at least not with his horses.'

'Really . . .' There was an audible note of hope in her voice. I didn't blame her. It was a relief to me, too. 'So what are we going to do?'

'Ride to Ashkabat and call it a day. What else can we do?'

'Ha!' she exclaimed. 'Really?'

'Really,' I laughed.

'Hoo-bloody-rah!' She clapped her hands and danced a jig, smiling from ear to ear.

'Hang on. I mean as far as the horses are concerned.' I pointed back to the railway line. 'We'll do the rest, as Geldie suggested, on the train.'

'Too bloody right. I'm not getting this close to the Caspian Sea without at least seeing it.'

'Sure.'

Suddenly she frowned. 'That means we'll be home in little over a week.'

'Possibly,' I said.

'Bloody hell,' she whispered.

By the time we were all loaded up and ready to depart, a blizzard was raging again. Except for one pair of trousers I hoped to keep dry, I wore every article of clothing I possessed. Sarah did the same. Loathe to leave the cosy hut, we squatted next to the stove, sipping a last cup of sweet, milky tea as slowly as we could, delaying the inevitable. Eventually we downed the last warm dregs, thanked our hosts and reluctantly rode away.

Driven by a perishing, easterly wind, as we rode on through the morning, snow began to drift against the railway line, the telegraph poles, the embankment and the scrub. With my frozen hand I tried to keep it from settling on my legs, but only succeeded in squashing it through the well-worn cotton. It felt as though the sky had crashed to earth. Now solid, flat, white-grey, filled with frozen down, the sky was no longer something above our heads but an omnipresent entity. The Kopet Dag escarpment, the great frontier wall that rose from the plain just a few hundred metres away, may not have existed at all.

By early afternoon the temperature had risen slightly and the harsh snow turned to sleet, hail and lashing rain. The next four days were the coldest I've ever known. Hour after hour we trudged on towards Ashkabat, with sweet reveries of a warm flat, a hot bath and ticket on the train the only encouragement to keep us moving on. Often we were soaked to the skin, and always cold to the bone. At times we rode, at other times we walked: it was the only way of preventing us from seizing up completely. With the days shortening, we often found ourselves riding well into the evening, praying for a light on the horizon that would lead to sanctuary for the night. The places we found to shelter – remote farmsteads and workmen's huts – had little food to offer, and the excess pounds we'd both accumulated on the trip began to fall away.

For all the hardship, inside we were happy. Approaching the City of Love for the second time brought to both our minds a sense of tired achievement. For the most part the crackpot adventure had been a disaster, but, despite the cold, the heat, the busy roads and lonely trails, the thieves, the broken cameras, the police, army, lame horses, angry horses, exhausted horses, and all the personal problems we'd endured, we knew we were at last near the end of our journey.

At two in the afternoon we rode into Ashkabat on the busy main road and up to the Hippodrome. We hadn't managed to find a phone to let anyone know of our imminent arrival and, with the exception of a couple of adolescent grooms mucking out some stables, the place was deserted. It was rather an anticlimax. Given what we'd just accomplished, we wanted, fancied we deserved, fanfares and bunting, tickertape and red balloons, a carnival parade. We wearily slipped from the saddle for the last time and, having handed the horses over to the stable lads, gave each other a celebratory hug. It was the first proper and relaxed physical contact we'd had since Pakistan.

Soon word spread that we were back, and after a few minutes Geldie appeared in his chauffeur-driven Merc. Wearing a smart, navy-blue anorak with an Akhal Teke's head embroidered on the chest, he climbed out, his usual broad smile creasing his handsome face. He kissed Sarah jovially on each cheek, and shook my hand.

'So you made it, huh?' he asked.

'Just about,' I answered.

He turned to Anah and spoke in Russian, checking that all had gone OK. Our guide of few words just shrugged and nodded.

'But that is it, no, I think?' Geldie glanced up towards the sky. 'Finish here, yes?'

'Oh yes,' said Sarah with a relieved smile. 'Believe me, I couldn't ride to the Caspian Sea if my life depended on it.'

'We'll do as you say and take the train the rest of the way.'

Geldie laughed. 'I think you English little crazy, now I see no. This good.' He pointed to the car. 'I have to go town centre, you want lift?'

'That's very kind, thank you.' I smiled. 'But unfortunately we just have a little more filming to do. We'll catch a taxi later.'

He shook our hands and expressed the hope that he'd see us before we left. He then turned to walk back towards his car. As he did so, I nudged Sarah and chuckled.

'Look,' I said, 'so we rode them after all. Not across the Mountains of Heaven . . . but across the Karakum Desert.' Emblazoned across the back of his jacket in large gold letters was written, 'Akhal Teke – the Heavenly Horse'.

'Do you think they are the real Heavenly Horses?' she asked.

I laughed. 'I guess we'll never know.'

We picked up the keys to the flat from Valerie. Aware that we both stank like a couple of vagrants, we made our excuses and rushed back to the apartment where we fought each other for the bath. Neither of us had washed for fifteen days. Needless to say, Sarah won. By five we were warm and washed in the set of clean clothes we'd left at the flat.

'Right,' said Sarah, 'I'm going to go round and see Makri and get our air tickets fixed. When shall we book them for? If we catch the train tomorrow night, stay there the next day, back the one after that, that'll mean . . .'

'About four days' time,' I said, smiling at her impatience. 'But listen, just book your own.'

'What? Why?'

'I'm not going to fly back. At least not from here.'

'Where then?'

'Well, I reckon any journey that sets out along the Silk Road from China should end in Istanbul or Rome. Call me an old romantic, but that's what I think.'

'I'll call you an idiot more like!' She pursed her lips, as though she'd just sucked on a lemon. 'You're going to go overland to Italy?'

'I think Turkey will do. But yes.'

'How?'

'Take a ship across the Caspian Sea to Baku. Ride the midnight train to Georgia – I like that, it has a nice ring to it, don't you think? – and from there get a bus all the way to the Bosphorus. I've been thinking about it for some time. It's pretty easy really.'

'Well, I'm not coming,' she huffed.

I laughed. 'Don't worry, I wouldn't expect you to. It's just something I want to do, Georgia, Azerbaijan . . . they'll be fascinating. It'll also give me a chance to wrap up the film.'

She shook her head and turned away. 'Rather you than me.'

Having bidden farewell to our friends, at six the following evening we returned to the railway station where we bought two tickets for a sleeper birth on the Trans-Caspian Express. We ate supper in the canteen – a last bowl of *laghmann* washed down with a half litre of vodka – and, as the train pulled in, moved out to the icy platform. Caught filming, we were almost arrested by members of the transport police. Sarah did little to help the situation by aggressively lambasting the sergeant for being an officious buffoon but, with a prod in her ribs and an obsequious smile, I managed to persuade him that we were just a couple of simple tourists who didn't understand matters of national security, and after a few minutes' hassle we were allowed to board the train. We found our carriage and compartment of four bunks, which we shared with a wiry electrical engineer from Tashkent and a young local woman on a trip to visit her sister. A few minutes later the train pulled out of the station and into the darkness of the desert.

When we woke we found we were alone. At some point during the night our travelling companions had left the carriage and alighted from the train. As the iron horse trundled slowly through the golden desert, once again under clear blue skies, we did our final personal video diaries.

It's amazing to have woken up today in the desert . . . the last leg of the journey, and my heart's brimming over with excitement that in five days' time I'll finally be on that aeroplane home . . . Really amazing.

I, too, found it hard to know what to say. How could we sum up concisely to a video camera all that had passed over the last four months, and what it had meant? On seeing the Caspian Sea for the first time, a thin slither of blue, sparking like a strip of steel beyond the yellow plain, I mumbled something about it being a bittersweet feeling finally to be almost arriving. On the one hand it meant that we had reached our goal, achieved – almost – what we'd set out to do, and that was great. But on the other hand it also meant that the dream that had driven me for so long was now at an end, and that was rather sad.

At eleven we climbed down from the train and found a hotel on the town's main square. Rising from a barren hollow, surrounded by a crescent of jagged mountains, Turkmenbashi – formerly known as Krasnavosk, until the President decided it should be named after himself – was a pleasant little town. With its pink and white buildings, many dating back more than a hundred years, – a rarity in Central Asia – facing the deep blue waters of the Caspian Sea, it reminded me of a sleepy Mediterranean fishing port. From our balcony we could see down into the harbour where ships of various sizes lay at anchor, including the *Dagistan*, which would carry me to Baku.

Wanting to make the most of the fine weather, without further ado we wandered down to the bazaar by the quay, and for our celebratory picnic on the beach bought, among other less salubrious items, a bottle of Uzbek champagne and half a kilo of caviar, the latter costing just $20.

Having been informed that the best beach was five kilometres up the coast, we set off in a cab through marshy coastlands of rough green grass and passed a small nondescript settlement and an ugly oil refinery. After ten minutes we pulled up onto a gravel carpark. There was nothing there: no beach huts or restaurants, no hotdog stands or ice-cream seller. On first inspection there wasn't even much of a beach, just pebbles, sandstone and granite rocks crafted by the prevailing winds into twisted, buckled sculptures. But there was the sea, stretching like a silver mirror towards the clear horizon.

Having asked the taxi driver to wait, we charged down to the water's edge, tore off our shoes and, like a couple of kids beside Brighton Pier, paddled happily in the surf. We hadn't ridden all the way from Kashgar to the Caspian Sea, as had been our original goal, but we had ridden most of the way, and that was good enough for us. We found a small area of sand, sheltered from the wind by an outcrop of rock and, having set up the camera, sat down to lunch. We cracked open the champagne, toasted the journey, each of our horses, deciding which had been the best and which had been the worst, and generally reminisced. We gluttonously pigged ourselves on caviar, which I'd never tasted before and thought exceptionally delicious, and, having filmed a few closing shots, lay down and smoked a cigarette.

Our 'Castaways on horseback' – undoubtedly one of the longest and most bizarre 'blind dates' in the history of the world, if that's indeed what it really was – had finally come to an end. Looking across at Sarah, it was hard to imagine that only five months previously we'd been sitting in a pub in London, meeting for the first time, flirting, chatting nineteen to the dozen about this great adventure. It was even harder to imagine that at that time I thought I might have found some emotional salvation in Sarah. But as she lay there, eyes closed, her pretty face calm and serene, turned towards the sky, I knew that my choice hadn't been so terrible. It was now clear to me why those early weeks had been so hard. With her forceful character it must have been a nightmare for Sarah travelling on 'my trip', making 'my show', always playing second fiddle. With less knowledge of the region, less ability with the horses, less experience with the camera, more by circumstance than any subversive design she had become infantasised – a situation she must have hated – and she'd dealt with it in her own individual way. But over the course of the journey she'd found her feet, had taken her share of the responsibilities – using the camera, planning the routes, looking after the horses, even learning Russian – to become an equal member of our team. Added to that, she'd seldom complained, had rarely been frightened, and though her intransigence had at times been annoying, and even slightly ridiculous, on other occasions it had helped to save the day. Moreover, early on she'd put up with my pensive moods which, regardless of the events that had caused them, could not have been easy to endure. And when all's said and done, she'd made it here, to the Caspian Sea: I wondered how many of the other girls would have managed that. Yes, I decided, I hadn't chosen so badly.

I sat up and filled my old tin cup with fizzy red wine and looked out across the sea. Beyond the sparkling waters lay Baku, a midnight train to Georgia and a long road through Turkey. It would be another interesting journey: the Caucasus, like Central Asia, was a place steeped in history that I'd long wished to visit. But what then? Would I really hang up my travelling boots? Wasn't that what I'd decided?

Well, no . . . not exactly. As the journey had continued beyond the Mountains of Heaven, through Samarkand and Bukhara and across the Karakum Desert, I'd begun to realise that it wasn't travel that was intrinsically the problem but the motivation that lay behind it. When I'd set out across Africa I'd done so with a clear heart and honest intentions, desperate to escape a world I was not brave enough to face to search for meaning in another I did not know. But as the travels led me into a career, with the travelling life becoming *my* life, with the books and films giving excuses for adventures, the reasons for the journeys had become spurious and confused. No longer was I travelling on heartfelt quests but trying to bolster a media career, and that had never been my goal. Though I knew I'd never regret the adventures that had filled the last ten years with all manner of interesting experiences, introduced me to many incredible people, taught me a great many invaluable lessons and ultimately helped to make me who I am, I also understood that this wandering lifestyle was coming to an end. When the plan to ride the old Silk Road had first been hatched, I'd hoped it would lead me to chronicle the *last part* of this traveller's tale and, though the story I'd gained was very different from the one of which I'd dreamed, I still felt that it had. Once that was over, and I'd written the book, I knew it would be time for a change.

And stop travelling completely? How could I do that? It was in my blood now. Over the last couple of months I'd been thinking more and more about my travel company, Wild Frontiers. Though I'd had some troubled times in much of Central Asia, there was no denying that parts of Kyrgyzstan, Tajikistan and even Uzbekistan had been wild and stunning and deeply fascinating, just right for adventure travel. Taking Dom's advice I'd spoken to Alex about possible joint ventures. I'd chatted to Saidullah and even Makri about tourism in their countries. Part of the motivation behind travelling home overland was to check out the Caucasus as a possible location for a Wild Frontiers holiday destination. I needed a home and a more settled life, and I'd find all that in London, but I also knew I needed a job, one that would allow me at least some travel. In Wild Frontiers I knew I already had the answer.

Before me the Caspian Sea danced and sparkled in the pale winter sun. I pulled my knees up to my chin, wrapped my arms round my legs and smiled to myself. I wasn't just looking towards Baku, Georgia and the road to Istanbul. Across the silvery waters lay a bright new future.

A Word from the Author

Before signing off with the inevitable lengthy acknowledgments, let me just add a couple of things I think you might find interesting.

Sarah and I saw each other once following the trip, a couple of weeks after I'd returned form Istanbul. I apologised for being such a jerk and placing too much of the hurt Rachel had piled on my shoulders on her; also for putting too much emphasis on the film and for being at times a grumpy bastard. She, in turn, insisted that she had been foolish and naïve and had not made the situation at all easy for me. We haven't spoken since. I'm not surprised, or especially concerned, by this. I feel sure that for all the drastic ups and downs – and let's face it they were mainly downs – we parted amicably. But I think on a trip as intense and demanding as ours, living as we were in each other's pockets for such a long period of time and through such trying conditions, we'd either end up married or not wanting to see each other again. And I think we'd both agree: not only are we not heading down the aisle, we've probably had quite enough of each other for one lifetime.

The film, having been turned down by both the BBC and Channel 4, was eventually bought by The Discovery Channel. As we had foreseen, there were some problems in the editing – filling the hole in the lead story – but in the end I think we managed to cut a relatively decent and representative film of our adventures. At least some people thought so, for when it was finally broadcast it received very favourable reviews and was 'Pick of the Day' in both *The Times* and *Daily Telegraph*. All that hard work was, it seems, worth it in the end.

Since undertaking this journey, Wild Frontiers has flourished. September 11 and the Kashmir issue sure knocked the stuffing out of the Pakistan side of the operation, but this simply forced me to expand the business into other areas, and now with a new partner and an office in London we are running tours to Northern India,

Bhutan, Central Asia, the Caucuses, Ethiopia, Morocco and Argentina; with Niger, Cambodia and Madagascar hopefully following soon. Taking people of varying ages and interests on carefully prepared itineraries, Wild Frontiers has not only proved a sound financial business, providing me with a stable future and an interesting new career, it has also allowed me the freedom to travel as much or as little as I want. A perfect balance, I feel. So if you fancy a trip to any of the places mentioned above – and will forgive a little bare-faced self-promotion – please get in touch via our web site at www.wildfrontiers.co.uk and we'll give you an amazing adventure.

And finally, on a sadder note, having recently returned to Kyrgyzstan with a tour group, I learnt that Kara, my irascible nag from the Kashgar bazaar, failed to make it through his first winter. On arriving in Bishkek I was informed by a thoroughly amused Murat that the smiling horse that had tried to kick and bite me at every possible juncture had become so fed up with the harsh conditions of his new, and no doubt unwanted, home in the mountains that he'd decided to end it all by throwing himself off a cliff. Surely the first horse ever to commit suicide. But as it turned out the truth, though no less sad, was somewhat less dramatic. On visiting Tash Rabat, Jergil, the caravanserai's caretaker, told me that Kara had become weaker and weaker as the weather grew worse, and eventually refused to eat. One cold, wintry morning, while struggling to follow Jergil up a snowy hillside, he'd slipped and fallen, tumbling slowly over a ridge to his death. Normally, Jergil and his family would have made good use of such a mishap by scooping up the carcass and turning it into steak or *kolbasa*. But not with Kara. Apparently his meat – at least what was left of it – was so rank that it was unfit for human consumption, leaving them little alternative but to cut him up for the dogs . . . a fitting end, I guess.

And so lastly on with the thanks. Journeys of the kind you have just read about inevitably rely on an immense amount of help and goodwill from very many people. This trip was no exception, and though some of these people have been mentioned in my tale – Dom, Alex, Zlatko and Valerie immediately spring to mind – others have not, and I should like to sign off by offering them my thanks.

Firstly I should like to mention all the women who took part in the auditions. Without them the story, and in particular the TV film, would not have had such an interesting and unusual beginning. Thanks to all of you.

Though there were many times on this journey when I wished my agent had never sent the original book proposal to Lion Television, I should like to thank Jeremy Mills for having confidence in the project's potential and giving it the green light. I'm just relieved that in the end Jeremy's courage and conviction did not go entirely unrewarded. At the same company I must say a huge thanks to Nick Catliff, Richard Bradley, Bridget Sneyd, Shahana Meer, Charlotte Markham, Launa Kennett, Josh Good, Bill Locke and Peira Cutica.

I would like to express my gratitude to Monica Whitlock, the BBC's former Central Asia correspondent, James Greenwood – the only man to have ridden a horse around the world – Richard Danziger, John Hare, Peter Hopkirk, Susie Dowdall, Maggi O'Sullivan, Shane Windsor, Michael Clayton and Nomad Travel, all of whom had a hand in the planning or gave useful tips about horse travel and the region in general.

I should also like to thank Jeremy Sheldon, Nicola and Guy Joseph, Bill Keeling, Laurence and Ruth van der Eb, Lavina Mills, Patrick Drummond, Henrietta Miers, Robert Sutton, Chris Bealby, Mark Nicolls, Katie James, Sarah Elder, Kerin Goodall and my parents.

Huge thanks to my agent, Mark Lucas, my long-suffering and brilliant editor, Victoria Hipps, Ravi Mirchandani at William Heinemann, and my old mate Andy Hobsbawm who, once again, took the time to read through the first draft and offer invaluable advice.

And lastly, of course, thanks to Sarah.

Apologies for inevitable omissions.

Jonny Bealby
London, 2002